The Rannock Legacy

The story of a remarkable horse

Jeanette Gower

PLATYPUS
PUBLISHING

Platypus Publishing

Image by Peter Gower

Cover design by Amy Curran

ISBN **Hardback: 978-1-962133-66-1**

ISBN **Paperback: 978-1-962133-65-4**

First edition published in Australia.

Dedication

To my family and the friends of Rannock, who appreciate good horses.

The Rannock Legacy is in many ways a compilation of the records of South Australian horses, not just Rannock, a scene which has long been regarded as an outlier by mainstream Australian Stock Horse enthusiasts. Hopefully this book will help to correct that oversight. It is an attempt to preserve information which would otherwise be lost. It also serves as a testament to those breeders who knew and upheld the traditions of breeding good horses, sadly, not always followed in today's world of specialisation, and desire for quick results.

Additionally, it is a record of the Chalani Australian Stock Horses, now celebrating 55 years of breeding the "breed for every need." We could not have done it without Rannock.

The bulk of the photos were taken by my husband Peter Gower (dec'd), myself, or my daughter Kim Ide. Where possible other photos in this book have been identified and credit given to the photographer. Some are not of good quality, but I felt they should be included anyway. If any reader has further details which I can use in future printings, I would welcome that information. The Rannock Legacy is as much a reference text as a photographic "coffee table" type record.

Thank you to all the people who have contributed in no small part by telling me their stories. You have enabled the dream of documenting the Rannock story, to come to fruition.

I do hope you enjoy this trip down memory lane.
– Jeanette Gower, April 2024

Background

Some definitions

The Australian Stock Horse Society records all registered horses, in capital letters, and others in lower case. This system is used throughout the Studbook, on the Website and in the ASH Magazine. In keeping with this tradition, I have used capitals when the horse is named for the *first* time. However, after this, I have simply used lower case.

ASH used throughout refers to horses registered in the Stud Book (1x, 2x and full Stud Book) of the Australian Stock Horse Society. Society definitions and any ASH horse's full breeding can be found by going to the Australian Stock Horse Society's website: https://www.ashs.com.au/

HSH used throughout refers to horses recognised by the Australian Stock Horse Society as being at least 87.5% Heritage Horses on breeding, regardless of Stud Book status. Heritage horses are those horses which descend from the same breeds as the original Waler or Remount horses prior to 1945 (WWII). These breeds were primarily Thoroughbred, Australian Pony, Arabian, Welsh, Hackney, polo ponies and 'station horses' (often crossbreds of those mixed with some cold blood).

Almost all the horses mentioned in this book are listed HSH in the ASH Studbook, where they are shown with their suffix. For the sake of brevity, I have not used the suffix after the horse's names.

A station horse was a general usage horse on cattle or sheep stations of outback Australia, which had a 'herd or station book' so its breeding could be traced. These herd books recorded most horses as being by a Thoroughbred sire bought from yearling or retired racehorse sales, since there was very little market for Australian sires in the Thoroughbred industry at that time.

Cold blood was sometimes introduced through the dam's side, occasionally Percheron or Clydesdale. Others would use full blood Arabian or Anglo-Arabian crossed over cold bloods to produce mares backcrossed to Thoroughbred. The resulting horses were nearly always 15h to 15.2h in height of very sound type, suitable for the tough conditions they were to work in.

Many were bought for the remount trade, and taken to New South Wales for handling, breaking and dispatched for military service to India, South Africa, and later Europe in WW1. Consequently, they became known overseas as 'Walers'. They were considered the best Light Horses in the world.

When the Society was formed in 1971, the idea was to preserve these bloodlines, as Australia was beginning to be swamped by other breed imports from USA and Europe. Upgrading often utilized Australian heritage mares, but without giving them any recognition. Australia was in danger of losing these valuable bloodlines, and people became concerned that the newly imported breeds would benefit without credit to the Australian foundation mares.

The Society did consider calling the breed 'Waler', but this was rejected due to the fact that the term 'Waler,' was not in use in Australia, only overseas, and it did not reflect the origins of the genuine station horse. The Station Horse at its heart, was an all-rounder, a work horse through the week, and on the weekend a campdraft, polocrosse or Pony Club horse. The whole family was involved, often travelling many miles to take part in each of these on the same weekend!

A Standard of Excellence was drawn up, and an Australia-wide Classification System instigated. This included the use of Thoroughbreds classified for inclusion, as the Thoroughbred is the foundation of the Australian Stock Horse. Thoroughbred blood is used to improve all horse breeds around the world except those with closed books. We have some of the best Thoroughbreds available here in Australia so it was thought Thoroughbred blood would help to continue the desired type and abilities, (especially speed, stamina, quality, and density of bone) and prevent genetic bottle-necking.

The Australian Stock Horse Standard of Excellence

- Head alert and intelligent with broad forehead, full, well-set eyes, wide nostrils. A fine, clean gullet, allowing plenty of breathing room.
- A good length of rein, well set into the shoulder.
- Sloping shoulder, not too heavily muscled, a well-defined wither slightly higher than the croup.
- Deep chest, not too wide in proportion, but showing plenty of heart room.
- Ribs well sprung and back strong and of medium length in proportion.
- In forelegs, forearms well developed, cannon bones slightly flat, pasterns short and slightly sloping.
- Hindquarters strong, rounded and well-muscled, nicely sloping to give a full line from croup to hock. Hocks broad, flat and clean, the cannon relatively short with well-defined tendons. The hind legs well under when standing.
- The hooves hard and in proportion to the size of the horse with a wide heel and feet straight.
- Preferred heights between 14 and 16 hands.

<u>The online stud book.</u> The listing of many of the early horses is fraught with inaccuracy, and many horses with known breeding were simply left blank by their owners upon registration. My husband Peter Gower, and the first Society Secretary, Mary Griffiths, spent hours sifting through the original records, and correcting them where necessary. Doubling up of names of the same horse, incorrect spellings, colour, birth-dates, or many other errors, were found along the way. Unfortunately, this was not incorporated into the stud book when it went online.

Attempting to correct obvious errors has become a frustration to many. One has to submit a statutory declaration, provide evidence, and pay a $200 fee to have anything changed. Just from my research for this book I have found errors and omissions. Where information comes to light, especially for key horses, it should be possible for the studbook to be updated in accordance with this information, without a charge to the provider of that information.

The online studbook is excellent for searching pedigrees of horses already registered, however one cannot search for an unregistered horse listed in a pedigree. That is a huge drawback for researchers. For instance, one cannot search for Radium, as he was unregistered, even though he appears in the majority of traditional Australian Stock Horses.

<u>The classification system</u> was to identify horses of the correct type. Here there was controversy, as type varied across the country, depending on topography. Some individuals of the newly imported breeds were accepted as being 'of the type, with outstanding performance.' It was feared that the Society was now being overwhelmed by these other breeds, in spite of the original aims to preserve the heritage horse.

Consequently, in 2020 it was passed unanimously and enshrined in the Constitution, that there was to be a bloodline requirement for entry, and a <u>Heritage Stud Book</u> established. Horses of heritage status are automatically granted this at the time of registration, and recorded as such on the Society website. Some members are now breeding and promoting their stock as Heritage Australian Stock Horses, and these automatically have HSH suffixed to their names in the Stud Book, and Society publications.

Of concern, is the demand for buying up HSHs to breed to non-HSH horses, (so their offspring can be accepted), which further dilutes the remaining pool of HSH horses available. It is up to breeders to decide if they really want to preserve the breed before it is too late. Competition with good prizemoney for the true heritage horses, might be an incentive.

From the Society's website: "The Australian Stock Horse Society is dedicated to preserving the heritage of the breed by recognising Registered Australian Stock Horses that have descended from the same *breeds* as horses ridden by the Australian Light Horse in WWI and *breeds* that resided in Australia prior to 1945."

Contents

Foreword

In 1975, I first met Jeanette Gower, a dedicated horse industry professional. At that time, I was a lecturer, and Jeanette an inaugural student, exploring the nascent realms of the Certificate of Equine Studies—a course crafted to cultivate expertise in the science underpinning the production and performance of horses, for those entrenched in the industry.

From the outset, Jeanette's fervour for the Australian Stock Horse, illustrated not only her passion for the horse, but also her exceptional grasp of Mendelian Genetics and its profound implications for the inheritance of equine traits.

The Australian Stock Horse—a paragon of versatility, resilience, and adaptability—has long been revered for its prowess across diverse terrains, from the rugged expanses of the Snowy Mountains to the sprawling cattle stations dotting our vast inland. It forged an iconic reputation in the theatres of war. It is a noble breed that evolved in the crucible of necessity—a stalwart companion equally adept as a pony club mount, a seasoned trailblazer, or a formidable competitor excelling in the arenas of campdrafting, polocrosse, and show ring spectacles.

In laying the cornerstone of the *Chalani* stud, Jeanette and her husband Peter, an equine photographer, selected Rannock—a majestic specimen epitomizing the exacting standards championed by the Australian Stock Horse Society. I saw him at his first dressage test: he had a presence that filled my eye. Rannock's lineage, intricately interwoven with that of the esteemed stallion "Panzer," endowed him with a genotype primed for perpetuating coveted traits in his progeny.

Within the pages of this wonderful book, unfolds the saga of Jeanette's unwavering dedication, meticulous planning, and triumphant collaboration with Rannock. Together, they have etched an indelible chapter in the annals of Australian Stock Horse heritage, leaving an enduring legacy that resonates particularly profoundly within the heartland of South Australia.

In the following pages, may you embark on a journey suffused with reverence for the noble steed and admiration for the extraordinary partnerships that have enriched the tapestry of a world with horses.

Ian Pickett
RDAT (Hons), Dip. T. (Tech)
Retired Educational Manager: TAFESA School of Veterinary and Applied Science.

***

"In 1973, the first horses were inspected in SA for inclusion in the registry for the newly formed Australian Stock Horse Society. Those horses were an amazingly diverse collection as there were virtually no members of the accepted Stock Horse, as found in areas of New South Wales, in the state of South Australia.

"When I encountered Rannock with his wonderful functional conformation and balance, and his outstanding mind, I understood what the fellows who were trying to get this ASH thing off the ground, were all about. Had I not been a totally committed Quarter Horse person, Rannock might almost have persuaded me to go in another direction.

"He was so different from the usual sort of TB around at that time. A great example that if you take Thoroughbreds, keep their positive traits and select for something not for the track, you end up with a Rannock." – Merrie Elliott.

Introduction

The story of Rannock is that of a horse which has been under the radar for a long time. This is partly because of his South Australian location, away from mainstream Australian Stock Horse activity and breeding, but also because so many of the resulting descendants have been unregistered, and unable to be traced. Yet the Rannock influence has been incredible, considering the lack of opportunity.

It is also the story of the families involved; families who knew the lines well and wanted to keep them into perpetuity. Perhaps not surprisingly then, the line is gaining new attention, due to its long-standing record of producing smart, good looking, trainable and reliable, traditional stock horses which are a true Heritage outcross to most Australian Stock Horse lines today.

The story of Rannock first began as a series of articles I wrote for the ASH Magazine. After six long years of research, there were five articles in the series. The first, published in June and August 2019 issues, were beautifully presented, and I received an excellent response to it. The Magazine declined to publish the rest, even though the Board had approved it for their 50th anniversary year (2021), as they were always needing articles for the magazine and it would be a good fit. The editor said "but I would need to edit the articles!" The CEO at the time said to me in an email, "if it is so important, go write a book."

I was not amused, but it gave me much fuel for thought. How would I do this? Would I do a complete story on the *Chalani* Australian Stock Horses, or limit it to an expanded and more complete story of the Rannock legacy itself? I realised there was so much I could write, including how we operated as a stud and trained our horses. This became the foundation for my book *The Thinking Horse Breeder*, published in July 2023, which has received excellent feedback.

Now I really had to focus on the Rannock story, and this is the result.

ASH members are now tending to specialize in show horses, or campdrafting or polocrosse, as prizemoney has led many into becoming professionals in their chosen discipline. Campdrafting and polocrosse are now HUGE. What happens to the horses which regularly compete in other open disciplines with the best of them, such as eventing, endurance or hacking, or regularly sire such horses?

They become unknown to the members and breeders, because they are not 'in the Magazine' being promoted by articles or in advertising.

Fact is, if I didn't put it out there 'for the record' there would be no one else to tell the story, and most of this information would be lost forever. Great horses deserve to have their stories told. The true heritage Australian Stock Horse *is* the *'breed for every need'* which can compete in the three main specialties *and* also in open disciplines, far outside the range of the traditional stock horse.

There are many people who now have Rannock blood in their Australian Stock Horses, yet Rannock's name is virtually unknown to all but a few. This then, is my attempt to record some of it, and to interest new buyers and breeders to this bloodline in their horses.

Rannock was a beautiful looking horse with an outstanding head, long arched neck, roomy gullet, well defined wither, great elbow room, short cannons, with strong, square hocks.

Despite being blind in one eye, he showed a natural aptitude and boldness over jumps. He could be ridden bareback amongst his mares and I would sometimes lead horses off him. If you introduced him to something new, he just did it; there was never any fuss or scariness. I even did a bit of sidesaddle with him as he had the type of back that would sit a side-saddle well.

His progeny were outstanding polo ponies; indeed, in 1979 Gold Cup, they played in three State A Teams.

In October 2023, Rannock was inducted to the ASH Society's Hall of Fame for his contribution to the breed as a foundation sire. I can think of no honour more befitting this horse. Time is now full circle to publish his story.

Chapter 1

Panzer

The start of it all

Panzer with Bob Mackay, 1973.

During 1973, the Gowers were returning to South Australia from a stud tour and the All-Breeds Congress at Gatton, Queensland. Peter and Jeanette decided to call in at the new office of the Australian Stock Horse Society, in Scone, New

South Wales. Scone was in the heart of the Hunter Valley, and indeed the heart of Australian Stock Horse country, where most of the renowned sires of the breed at that time, were either foaled, or found their homes. They asked if they could be pointed in the right direction to visit PANZER, now an old horse, and one of the remaining living foundation sires of the breed. RJ MacKay of *Tinagroo*, Scone was Panzer's breeder. The Secretary immediately said, "hold on, I will ring to let Bob know you are coming. When you enter the gate there is a long driveway and you will see the house on the top of the hill." Little did we know that this would change our lives.

By this time it was late, about 5pm, and when we entered the gate, it turned out the driveway was about 9 miles long, and the 'house' was a large, elegant old colonial homestead, of the type one sees in movies. We were duly greeted at the front door by Mrs Mackay, who welcomed us into the gorgeous huge reception hall, decorated with all kinds of Scottish and WW II memorabilia.

As it was late, we were invited to stay the night, and we were quickly taken to the guest quarters at the opposite end of the hallway, to rejoin them for "dinner at 8". And what a treat that was! Bob was totally at home, talking horses, and in particular Panzer. He advised us he had recently sold a youngster to South Australia, which he'd called Rannoch, after Loch Rannoch in Scotland. Most of his horses were given Scottish or WWII names. Then we poured over his photo albums, learning the history of the various horses. Most were straight Thoroughbred.

Next morning we were taken to see the great Panzer, then 29, and still in wonderful condition. Bob was immensely proud of the old horse and the bond between the two was evident. We felt very privileged. We were then taken to see many of his stock and other relatives around the station. There were some 'taffies' (now recognized as the silver gene) by Panzer, which although not pure Thoroughbred, were kept as working stock horses, in addition to the Thoroughbreds used. As was the custom in those days, Bob MacKay rarely sold a mare, preferring to sell colts, and used well performed stallions from neighbouring stations when breeding out. The Mackays bred Thoroughbreds to race, and once retired, many had a second career working on the property.

Finally, we were taken 'down the road' to see the stallion Dundee at the Munro's place; all the while Bob was filling us in on the lineage and performances of the horses. Just as we were leaving Bob turned to us and said "take the album, and copy any photos you want". This was just done on a handshake and a promise to return when we'd finished! We couldn't believe it. We'd started out as complete strangers and ended up lifelong friends.

The ensuing information is taken from that visit and letters in our possession from him:

"Panzer began his polo career as a rising five year old in 1949 and played until 1956 when he was 11 years old and about reaching his prime. I say this because each chukka he played was better than the one before.

"That year we won the Northern Challenge Cup at Quirindi for the third successive year but my health forced me to give up polo. Panzer retired with me, as did two of his daughters Mersa and Misra, both of whom had been playing beside him for the past two or three years. It was unfortunate for Panzer, as he would have played on for another four or five years at his top. He never developed a heavy neck as stallions do and become heavy to handle, but remained a very orthodox polo pony. He never pulled or ran on and always played off the single bottom rein of the curb.

"Although Panzer was a brilliant horse cutting out on a camp (I always used him for this work on the property) I never allowed him to compete at campdrafting, as for me he was a specialist polo pony."

This information and photos were reprinted many times by journalists in articles for the Society Magazine and various histories of the ASH. The Panzer influence is widely documented and a complete story on Panzer can be found on the Society's website. Panzer quite rightly appears in both the Australian Polo Hall of Fame and the Australian Stock Horse Society for his huge contribution to the depth and talent of Australian Horses. He is listed as a Waler Horse of Significance, and is mentioned in Peter Gower's *ASH Pedigree Book* as one of the 14 foundation sires of the breed.

Panzer upon his retirement from polo, age 12.

Panzer produced great sires such as: MYRA BRONZE (1951) sire of the well-known MYRA SUZIE, NABINABAH THE GUN (1957), himself one of the most influential ASH sires, and sire of the great Impact Mare BREEZETTE, CAIRO (1957), Dundee (1959), BERRICO MATRUH (1962) a full brother to Cairo, MR TARA KING (1964), CHECKERS ALAMEIN (1965), PRANCER (1966), TINAGROO ROMMEL (1973) which Bob MacKay kept himself as a replacement for Panzer, and PICARILLI BENGHAZI (1974).

The great Nabinabah Breezette, owned by the Palmer Family.

Myra Suzie with Ted Hooke, Expo 75.

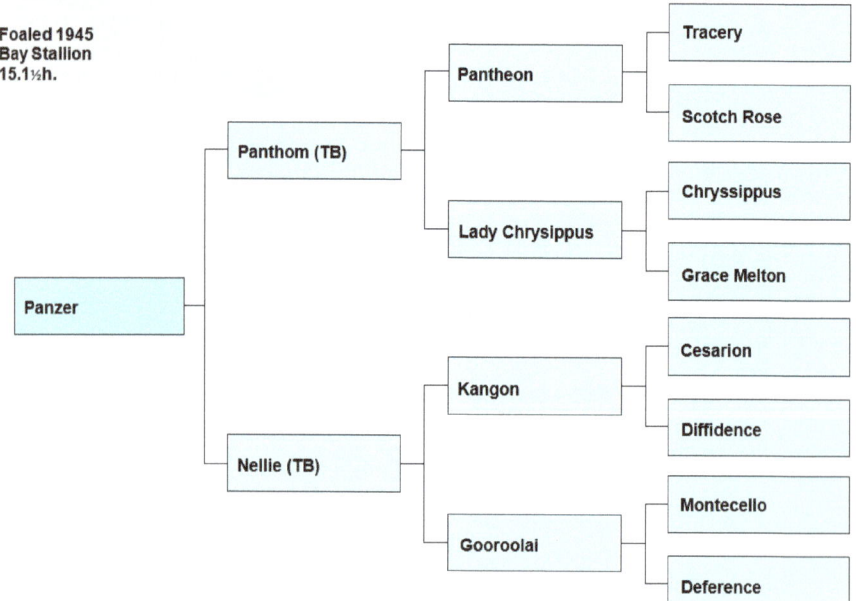

PANZER

Foaled 1945
Bay Stallion
15.1½h.

Panzer
- Panthom (TB)
  - Pantheon
    - Tracery
    - Scotch Rose
  - Lady Chrysippus
    - Chryssippus
    - Grace Melton
- Nellie (TB)
  - Kangon
    - Cesarion
    - Diffidence
  - Gooroolai
    - Montecello
    - Deference

Deference is also a granddaughter of Diffidence.

Australian Polo Hall of Fame inductee Panzer, sire of many great Australian Stock Horses including MYRA BRONZE - FS HSH and NABINABAH THE GUN - FS HSH.

Eight Australian Stock Horses inducted into the Australian Polo Federation Hall of Fame

The Australian Polo Federation recently announced the establishment of the Australian Polo Hall of Fame, which will formally recognise the greats of the game. An inaugural dinner took place on Thursday 28th March 2013 in Sydney, and 8 of the 14 polo ponies inducted into the Hall of Fame were Australian Stock Horses, including the following:

- Panzer (Pantheon/Nellie) sired many great horses including MYRA BRONZE - FS HSH and NABINABAH THE GUN - FS HSH. 'Without doubt, the most influential stallion in Australian polo,' said James Archibald.

- TERLINGS MARTINI - HSH (TERLINGS DEO JUVANTE - FS TB/ Nightcap), grey mare bred by AR & CL McGilvray. An outstanding mare with a beautiful temperament, she played mainly in a snaffle. At stud, TERLINGS MARTINI produced two quality stallions in BOLINGER - HSH and TERLINGS TAITTINGER.

- TERLINGS JESSICA (CAIRO/TERLINGS JEWESS), light bay mare bred by Sinclair Hill. She was an extremely agile mare that won numerous pony prizes, including Champion Pony in the 1973 Easter Gold Cup, and was in the team of ponies that played the 1971 Queensland Gold Cup. TERLINGS JESSICA was a mainstay of Sinclair Hill's famed pony string, winning most of the major tournaments

in Australia during the 1970s. 'You didn't just ride this pony, she played the game with you,' Sinclair said.

- GILGANNON TUESDAY (The Colt/ Emblem), bay/brown mare bred by Stuart Gilmore. A striking looking mare, GILGANNON TUESDAY took Stuart to the top of high goal polo in the 1980s, and won many pony prizes. 'Stuart would usually play two chukkas on her, and she was as good at the end as the beginning,' said Anto White.

- CANGON CASTINETTE (Rapid Hour/ Castina), gelding bred by the Mackay Family. At 16.1hh, CANGON CASTINETTE had raw power, strength and speed, which he combined with immense athleticism. He formed the backbone of Jamie Mackay's high goal string, and retired from play after 15 years.

- CLAREMONT TRESCAA (BAJO - HSH/ PENELOPE), 15hh brown mare bred by Peter Cudmore. She played 10 seasons of high goal polo with Jim Gilmore, winning 24 champion pony prizes, including Champion Pony at the 1987 Easter International.

The Polo Hall of Fame is a terrific initiative to recognise the achievements of polo ponies. The Australian Stock Horse Society is proud to see these brilliant Australian Stock Horses succeeding at the highest level of this demanding sport. ◐

HALL OF FAME

Panzer

Pony to Remember

Owner: Mr Bob Mackay

Born in 1945, Panzer was by Pantheon from the thoroughbred mare Nellie. He was played by Bob Mackay in the Wirragulla team, with wins in the Countess of Dudley Cup in 1950, '51 and '52, the Australasian Gold Cup of 1952 and the Northern Challenge Cup in 1956. In 1956 at 11 years, Panzer was retired to full time stud work, although he already had a number of talented polo playing offspring on the ground. Bob Mackay described Panzer as being blessed with amazing speed and agility and with a superb temperament, a trait passed on to his progeny. The Panzer legacy resounds through Australian polo. His sons dominate polo bloodlines including The Gun, Alamein, Cairo, Dundee, Myra Bronze, Mocket, Mountbatten, Gunfire, Rannock and Montego. Another grandson Gillette carries a double cross of Panzer and continues the bloodlines at Cangoi. Panzer died at Scone in 1974.

"An exceptional playing horse with a significant influence on the Australian breeding scene." Pat MacGinley

"Without doubt the most influential stallion in Australian polo." James Archibald

"His influence has been enormous over decades." Andy White

Chapter 2

Rannock

The one-in-a-million horse

RANNOCK was sold as a yearling, to Mr Alan McGregor of *Roskhill* Mt Pleasant, in the beautiful Adelaide Hills of South Australia. He was to be used for polo and as a sire. Unfortunately, shortly after being broken in, he received a paddock injury which blinded him in one eye. A blind-eyed horse is not permitted to play polo, so he was sent to another McGregor property, *Willalooka* in the South East of South Australia.

"He ran with the station mares who were a rather rough bunch. One day a station hand rode through the paddock and his gelding was chased by Rannock, resulting in injury to the rider's arm. Rannock acquired a 'reputation' from this, and that, together with his 'thoroughbred breeding' was something he had to overcome in conservative stock horse circles of SA, for the rest of his life.

"I brought him back to *Roskhill* with a couple of the better progeny, and turned him out with my polo mares. When I saw the first foals I thought "what have I done! – they were all 'pretty' chestnuts, with no neck, but I soon learned they would stretch out later and have lovely rein." – Alan McGregor.

Rannock was foaled in 1967. He was by Dundee (by Panzer) x TINAGROO MERSA (by Panzer) a half-brother/half-sister cross. All the immediate ancestors were high class polo ponies in their own right. Panzer's dam, Nellie was a polo pony, foal recorded in the Australian Stud Book in 1933 but never raced due to the outbreak of WWII. She too was inbred, to the Sydney Cup winning mare Diffidence which was purchased as a 17 year old by JK and WH Mackay for 900 guineas in 1913, a princely sum!

Rannock, 'look of eagles,' in his paddock with mares, at Roskhill.

"Mersa's dam, Ranmena, was a successful racehorse, which also went on to become a good polo pony. Mersa, Rannock's dam, was the first of Panzer's progeny to play and was a beautiful mare to play on, being completely orthodox and simple to play in a single rein curb off the bottom ring only. Literally a finger-tip control! Her dam, Ranmena, was the best of three sisters I played in the 1930's." – Bob Mackay.

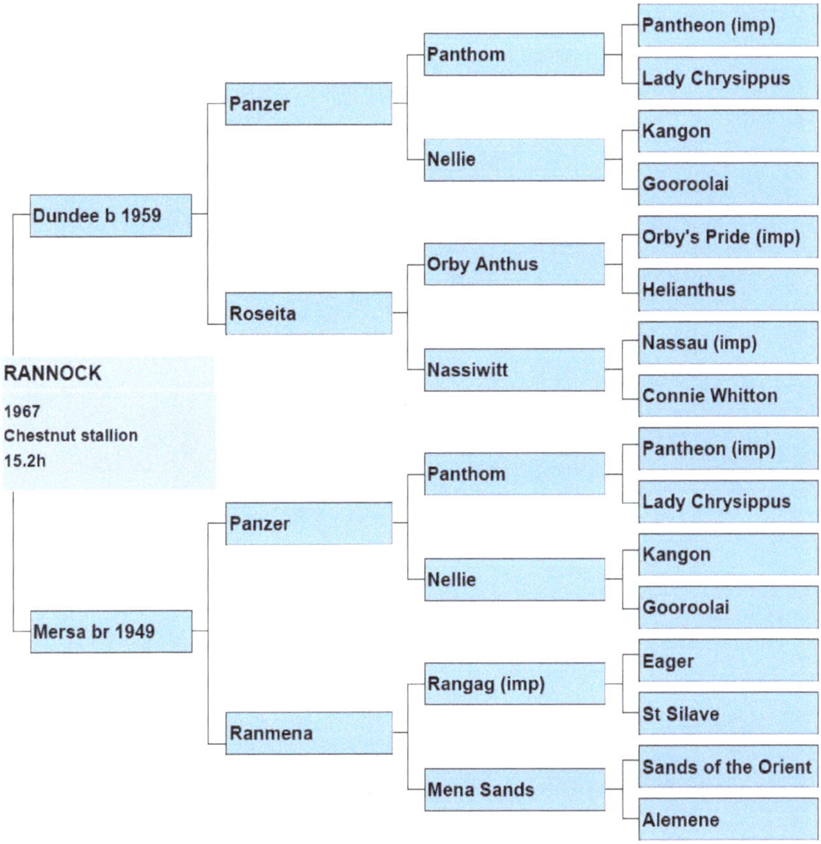

			Pantheon (imp)
		Panthom	Lady Chrysippus
	Panzer		Kangon
		Nellie	Gooroolai
Dundee b 1959			Orby's Pride (imp)
		Orby Anthus	Helianthus
	Roseita		Nassau (imp)
		Nassiwitt	Connie Whitton

RANNOCK
1967
Chestnut stallion
15.2h

			Pantheon (imp)
		Panthom	Lady Chrysippus
	Panzer		Kangon
		Nellie	Gooroolai
Mersa br 1949			Eager
		Rangag (imp)	St Silave
	Ranmena		Sands of the Orient
		Mena Sands	Alemene

Rannock, due to his inbreeding to the prominent foundation sire Panzer, was able to reproduce his concentrated genetics time and time again. His consistency, type and quality can be recognised in generations down the track.

Tinagroo Mersa, in 1973.

Tinagroo Mersa at 29 years of age.

Dundee when we saw him in 1973.

Kangon, son of Diffidence.

Ranmena

Dundee was purchased from Bob Mackay by the Munro family in 1962, and played A grade polo for a number of years until so many of his stock were playing that he was retired to stud. Progeny of this great horse formed the nucleus of all teams of polo ponies played by Angus and Hamish Munro. Some of the most noted were Swallow (twice Champion at Quirindi), Mandy, Sarich (played two chukkas in every international match by Hector Grotto for Argentina) Rommel and Sonny (a Sydney Royal Champion Pony and played in all International tests by Joe Barry for USA). Two full brothers to Sonny were used as sires on other Munro Properties.

Of Roseita, Dundee's dam, Mr Mackay said, "I played her first chukka for several years; a very fast 15.1h mare and top quality. Her dam was also a polo pony by Nassau (imp)." Roseita was by Orby Anthus, a 16h Thoroughbred which sired good polo ponies and drafters, such as Ken Mackay's Radar. *(An article on Orby Anthus appeared on page 29 of 1979 The Stockwhip annual.)* This makes Rannock a full Thoroughbred on bloodlines, though every bit a true Hunter Valley stock horse on breeding and type.

Having received only minimal amount of riding as a two-year-old, Rannock was not ridden again until rising 7 years. In May 1974, he was ridden for inspection by classifiers of the newly formed Australian Stock Horse Society at *Roskhill*. He was mistakenly recorded on his paperwork with the spelling 'Rannock.'

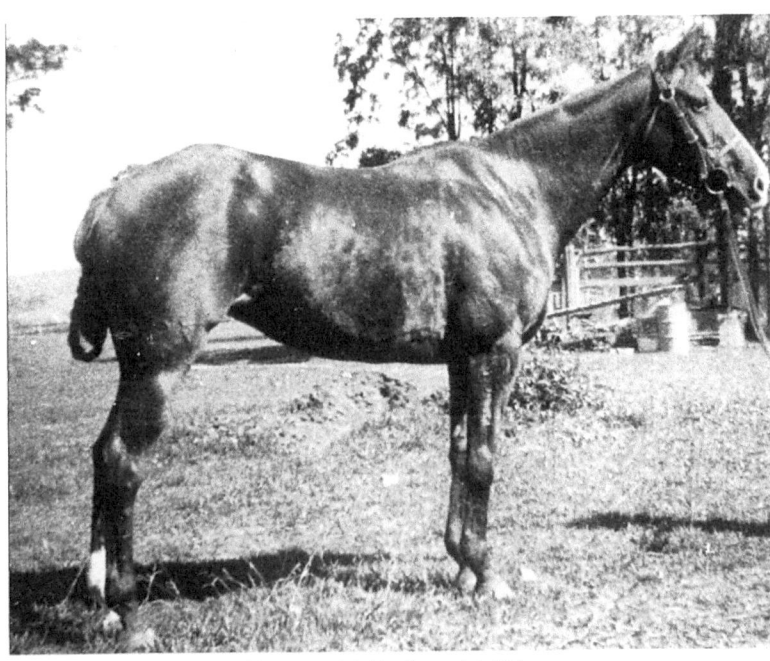

Roseita, 1949, ch m 15.1hh.

Orby Anthus (TB) (Orbys Pride x Helianthus) ch h 16h.

*Pantheon (TB), (Tracery x Scotch Rose) grandsire of Panzer, and sire of
Peter Pan, winner of 1932 and 1934 Melbourne Cups.*

At that time horses had to be inspected for suitability on a scale out of 100 points, for type, breeding and ability (or a performance record). Brenton Matthews who rode him, stated how impressed he was with the temperament of the horse and that of the progeny he had been breaking in for Mr McGregor, the oldest of which were rising 4 years old. "They were real naturals, you could just play them right from the start."

By a rare quirk of fate, Jeanette and Peter Gower (as Secretary of the Branch, and photographer, respectively) attended that classification day. Jeanette said "In spite of his paddock condition, and obvious lack of education, he was cool, relaxed and friendly. We instantly fell in love with the horse. He was in fact the most magnificent quality horse we had ever seen, true to type, and we couldn't believe it when we saw his classic breeding. Better still, that he was *inbred* to the mighty Panzer! The progeny were peas in a pod, with his same head and compact type. To me, Rannock was a 'once-in-a-million' horse.

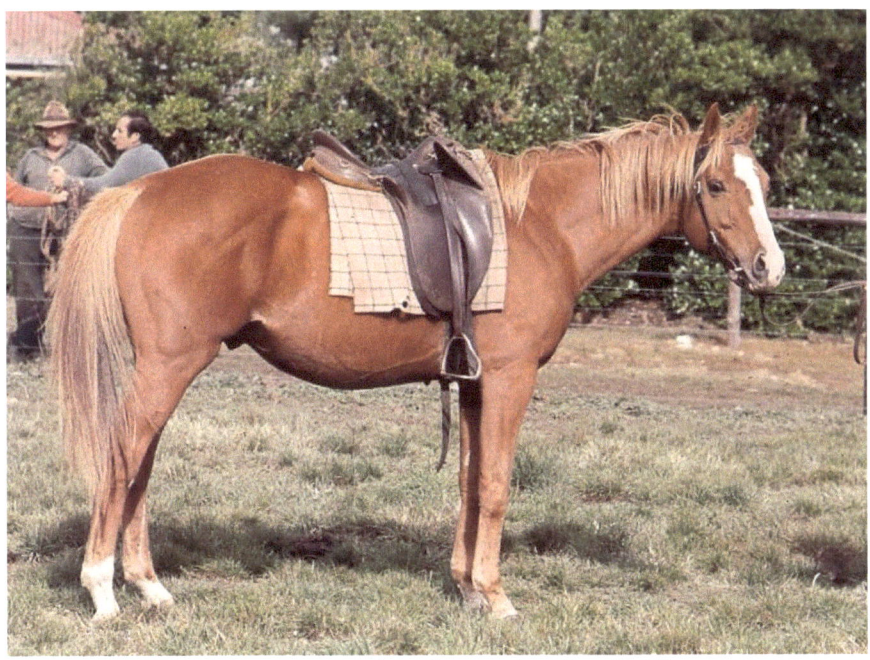

Rannock at an ASH classification day, "Roskhill" 1974.

Author's note: My knowledge of genetics told me that this was the horse to send a mare to, inbred horses having high capacity to reproduce their likeness; little did we think we might ever be able to purchase him! As Rannock was unavailable to outside mares, we did manage however, to convince Alan McGregor to take one of our mares. Rannock was not ridden again until purchased by us in September 1975, as an eight year old.

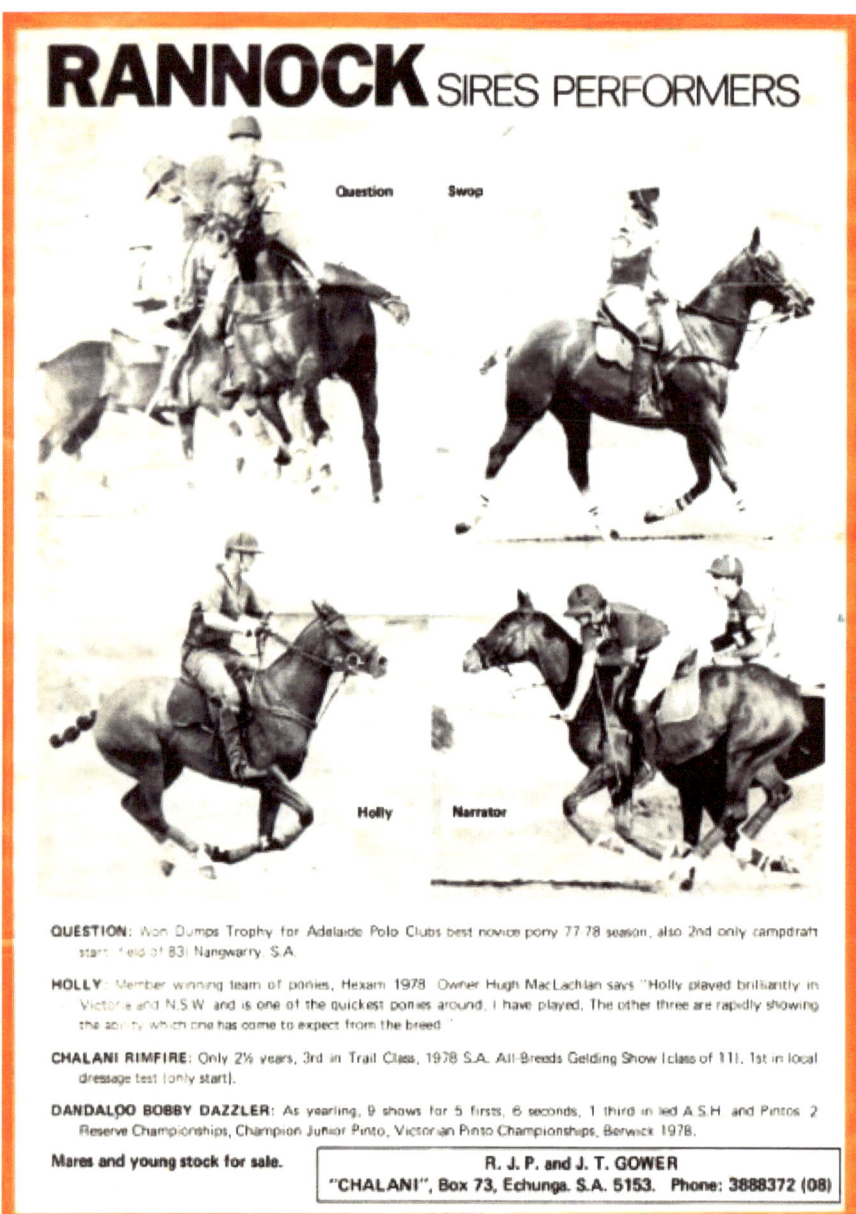

Early advertisement, Australian Stock Horse Magazine, July 78.

Chapter 3

Rannock

His life at Echunga

Rannock shortly after we purchased him in 1975.

One day, Peter received a call from Alan McGregor asking if we knew the best way to advertise Rannock. Without even discussing it, or asking a price, Peter said "look no further, we'll buy him!" It was done. Alan had bought another stallion, the Thoroughbred/reg ASH ROMANTIC GENTLEMAN, which later proved to be a good cross over the Rannock mares. However, when the first of Rannock's progeny hit the polo field, Alan realized he'd made a mistake and asked to buy him back, then sending mares on several occasions. John (Patto) Patterson, who started and played many of them in those early days, described them as "easy to play horses and very tough. No matter the question, they would rise to the occasion."

At that time, we only had our horses on agistment, so we made arrangements to keep him at the *Woodlands* Riding School of Peter's mother, Mrs Nancy Gower, at Echunga, SA. We set up a paddock where he could run with his mares.

Rannock at Echunga in 1975. We used this photo in most of his advertising.

I'd never struck a horse with the quality that still had the temperament of a kid's horse, and a stallion to boot! Not once in all those years of owning him did he put a foot wrong, being ridden or tied up amongst the school horses and children. Despite being blind in one eye, he showed a natural aptitude and boldness over jumps. He could be ridden bareback amongst his mares and I would sometimes lead horses off him. If you introduced him to something new, he just did it; there was never any fuss or scariness. I even did a bit of sidesaddle with him as he had the type of back that would sit a side-saddle well.

He was a beautiful looking horse with an outstanding head, long arched neck, roomy gullet, well defined wither, great elbow room, short cannons, with strong, square hocks. He had no feather, a fine silky mane, almost no forelock and always kept a smooth coat.

Although 15.2h, he felt like a 16h horse to ride, with a brilliant walk and long easy gallop. He had a smallish hoof, unusual in a thoroughbred, which may have contributed to his sure-foot-edness. He was never known to disunite at the canter and his progeny inherited this attribute. They were easy to sell, as they were kind, sure-footed, smooth down hills and consistently of the taller 'polo height' 15.1-15.3h, which fitted so well into the South Australian scene.

We would show him straight from the paddock, unshod, unrugged, only washing him the night before. Shown only in led classes in his first season, he was Champion or Reserve ASH or

This photo, taken by Keith Stevens, Editor of Hoofs and Horns, at a Light Horse Breeders Show, 1975 shortly before winning the Champion Open Stallion, under Maurice Wright. Maurice spoke on the microphone, stating in his opinion, this horse represented everything that a true to type Australian Stock Horse should be.

Open Stallion at all shows in which he competed in 1975-76, perhaps the two most prestigious awards being under judges Maurice Wright and June James. I remember him yawning in his classes, he was so quiet to show.

One time a well known competitor in the line-up next to us came very close with his fiery Arabian stallion so as to intimidate Rannock into misbehaving. Rannock stood rock solid, and his own horse swung around dangerously with an impressive roar. With that the man yelled out "keep your horse away from my stallion!" Rannock took the Championship. Another time I caught a loose mare, while holding Rannock in his Led class. Again, Rannock stood rock solid.

Peter Gower on Rannock at Willomurra circa 1976. Below, Jeanette in the hunt field.

In the next season, he won and placed at dressage, English and Western pleasure, trail and Western Riding, always giving a relaxed and comfortable ride. He went in everything a one-eyed stallion could compete in. As there were no stock horse type events at that time, he competed in big open western classes against imported horses, showing his temperament and versatility.

At one show I was getting changed inside the horse float, when I heard a conversation outside which went something like this:

> "That's a really nice horse there. Is it a stallion? (looks underneath). Gee, you'd never know, he is just standing there half asleep. I wonder what breed he is?"

> "I'd say he'd be Anglo-Arab. Look at his beautiful head and neck, the substance, his kind, big eye, and the width of his forehead."

> "I'd doubt that. Look at his strength, the muscles above his eyes and round jaw, his neat ears. See how he stands square? I'm guessing he is a first cross Quarter Horse."

Imagine their surprise when I appeared from the float, and told them he was full Thoroughbred by breeding, and a true to type Australian Stock Horse!

We enjoyed spending hours watching Rannock with his mares, snaking his neck to direct them where to go, like a cutting horse, or being 'dad' to the foals. There was never doubt as to who was in charge. It was a wonderful learning experience to observe natural stallion behaviour. Although Rannock had paddock-served all his life, we could hand serve by teasing at his gate, then taking the mare into his paddock, and holding her.

One particular mare had us baffled, because when she arrived, we'd been told that she had been running with a stallion for 5 years but never got in foal. As soon as we teased her, we realized the problem. She was unbelievably ticklish around the flanks. We threw a rug on her, and despite a few 'wriggly' moments, the service was done. She bled just a little. She was obviously still a maiden mare! Best of all, she went straight in foal.

Another time, a well known polo player sent us an old maiden mare. She was 28 years of age and we very much doubted our chances, but she was very special to him. She arrived as many old mares do, looking a bit scrawny, long coated and frail, but showed 'in season' the next day. We decided we wouldn't run her with the others and hand served her, whereupon she almost collapsed. We asked her owner to take her home. We thought it just wasn't fair on her. Lo and behold a few months later, he rang to say she had really 'bloomed.' She looked like a young mare again and had a belly. He thought she might be in foal.

Sure enough, she produced for him a 'special' filly, which played polo for some years.

Rannock had great elbow room, and defined muscling. He was compact, strong over the loins, and in the hocks, with short cannons.

Rannock at home with some of his mares.

Chapter 4

Rannock

Progeny start to shine

During the 1975-76 season, Rannock's oldest progeny began playing. **GLEN DEVON HOLLY** (1972), owned by Hugh MacLachlan proved an outstanding novice pony and went on to play brilliantly for many years in Victoria, and NSW, being one of the smartest ponies around, very quick on her feet. She was out of Rosalie (TB), by Emborough.

Holly with Hugh McLachlan, Adelaide Team Captain.

Others soon followed: **ROSKHILL QUESTION** (1972) played by John Kelly, was Adelaide Club's Champion Novice pony, 1978 and was second in an Open campdraft at Nangwarry, her only start, for Brenton Matthews.

Roskhill Question, with Johnny Patterson, 1978, later with John Kelly (Vic).

ROSKHILL SWOP (1972) played brilliantly for John Patterson and was a finalist at the SA Open Campdraft Championships, Tintinara 1980. John Patterson (now at Wondaby, Vic) played many of the Rannock progeny in those early years, describing them as horses that would "always rise to the occasion, no matter what was asked of them."

ROSKHILL NARRATOR (1973), played 1981 Easter International Polo Tournament under Aust Team Captain and coach Jim McGinley; others to make a name were ROSKHILL BRIQUET (1972), ACTION (1974) and BRITTLE (1975).

Roskhill Narrator, started by Johnny Patterson, then with Australian Team Captain Jim McGinley, and was part of his best team of four.

*Roskhill Briquet, Dumps Trophy winner, and used by
Alan Mcgregor's son Stirling for polo.*

Soon to follow were WOODCONE GENIVEVE (1978), who played from 1983-1990 for Nick Simpson, CHALANI GYPROCK and LITTLEWOOD MONTEGO, both stallions which played alongside one another for Andrew Gray. They were later to make their mark as sires. Their stories are to follow.

The Gowers donated a service to Rannock for the Champion Novice Polo Prize presented at each State Tournament, the first of which was won by the Reids of Kojunup WA and later won several times by Rannock progeny.

At the 1979 Australasian Gold Cup, Rannock progeny played in three State A teams.

Roskhill Question, Dumps trophy winner, 1978, 'Patto' riding.

Chapter 5

Rannock progeny

From the Gower's first crops

Rannock was often used as a lead horse, here with a son, Chalani Gunfire, (1976).

When the ASH Society formed in 1971, Peter called the inaugural SA branch meeting. This ensured the ASH would be recognised in our state. The committee organised many events, demonstrations and shows. The first classification day was held in 1972, with Bill Reid's stallion JERILDERIE MIDNIGHT (by Charble TB) the first horse to be classified.

Rannock progeny soon began to dominate the South Australian ASH performance scene. In 1980 he sired no less than *half* the winners of the 22 classes at the SA Central ASH Branch's Championship Show, including the Supreme Led Exhibit, three Champions, both Yearling Futurities and the Three Year Old Maturity. This chapter is a listing of some of the progeny with their major achievements:

CHALANI RIMFIRE (1975) ex Chalani Ricochet: Winner 2 years running Trail Class at the All Breeds gelding show (79-80), winner of the huge Expo 80 Hack Show, and an outstanding performer for some years.

Chalani Rimfire with owner Jane Cannon, Expo 80, and below.

CHALANI GARNET (1976) ex Chalani Anna: Winner of the first SA Reining Futurity 1980, and undefeated in open reining patterns over a two year period, before being sold for polocrosse.

Chalani Garnet, sliding stop with Neville Fennell aboard, 1980.

CHALANI WILDFIRE (1977) ex Chalani Ricochet

Chalani Wildfire (grey) ex Chalani Ricochet, Dumps Trophy winner 1984, Adelaide Polo, with Paul Angerson.

CHALANI SKELTER (1975) ex Paradis: Winner Expo 80 Trail Class, and High Point Snaffle Bit Horse for 1980, runner up to Garnet in Reining on numerous occasions, and defeated only once in a two-year career in Trail class. (Also p168.)

Chalani Skelter with Jeanette Gower, at the letterbox during the Expo 80 Trail Class which she won.

CHALANI ASPEN (1978) ex CHALANI CAT BALLOU: A grade polo pony for 5 years, Champion Led mare Adelaide Royal 1987, whilst heavy in foal. Always hunted during the winter for Whipper-in, Andrew Gray, who described her as a "very fast, go anywhere mare with an amazing constitution." At the age of 20 yrs, under the tutelage of stunt-master Bill Willoughby, she was used in the making of films for the SA Film Corporation. She was one of the favorites at Chalani.

Chalani Aspen, with Pat McGinley umpiring in SA during a Gold Cup and below, broodmare 1987 at Chalani.

DANDALOO BOBBY DAZZLER (1973) ex Gay Princess, bred by Rosemary Hill, Macclesfield, SA, and stood at stud at Trafalgar, Victoria for a number of years promoting the ASH in parades, carriage driving and demonstrations. He took out numerous Championships at Victorian pinto shows.

Dandaloo Bobby Dazzler with John Bechaz

Giving regular displays at the Swan Hill colonial village.

PEREGRINE (1977) ex Nangkita, bred by Robbie Douglas, frequently took out both open and heavyweight divisions in Endurance under Michael Heffernan. In 1986 at Mt Crawford SA, Peregrine recorded a State Heavyweight Record for 80ks which stood for many years.

LORD TYSON (1978) ex Saras. Tyson's dam was part Clydesdale, about 15h, but very heavy. Her first breeding to Rannock resulted in a stillborn foal, so she was re-bred, and sent to foal down at *Chalani*. This foal was enormous, and had to be forcefully pulled by Peter Gower.

He was bought by Barrie Stratton to be trained for dressage, then bought by Sharyn Edwards for competition purposes.

"After I bought him, I had extensive coaching from Barrie, and Barrie helped train him. Basically we learnt together as I had not competed at that level at that point. I also did some stock horse classes on him, in which he did very well. He was a very versatile horse. I had fun swimming on him in our dam. He was a gentle giant at around 16.3h.

"He was about 8yo when I bought him. I trained religiously four times a week with Barrie at *Monserrat*, Bridgewater SA, to get him to Medium and Advanced within 3 or 4 years, (back in the day when I had no other money commitments!) I stabled him there whilst training and brought him home later. Barrie has fond memories of Lord Tyson, as he enjoyed riding him also. This training was invaluable knowledge. It helped with me training Chalani Paper Note. (See p199).

"When I started competing in dressage on him, we went straight out and started at Medium and won his first ever dressage competition. He was very competitive in Medium and Advanced dressage, and we were selected for the State dressage squad. I sold him when I left for overseas for a few years, whereupon he became a schoolmaster in his new ownership."

Lord Tyson with Sharyn Edwards circa 1988.

Several Rannock progeny went on to become very good eventers, as despite not being the typical height, they were bold jumpers and had a lot of scope.

CHALANI RAPID FIRE (1982) ex Chalani Romantic Fire (a Romantic Gentleman mare). Following a tip-off, this horse was rescued from the doggers as a yearling, by the Bagshaw family. He was rarely defeated in Led ASH gelding classes and working events, including 1990 Adelaide Royal Working ASH winner, and was a Rannock Trophy winner. He also did dressage and eventing, all under junior rider, Ann Bagshaw. He was later sold to Sarah Chinner for eventing.

Reynella Horse Trials, Adelaide, Sara Chinner aboard. Photo: Julie Wilson.

CHALANI CATLOW (1983) ex Chalani Cat Ballou: Barry Sawyer's brilliant mare was Champion Working Melbourne Royal inaugural Alistair Irving Memorial 1988, and Barastoc Working and Led titles 89-91. Barry said "she is such a docile mare, I call her *Pussycat*."

Ken Robinson added "She was given to me as a broodmare. When I rode her one day to move some cattle I thought she was too good, so I got her fit and started to campdraft her. She has since won many Working Championships, and in 2001 she was placed in the Alistair Irving at Melbourne Royal. *See Australian Stock Horse Journal-March/April 2009 for a full article on Catlow.*

She came out of retirement as a broodmare and repeated her successes at the age of 24 and 25 years at Barastoc 2008, with brothers Stuart and Peter (11yo) Robinson winning the Working Mare class, in 2007 and 2008. Stuart is now a professional trainer of show horses and his mother said "Catlow was our first ASH. She started it all."

Catlow with Barry Sawyer

Catlow at 25 years, with 11 year old Peter Robinson.

CHALANI PAGEANT (1977) ex Bevlyn Casscade. "I was privileged to own Chalani Pageant for many years, winning many Paint classes. She was 7 when I bought her and almost 30 when I lost her." – Karen Bakker.

Not to be forgotten were the exceptional mounts Mrs Nancy Gower bred for her riding school, which gave children pleasure for many years. One of these, **REXSHEEM** (1981) ex Pesheem, went on to become a very successful competitor in ASH and EFA Dressage with owner Cathy Beer, retiring only in his twenties.

Three full siblings, ex Pesheem, bred by Mrs Nancy Gower and purchased by students. L-R Panseita, Rexsheem and Panrosie.

"Rexsheem was a sweet boy with an amazing elastic stride. He won many championships at Stock Horse shows in English classes. He inspired others to give ASHs a go at Dressage (competing Medium and Advanced) because of his amazing soft, beautiful, extended trot. He took me on many lovely forest and beach rides, and carried one of my attendants at my forest wedding, together with CHALANI WINSTON (by Chalani Mystic)" – Cathy Beer.

JULIE MAY (1978) ex CHALANI KISMET.

Kismet, an ex SA Police Mare was sold in foal to Rannock at the second Melbourne ASH Sale. She produced a filly called Julie May. Her then junior owner Donna McCall said "Julie May was 15.2h and very smart on her feet. I did everything with her in 1984-85, from Hacking to Novelties with success. In 1985, she got a couple of B grade showjumping wins and qualified for the NE Zone Pony Club State Championships in Melbourne, where our team came third. Then on to our first Pony Club A grade ODE, coming in first!

"Through the Spring show season, she was winning everything including a Reserve Champion Hack and Reserve Champion Led Mare at Albury. So we stepped up to ASH classes at Canberra Royal. To my surprise we went really well, defeating some of the name horses, like QUIDONG BRIGADIER, winning the High Point Ridden ASH and qualifying for Barastoc."

WIRREANDA CANDI (1980) ex Wirreanda Charisma. Mare bred by Grant Waterman. Placed in numerous ASH and local open Hacking and Working events in Mid North, South Australia, with Jo Cullen.

PASCALI (1977) ex Silver Seas. Mare bred by Robbie Douglas, Team Winner Aust Dressage Champs 1981, and hack winner, Alice Springs Show 1981, with numerous Hack and Dressage wins in the Northern Territory, 1981 to 1985.

CHALANI ORAN (1976) ex Tano Mundano, gelding sold at the first All-breeds sale, *Hazelmere Park*, 1980, to SA Team Captain Gary Gurney, who played polocrosse on him for years, which included a trip to the Northern Territory National Championships.

TIMPANI, a most exquisite foal, 1978, with the Panzer 'look'.

Chapter 6

Timpani

A most successful mare

When this lovely filly was born she stood out for her beautiful type and elegance, true to the Panzer mould. She went on to become the SA Central Branch's most successfully performed mare of the time, in both ASH events and multiple disciplines.

TIMPANI was bred in 1978 by Mrs Juliet Bleby of Nairne, who had sought the right sire for her highly performed mare, MISS TIFFANY.

Juliet says "Miss Tiffany was a little black Thoroughbred mare, my first 'good' horse and a wonderful all rounder. I bought her from her breaker, Robby Murray. She died at my place at the age of 31 years. I saw Rannock multiple times at the riding school *Woodlands* of Mrs Nancy Gower and I thought he was the most magnificent horse I'd ever seen. I had watched him numerous times under saddle and with his mares. So far as I was concerned, he ticked all the boxes.

"Timpani was the first Australian Stock Horse that I bred and she was an exquisite foal. She was a very intelligent horse with great character. She learnt to lunge by watching me lunge other horses. She really hated her neck rug and if it was off her for the day and somewhere she could reach it, she would take it and throw it over the neighbour's fence!

"She started her show career by winning the Foal Class at the SA Central Branch Feature Show. Next year she went back and won Supreme Led Exhibit as well as winning the Yearling Futurity. She followed this up by winning Champion Junior at the huge EXPO 80 Australian Stock Horse Show – (which saw competitors arrive from all over Australia, including that great horse RIVOLI RAY.)

"She was Champion Exhibit All Breeds multiple times at major open shows, and Supreme Champion ASH at Branch and State ASH Shows almost every time she competed, through to 1988.

"Timpani was broken in by Peter Gower. In 1983 she won the Three Year Old Maturity trained and ridden by Neville Fennell, and again, the Supreme Led Championship. In the same year she took out Champion Led ASH at Adelaide

Royal Show (still a Junior) and did so on no less than 3 occasions, namely 1983 (did not compete 84), 86 and 87 and Reserve Champion on two other occasions. As far as we know, she is the only mare to have achieved this honour, never being unplaced in her led classes at any of the Royal Adelaide shows at which she competed.

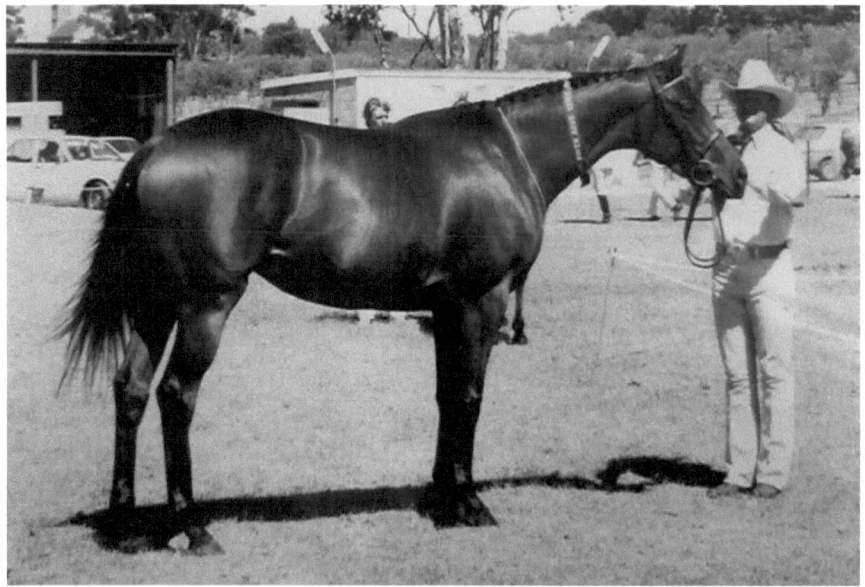

Timpani, winner of the 3yr old SA ASH Maturity, 1983.

"Timpani continued her wonderful show career under saddle , regularly winning Open Hack classes, working, challenge, time trial and reining competitions, often achieving High Point of the Show locally, in the SE of SA and Western Vic, always against good horses and strong fields. In 1987 she won SA Central Branch's highest honour, the year end high point Rannock Trophy."

Due to Ms Bleby's personal circumstances, Timpani spent much of her time leased to other people. First was with Valda Prideaux who won many hacking awards at major Agricultural shows, then Peter Hill, who campaigned her for most of her working wins, including Adelaide Royals. Amongst them, in her thirteenth year, she won the 1991 Adelaide Royal Time Trial.

Author's note: I travelled to Melbourne Royal to watch Timpani compete with Peter Hill one year. We slept on the grounds and I well remember being kept awake in the early hours by Timpani snoring in the box next to us. This was the same year Chalani Catlow (see p35) won the inaugural Alastair Irving Memorial Working Stock Horse with Barry Sawyer on board (1988).

From 92-94 she was with the Hartwells, during which time she was a family horse to three young girls. Caroline Brokus, continued with her after that.

Timpani with Neville Fennell, 1983 ASH Maturity, Strathalbyn, SA

"As well as ASH events, I did two full seasons of Pony Club at Mt Pleasant and Interschool gymkhanas as Captain of Walford's equestrian team. She won pentathlons and also played polocrosse. Timpani was a very clever mare, allowing me to win quite a few Junior Awards, including SA C Grade Polocrosse State Champs 1993 and National Zone Championships (junior) in 1994 - both times runner up in the final. It broke my heart when it was decided to retire her for breeding after the 1994 Adelaide Royal. She was my absolute favourite horse, a delight to handle, and such a pleasure to ride. I adored her" said Caroline.

Timpani went on to produce 3 beautiful foals and lived out her retirement at Ms Bleby's property in Nairne, SA. Due to the unfortunate flooding of records, much of Timpani's remarkable achievements are incomplete, though it is certain they were much more than I have managed to piece together for this story.

***

From Fiona Waddy – "As young people, we had Rannock in our lives [at *Woodlands*]. Such a wonderful lesson for us. I had no fear of him as a child and I had a deep respect for him as a stallion. He always had a calm and reliable attitude, and beautiful conformation, with a classic head. The Rannock progeny were all sound, virtuous and reliable, with a strong athleticism enabling them to perform in many disciplines.

"I had the good fortune to have two Rannock mares, Charm (p194) and Aspen (p31), to ride for a period of time. They were bold, free, straight moving, and willing to work. It was a pleasure to ride Charm as a three year old through the stubble of

Carolin Brokus with Timpani, approx 1994, as a 16 year old.

the wheat fields of Jamestown at a steady rated canter, and to ride Aspen through the Kuitpo Forest near Echunga.

"Rannock's virtues continued in his progeny to be passed down to the next generation by his daughters, such as Chalani Skelter, the dam of Chalani Pacesetter (p167). I purchased a mare, CHALANI MOONLIGHTER (Pacesetter x Chalani Cat Ballou), and it was undoubtedly the most reliable riding horse I had.

"I also remember Rannock's daughter Timpani with awe, because of her beauty. I remember Timpani's sister, TIMBAL, which was acquired by my close friend Tony Brooks, to work on McTaggarts stations, and for polocrosse. The mare was treasured by Tony."

Timbal, full sister to Timpani, playing for Penola, with Michael Devitt.

WILLOGLEN SYDNEY, (CHALANI CHAPPARAL x WILLOWGLEN MYSTIQUE) 2015 gelding grandson of Timpani, schooling with 11 year old Ashton Ide.

Kirsty Foster and WILLOWGLEN SYMPHONY (2017) gr m, granddaughter (CHALANI TEMPO x Willowglen Mystique, by CHALANI MYSTIC, see p193) owned by Juliet Bleby, placed equal 4th of 125 at the 2023 Ranch Sorting National Championships at Dubbo, NSW.

Chapter 7

Rannock's record

Rannock's record as a sire is unequalled by any other ASH stallion in South Australia. In 1986, the only year ASH Sire Ratings were published, he was listed in the top 20 sires of the country and was the only SA stallion on the list. He sired National and State polo ponies, Champion Led, Hacking, Dressage and Working Horses at all levels, including Adelaide, Canberra and Melbourne Royals, and a State Endurance Record Holder. At least ten on this list appear to have had a lasting influence on the breed. They are Rivoli Ray, Elliotts Creek Cadet, Quidong Brigadier, Cecil Bruce, Valentine Stud Master Luke, Jaipur, Rosebrook Abou, Daleys Rio, Rannock, and Scrumlo Victory.

Stock Horse Journal Sires Ratings 1986

Below is the list of sires who scored 10 or more points from the shows nominated for consideration.

Basically, the points were allocated on the basis of 3 for first, 2 for second and 1 for third placing in all led and ridden classes at the nominated shows that were restricted to registered Stock Horses.

You will note from the results that only 4 horses managed to get a rating of more than 20 and all the horses between 10 and 20 could be considered, under the variation of conditions which occurred, to be of more or less equal rating.

And then were others such as Trio Pal, Rannock, Scrumlo Victory and Jet Straw, who built up points with consistent placings by progeny at a number of shows.

Please feel free to contact the Journal with any questions or suggestions you may have about the Sires Ratings.

Ratings

Sire	Points	Sire	Points
Rivoli Ray	62	Cecil Henry	12
Elliotts Creek Cadet	45	Dyamberin Richard	12
Cardinal	26	Jaipur	12
Quidong Brigadier	21	Rosebrook Abou	12
Cecil Bruce	19	Trio Pal	12
Hillinview Black Panther	18	Daleys Rio	11
Sharif	15	Rannock	11
Quidong Tobruk	14	Wansev Leon	11
Valentine Master Luke	14	Convamore	10
Jet Straw II	13	Dalintober Kimberley	10
Raimondo	13	Scrumlo Victory	10

ASH JOURNAL JULY 87

In 1983, Rannock was sent to polo player Anthony Baillieu of Mt Elephant, Victoria, to be given better opportunity at stud through a wider range of breeders than in SA. Tragically he died from colitis X, before siring another foal, a result of a kick from a mare. He was just 16 years of age. We bought a block of land from the insurance payout and couldn't talk about it for months.

Rannock at 15 years on his hill paddock, overlooking the mares.

Saddened by this loss, the Friends of Rannock donated an end of year High Point Ridden Trophy, a Mary Pinsent bronze, to the Branch, called the *Rannock Trophy*. Several of Rannock's progeny have had their names on this Award. It had been the most prestigious achievement for South Australian Stock Horse competitors until the Branch's unfortunate closure in 2019.

The Rannock Trophy, a Mary Pinsent bronze 'Mountain Man'.

Later the ASH Society honoured three SA horses with inclusion on the Society's *Wall of Renown*. These were the mare, Chalani Cat Ballou, and Rannock, both owned by the Gowers, and the stallion, Jerilderie Midnight.

***

In October 2023, Rannock was inducted to the Society's *Hall of Fame*, for his contribution to the breed as a Foundation Sire. This is a wonderful honour to be given to a breeding horse by the Society.

Australian Stock Horse
SOCIETY

THE AUSTRALIAN STOCK HORSE SOCIETY LIMITED

HALL OF FAME

RANNOCK - HSH

Registration Number: 9973
Owner: Chalani Australian Stock Horses - 33704

FOUNDATION SIRE

Registered Australian Stock Horse Stallions, registered in the first ten years
(Registration Numbers 1 - 65,000), with over 1,000 Registered
Australian Stock Horse Descendants within 5 generations.

General Manager
THE AUSTRALIAN STOCK HORSE SOCIETY LIMITED

With the loss of Rannock, the Gowers decided to concentrate his blood in their stud, so as not to lose this valuable line. His characteristics have flowed down through the generations – the beautiful fronts, athletic ability, muscle definition, strong coupling, square stance, quality and heart. Notably, his blood has withstood the test of inbreeding with no deleterious effect.

Even now, 40 years on, Rannock is largely unknown outside a few circles. It is extremely important for versatility and diversity of the breeding pool and the direction of the breed, to ensure such proven lines are not lost to the Society. They are a valuable outcross to more fashionable strains which can easily saturate a breed and lead to genetic bottle-necking.

Rannock is the type of Hunter Valley horse that the founders of the breed imagined when they started the ASH Society. Every breeder dreams of having a successful stallion that leaves its mark on the breed. We were honoured to have owned such a horse. – Jeanette Gower.

Rannock's meaurements

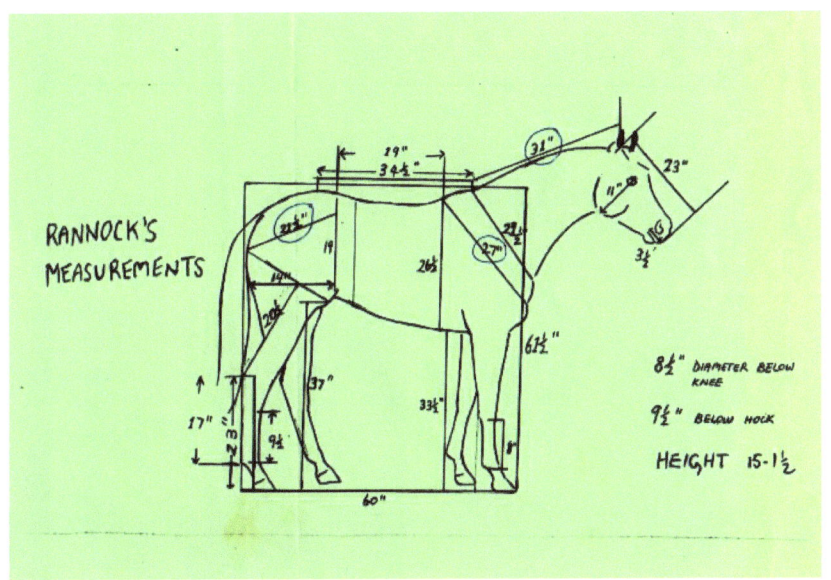

A couple of years after purchasing Rannock, an article appeared in the US Horseman magazine regarding the measurements of Secretariat, the great TB racehorse. His exact measurements had been taken for the commissioning of a sculpture and had been printed in that article.

The author concluded that the horse's greatness could be attributed to his faultless conformation. In particular, his length of rein was remarked upon as extraordinary. Secretariat was 16.1½ h high. The Gowers immediately decided to measure Rannock. Remarkably, though Rannock was an exact hand smaller, his length of rein was identical to that of Secretariat.

The following pages show samples of old advertisements which appeared in the Australian Stock Horse Magazine.

RANNOCK 9973

Sire: Dundee (by Panzer)
Dam: Mersa (by Panzer)

Photo taken straight from paddock.

R.J.P. & J.T. GOWER,
"CHALANI",
BOX 73, ECHUNGA, 5153.
Phone: 3888372 (08)

FEE: $250 L.F.G.

S.A. FEATURE SHOW 1979

Rannock sired:
1st and 2nd foal class
1st and 2nd yearling filly
2nd Yearling colt/gelding
THIRD YEARLING FUTURITY
    (filly section)
WINNER YEARLING FUTURITY
    (colt/gelding section)
Equal High Point
WINNER THREE YEAR OLD MATURITY
(oldest Rannock in Showring)

GOLD CUP POLO 1979

Rannock progeny played
in 3 state teams.
Also 2 used as Umpires
ponies.

QUALITY IS OUR STRENGTH AND YOUR PROTECTION

The Australian Stock
May 1979.

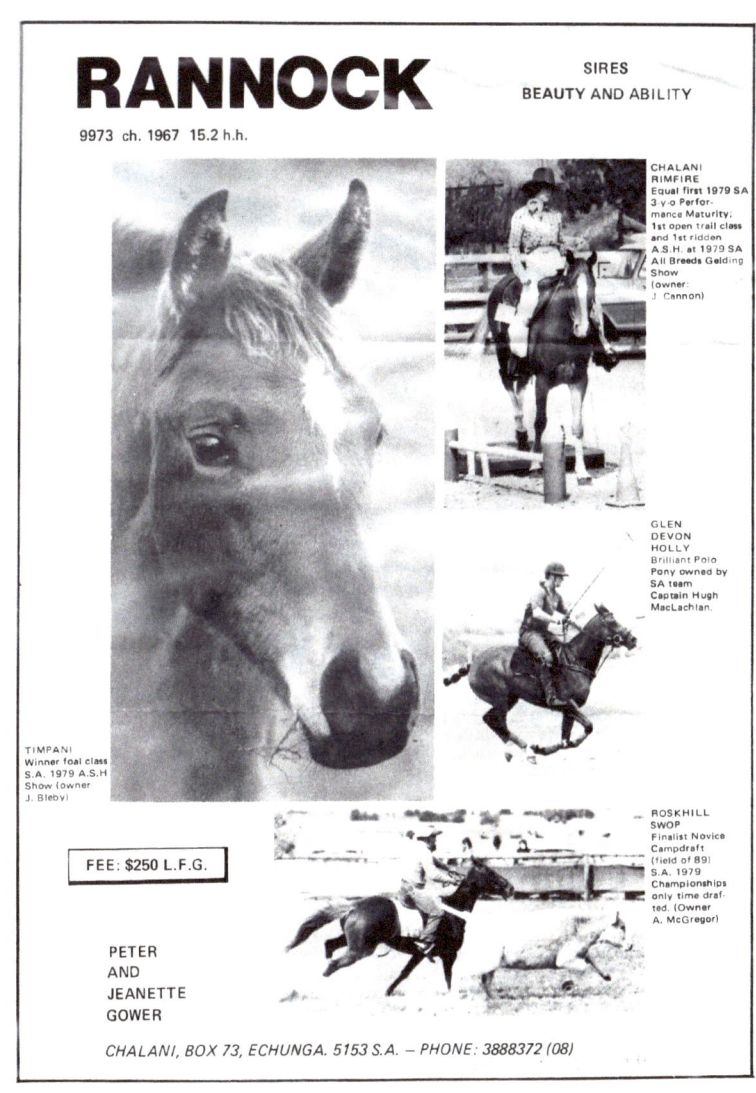

RANNOCK

SIRES
BEAUTY AND ABILITY

9973 ch. 1967 15.2 h.h.

CHALANI RIMFIRE
Equal first 1979 SA 3-y-o Performance Maturity; 1st open trail class and 1st ridden A.S.H. at 1979 SA All Breeds Gelding Show (owner: J. Cannon)

GLEN DEVON HOLLY
Brilliant Polo Pony owned by SA team Captain Hugh MacLachlan.

TIMPANI
Winner foal class S.A. 1979 A.S.H Show (owner J. Blebyl)

FEE: $250 L.F.G.

ROSKHILL SWOP
Finalist Novice Campdraft (field of 89) S.A. 1979 Championships only time drafted. (Owner A. McGregor)

PETER
AND
JEANETTE
GOWER

CHALANI, BOX 73, ECHUNGA. 5153 S.A. – PHONE: 3888372 (08)

The Australian Stock Horse, July 1979 – 35

This is a better photo of Holly than the one on p 23, but unfortunately I was unable to find it for this book.

RANNOCK

Sire - Dundee by Panzer.
Dam - Mersa by Panzer.

PROGENY WIN

11 of 22 events at
1980 S.A. Central Branch
A.S.H. Show.

1st Foal Class
1st Yearling filly.
1st Yearling colt or
  gelding.
1st 2yr old filly.
1st & 2nd Yearling
  filly **futurity**.
1st & 2nd Yearling colt or
  gelding **futurity**.
1st Gelding 3yrs & over,
  15 hands & over.
1st Hacking section 3yr
  old **maturity**.
1st & 2nd Working section
  3yr old **maturity**.
1st & 2nd High point
  3yr old **maturity**.
1st & 2nd Educated stock
  horse. (16 entries.)

Champion filly.
Champion colt or gelding
  under 3yrs.
Champion gelding 3yrs
  & over.
Supreme Champion A.S.H.
  of show.

FEE: $250-00 L.F.G.
($50 reduction if booked before
 1 August, 1980)

Progeny for sale.

R.J.P. & J.T. Gower,
"Chalani",
Box 73,
Echunga, S.A. 5153.
Phone (08) 388 8372

QUALITY IS OUR STRENGTH AND YOUR PROTECTION

This photo also appeared on the front cover of the book "The Great Book of Australian Horses" published by Rigby in 1976.

Part II - The Sire Sons

Four stallions carry on the line

"I remember Rannock at *Woodlands*. Such a wise, beautiful gentleman. This is why I have owned 4 of his line. His presence is (or was) in them all. My beauties, Rexsheem (by Rannock), Chalani Winston (by Chalani Mystic), Auster (ex Aurora) and Zenith (by Chalani Tempo)." – Cathy Beer

"I remember Rannock at *Woodlands*, I remember thinking how beautiful he was and such a lovely calm boy." – Shannon Roberts.

"I remember seeing Kim [then a toddler] wandering around between his legs one day at Nancy Gower's *Woodlands*. A friend of mine was meant to be watching her, but he got distracted and she wandered off. Gave me the shock of my life. He was just standing there calmly, as if it was quite normal. Such a beautiful, kind fellow."– Anita Killmier.

"I saw Rannock at the first campdrafting school held at *Hazelmere*. Peter rode him. He was a lovely, calm, athletic stallion and did well, despite having one eye. Tried his heart out." – Lorraine Micke.

Chapter 8

Chalani Gyprock

The small horse with the big heart

(Rannock x Chalani Anna), 1978, b h 14.3h.

Gyprock at 3 years.

Chalani Gyprock was bred by the Gowers out of a little brumby mare born on *Peak Hill*, Anna Creek Station. She came down to Adelaide as a wild, unhandled 3yo, to be used in a demonstration of the 'Jeffrey Method of Horse Breaking' by Maurice Wright. Her breeding was unable to be traced, though it was known to be a cross of TB/Arab/cold-blood. Maurice described her as the most tricky horse he had ever used in a demonstration, due to her sensitivity and determination.

CHALANI ANNA with Peter Gower, 1975.

Bought by Peter Gower a week later, she proved an outstanding mare, winning multiple championships led and under saddle. Barely 14.2h, Peter gave many stock horse demonstrations of her without a bridle, even doing so on Adelaide Oval for the opening of Expo 75. This is the first and only time, horses have been allowed on the Adelaide Oval. Anna's first foal by Rannock was Chalani Garnet, mentioned in chapter five. Anna produced an incredible four individual winners of the SA Yearling Futurity!

Gyprock was first shown as a yearling to win the 1981 Yearling Futurity at the ASH State Feature Show. He became a Clerk of the Course horse at the SA sprint racing at Willomurra from 1982 through 1983, then was bought by Andrew Gray for polo.

"He went straight to polo; he was just a natural. When schooling him and he's cruising around like a horse that knew what he was doing, I remember ringing to ask what education he'd had, and was told "nothing much, he's just a natural." He just schooled like a made horse from the first few circles he did and just went out there and played. He just did everything you asked of him first off." – Andrew Gray.

Shortly afterwards, Andrew broke his arm, so Jeanette borrowed Gyprock back for the show ring. "I only had 4 weeks to get him ready. He was polo-fit and very showy. I was called to work first in the 1984 Maturity workout, and the way the course was laid out, you could choose whichever direction to go through the gate. I knew I had the horse, so I chose the hardest way, backwards through the gate, swinging around to close in one motion, expecting the others to copy. Sure enough, they did and messed up! It was an easy win, and he won all sections. Gyprock won everything he was entered in, completing the season undefeated under saddle."

As a polo pony he proved outstanding even though he was barely 15h. An agile and tough horse, Andrew was known to have played him 3 chukkas, retiring absolutely sound! Andrew described him as a "dead quiet horse, a great competitor with fantastic heart for the game. He would never give up and would always play the next chukka as though he was fresh."

With limited opportunity, Gyprock had few registered progeny. Andrew's only mare was Gamma, (dam of LITTLEWOOD MONTEGO), to which Gyprock produced the top pony Anto. "I played Anto for about 15 years after umpiring with him a couple of years. Another full brother was Hughie, which I hunted. Breeding was too expensive and you'd end up with too many horses. I seemed to acquire good horses easily, so I never used either of the two stallions."

Having limited use as a sire, Andrew gave him to Philip Clarke, Wrattonbully (near the Victorian border), for a couple of years, then to well known endurance rider Jill Bourton at Mylor, for a few more. Brought out of retirement, at the age of 15 and with the battle-scars of a paddock stallion, Gyprock competed favourably against his much younger rivals. Rarely out of a place, he won from long-reining to hack, trail and working events, with many Championships to his credit in ASH classes.

With Jill, he came to endurance as an 'old' horse. His swansong at the age of 17 was a completion in the 1996 SA State Championships 160km.

Chalani Gyprock with Andrew Gray, circa 1983

CHALANI WILDSTAR (1988) ex Chalani Wildfire, b m 14.1h.

The first foal by Gyprock was Chalani Wildstar (1988), out of the polo mare Chalani Wildfire (by Rannock, p 29), making her a double cross of Rannock. Wildstar was only small, 14.1h, and Kim insisted on breaking her in. Even though she was only 9 years old at the time, eventually we relented. The two formed an undeniable bond.

Wildstar was only the second horse in the 21 year history of the SA Central Branch to have achieved the ASH Society's one thousand point Supreme All-round Award. (These awards are now discontinued.) The two achieved this award over a mere two and a half year period. Chalani Wildstar won the National ASH Director's Trophy for Youth High Point of the Year three times, in 1991, 1992, and 1993.

Mountain Pony Club ODE with Kim Gower, circa 1993.

Many times they won the High Point of the Day when Kim was the youngest rider competing. From three ODEs they were first twice and second once. Wildstar won the Open Novice Dressage at the 1994 ASH National Championships (Geelong). Kim was only 13 years old at the time. The combination won Led Championships, Hacking, Western and Pony Club, Educated and Open Working classes, including the Open Time Trial at the 1993 Adelaide Royal show. After this win, Kim and Wildstar graced the front page of the local paper "*The Courier*" (pictured overleaf).

Showstopper

YOUTH THE BIG WINNER

Youth was certainly the winner over experience in the stock horse time trial class at the Royal Show last week.

At 12 years old Kim Gower from Wistow was the youngest rider in the class and at five years old her horse Chalani Wildstar was the youngest horse.

But together they combined to overcome their nerves and win their first Royal Show ribbon.

Kim and Chalani Wildstar have been together since Kim broke the mare in three years ago.

"It is a dream come true to win at the Royal," Kim said.

The time trial class is a timed event where competitors show just how versatile, fleet footed and responsive their horses are.

Kim Gower of Wistow with her winning mare Chalani Wildstar

Veloce Orlando (1996) ch m 15.1h ex Wortanda Matilda

Bred by Jill Bourton, this good looking mare was purpose-bred for endurance, inheriting her sire's good looks, grit and determination. She started competition in October 2001 putting in a fairly solid season, with mainly Jill's daughter Layla on her back, gaining runner up Lightweight Points Horse, 1023km total in competition completed, including 160km Tom Quilty Gold Cup in 2002. She was described as a tough horse, with excellent recoveries and a very smooth 'no fuss' ride. She is the dam of Veloce Finale, (sire Centre Braveheart, Jill's Arabian stallion) which completed 811km total competition in 2017, in good times, his first season.

Veloce Orlando, pictured on the right

Finale at the 2019 Easter Marathon at Mil-Lel over 240Kms. The rider is 70year old Trish Smith from Tasmania competing in her 12th marathon for =2nd lightweight. Photo credit is Sallyann Duke.

This included his first 160km Championship gaining 8th place. In June 2018 Veloce Finale won the 160km State Championship at Mt Crawford on the long weekend in just over 12 hours.

He took line honours, 1sr SA Arabian bred & Best Conditioned Middleweight Horse. He did it with ease at only his second hundred miler. Says Jill, "I am very happy with his performance and have high hopes for his competitive career in the future. He is very much a tough 'waler' type."

Veloce Mamma Mia (1997**)** ex Wortanda Matilda, b m.

A full sister to Veloce Orlando, Mia was a big striding and strong type mare, fabulous to ride, easily completing her first three novice 80km rides in 2003 with very impressive heart rates of 40 / 44 / 44. Completed 25 x Rides, 2478km total in competition, including the 160km Tom Quilty Gold Cup in 2004 . A competitive, good solid consistent horse, she had 6 years competing in Australia prior to export to Dubai in 2007.

Veloce Mamma Mia, with Jill Bourton.

YOOROONA TINKA (1998) ex YOOROONA THERESA (by Master Herbert) ch m, with Scott Roberts. Shown here at Polo in the City, Adelaide 2012. Photo by Marscar.

There were a number of ponies by Gyprock bred by the Clarkes which went on to play both polo for Penola and polocrosse for Naracoorte Club, among them Granite, and the very smart 18-goal mare Impulse, played firstly by Phil Clarke, then Rob Archibald, before being sold for $40k to England around 2007. Both were still playing ten years later. Gyprock spent his final days with Phil Clarke and died in 1997.

"Impulse was a natural. She just turned it on. Lethal, a full brother with a "ton of guts", is still playing polocrosse on Yorke Peninsula. Locket, and her full sister Jingle, owned by President of the Naracoorte Club Justin Schultz, won best horse trophies in both polo and polocrosse. They were known for their massive heart. Their dam was Ella, a mare I bred by HILL. Locket's first game occurred because my main horse was out with injury, and she had only had practices. She won best A-grade horse at this, her first tournament, and went on to win many more. She retired at 15 years and is now producing foals for me.

"Gyprock's progeny were very smart and athletic but they could put it over you if you were too casual. They always performed well. I took them to polocrosse practices for training, then to polo for the season, and back to polocrosse when the season wound up. They were all beautiful looking and mostly around the 15.1h mark or bigger." – Phil Clarke

"It takes a good horse to play both polo and polocrosse. The games have different demands, and they must be calmer for polo. There is more pressure on them because of all the galloping, so they cannot run through the bridle. They must pull up and go in the opposite direction in an instant, away from the others, which is against their natural instincts.

I like to stick to proven lines, as I have found that many of the campdraft lines can't handle polocrosse or polo. Polo is a great test of a stallion. All the ones I have known that played could also be ridden by children." – Phil Clarke

Chapter 9

Witchetty

The forgotten sire

(Rannock x Glen Devon Candy), 1979, Ch h 15.2h.

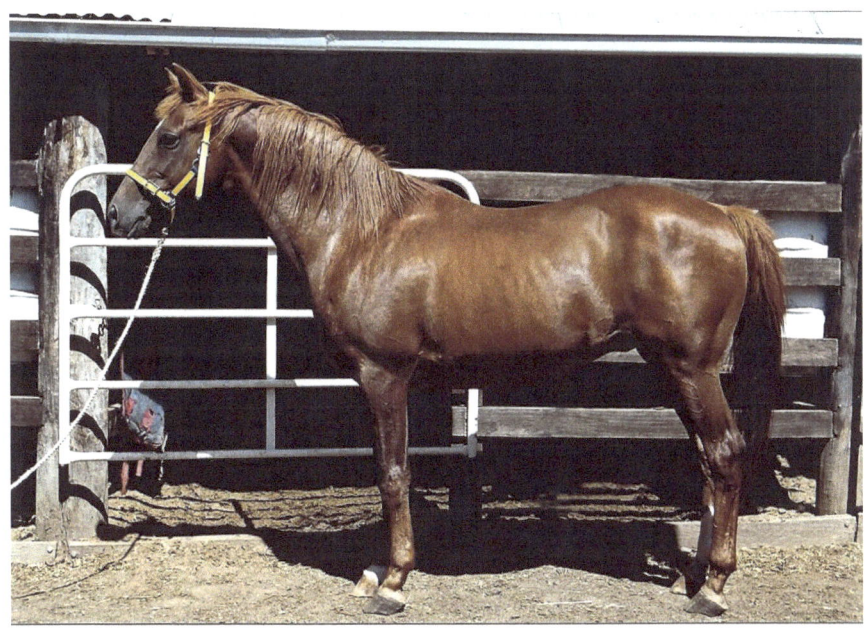

Witchetty, photo taken at about 19 years of age at Hampshire.

WITCHETTY had a remarkable career as a sire of top polocrosse horses. This largely forgotten horse was bred by polo player Hugh MacLachlan on his *Glen Devon* Mt Pleasant, South Australian property. The continuing survival of the Rannock line goes hand in hand with the foresight of Mr MacLachlan in acquiring the very best polo lines and breeding the best to the best.

Mr MacLachlan played polo for 25 years from 1965 until 1990, holding a 5-goal handicap for some 7 years for South Australia. The highlight was playing 'back' with Sinclair Hill for the Australian Emus in 1972, beating New Zealand two tests to one in New Zealand and winning the Gold Cup.

In 1978, Hugh sent 8 of his best mares to Rannock for 6 live foals, all of which were foal recorded ASH as 'no name' but included the very good ponies Belar and Gidyea. One of these mares was GLEN DEVON CANDY which produced a handsome chestnut colt, later known as Witchetty. Because he was unnamed with the ASH Society until he was 19 years of age, little was known publicly about him.

Author's note: Candy was a Thoroughbred mare, sold as being by Night's Romance x Mary Chieftain. There are no horses of these names in the ASB / NZ Stud Books. I suspect the names were incomplete or incorrect spelling. Maybe the dam was by Merry Chieftain? I tried many configurations to no avail.

Hugh says "Candy was a very good polo pony and very agile. I played her in New Zealand and I liked her so much I bought her. Her sire was a highly regarded Irish TB in NZ by Royal Charger. She was one of my best broodmares, at least until Kintra came along much later. Witchetty was Candy's first foal, following which she produced nine foals, including Money Penny, Fudge and Bullseye. She bred very clever horses."

Mr MacLachlan then went on to buy TERLINGS GOLD FINGER, so Witchetty was no longer required. As was his custom, Hugh would send well bred horses to top up the breeding programmes of other MacLachlan properties in the Kimberley, North Queensland and the Hunter Valley.

"Witchetty was bred and owned by me for his entire life. I used him at *Gunbar*, north of Hay, *Hampshire*, Merriwa, and *Narrangullen*, Yass, (NSW) in that order. In between in 1992 and 1993, I used him sparingly at *Glen Devon* (SA) where he sired two notable polo ponies, Meteor (out of a marvelous mare called Telstar) and Pinde (out of another wonderful mare called Tekki which goes back to Emborough).

"Whenever I went to *Hampshire*, which is very steep country in the Liverpool Range, I rode Witchetty myself. He was a true gentleman with fluid drive. He always knew when to produce extra effort without needing to be invited to do so."

Witchetty was sent to Hampshire, in February 1983, along with 2 geldings and a filly, where he resided as a station sire until he was 19 years of age. The only mention in the station diary is of him "having shoes after being worked for a few weeks" in July 1983.

Hampshire Station was owned by the MacLachlan family, trading as BH MacLachlan Pty Ltd. When 'BH' died, ownership of Hampshire was taken over by Mr MacLachlan's sister, Mrs Susan Morgan, who still owns the property today. John Halsted, station manager from 1998, got a call in 2002, to send

Witchetty down to *Narrangullen* owned by the Reid family. (George Reid is Hugh MacLachlan's nephew).

John Halsted said "That was the last we heard of the horse. I knew him well. All the station horses were by him. Most of his progeny never left Hampshire and were only used as station horses, so never got a chance to show what they could do."

"We have used his daughters to continue breeding horses for Hampshire as all stockwork here is done on horseback. Hampshire is 24,000 acres, running 14,000 Merino sheep and 2000 cattle on very rough terrain. Most of these daughters are from Terlings Gold Finger mares, which were sent here by Mr MacLachlan after playing polo. This puts Panzer in their offspring's pedigrees 4-5 times. The old horse was a true gentleman and his good manners and ability still live on here in the progeny.

"We have used five of his daughters to play Polocrosse and they have performed very well. One mare represented NSW at National level in Polocrosse.

"A son of a Witchetty mare was the Champion horse at Muswellbrook carnival (2017) and one of his daughters Raindrops was recently retired from producing foals at 25 years. – John Halsted.

Mrs Georgina Reid, of Narrangullen remembers Witchetty well. "He was about 15.2h and the quietest horse on the place. I always rode him myself, except when Hugh came along. He left masses of foals, which were mostly out of DARTH VADER (by ABBEY), mares that my father-in-law, the late Sandy Reid had accumulated."

Darth Vader was well known locally as a sire of good polo and campdraft horses. He carried the same female line of McNAMARA ACROBAT, REFUND, and DIGNITY. Later he was exported with a few mares to a property in Vanuatu, as Sandy was setting up cattle interests there.

A couple of his sons have produced offspring, such as the grey NARRAN-GULLEN PHAROAH who has established a strong branch of the family, including a number for Bill Peadon's *Bibbenluke* Stud, the *Hannaford* stud, Ben Salmon's *Fernloff* prefix, and for the Brewer family.

Sandy Reid also stood CAIRO (by Panzer), so most of the Darth Vader mares were out of mares by Cairo. The best mare of this cross was Kareeba, of Shane Piper's, and Shane's best polocrosse ponies were out of her by Witchetty. Darth Vader also sired RIVERDALE INVADER (46 reg progeny including RIVERDALE RECRUIT) and CAREYS WEE JASPER which bred some useful horses out of SIENNA, a Witchetty daughter from NARRANGULLEN MECCA by Cairo.

"Witchetty crossed really well over those mares imparting calmness, athletic ability and quality. As we transitioned to motorbikes, most of the progeny were bought by polocrosse players, so that was when he was named and adult registered with the Society. He looked fabulous for his age. He sired his last foal at age 31 years and died a few months later at 32 years. He was such a fantastic horse; we really enjoyed being his keepers."

Cairo

(Panzer x Mena) 1957 b h 15.1h

Cairo was a bay stallion bred by Bob Mackay who bred and owned Panzer. Not a lot is known about the horse's history and no photo was available for this story. However, he consistently appears in pedigrees of top horses as a broodmare sire and would have to be regarded as a most underrated sire. He is a full brother to another sire, Berrico Matruh (1962).

Interestingly, Cairo is out of Mena by Richard. Mena and Mersa (dam of Rannock) were half-sisters, both out of Ranmena. Mr Mackay told the author in 1973 that he really valued Richard for the Carbine influence so close, being by his last son Cavalry. He believed you had to have the speed and stamina close up. Richard sired some of their best ponies and camp horses. His potential was never fully realized as a sire, as he was killed in a fence in the Mackay's absence during WWII. A full article on Richard appeared in *The Stockwhip – ASHS Eastern Branch annual – 1976 p7.*

In a *Terlings* station book entry, it states "Cairo was lent to Sinclair Hill as a two-year-old by Bob Mackay." He was broken in and used as a paddock stallion until 1965. Mr Hill described him in 2018 as "an unremarkable yellow bay, so I didn't use him a lot, though he bred some good horses. I just wanted his genes, that Panzer blood."

John Allison, who worked at *Terlings* and *Boonaldoon,* broke in a lot of their horses. He recalls: "At that time John Mackay was a jackaroo at Terlings, and when John left Terlings to go and manage Boonaldoon, owned by the Munro Family, John took Cairo with him. Cairo had a twisted leg, but was a good horse, bloody good to ride. It was because of this, he was moved around a lot, and because of his breed. Everyone wanted the Panzer blood."

In 1972, Cairo was transferred to *Narrangullen* for the Reids who registered him, then he returned to Boonaldoon (1975 to 1977) and was later sold to I.T. Reid in Western Australia.

Cairo sired the champion mare TERLINGS JESSICA, (Polo Hall of fame and granddaughter of that great mare TERLINGS JEWESS which Sinclair Hill rated an outstanding mare, second only to that other all-time great mare of Sinclair's, TERLINGS MARTINI.) Jessica was inducted into the Aust Polo Association's *Hall of Fame* in 2013. She always played in a snaffle and gave her all. She would frequently play 2 ½ chukkas.

RICHARD

BAY HORSE · Foaled 29-10-30

(Ref. A.S.B. Vol. xvii   Page 756

RICHARD was broken in by me in 1933 and ridden about doing stock work for about two months, then sent to the late Jim McCurley then a trainer at the old Moorfield racetrack. He showed great promise, given one start and sent home for a spell and time to fill out. After his spell I rode him about again, and he was so promising as a polo pony, that I took him to Cobbity in 1935 and played him his first chukka the first day of the Polo Carnival there. The ground in those days was very rough, and he unfortunately broke his off side front pastern right at the end of the game. There were virtually no vets about then, and his leg was put in plaster on the spot by Dr. Crookston of Camden, and conveyed to Mr. Curtis Skene's home Kilbride at Campbelltown, where he was slung in a crush for three months, then brought home.

Richard sired some of our best polo ponies and camp horses, prior to World War 11, among them Leeward 11 a brilliant mare at polo and campdrafting, Mena who R.T. Mackay probably considered to be his best mare at anything, Ellen, brilliant polo pony and many others, including C.W.Hooke's Peggy, a brilliant horse also.

When R.T. Mackay and myself left for the War, we sold most of our young unbroken horses including about 20 sired by Richard, but unfortunately lost their breed forever, as Richard died in a fence in our absence about 1942.

One of the greatest mares I have owned WESTWARD HO — from Leeward 11 by HIGH CASTE, is still breeding here at the age of 22 years. Her daughter by SUNNY HOUR, Nancy Lee 11, is a brilliant polo pony, having won many trophies playing. WESTWARD HO, was taken to the Royal Show in 1960, and ridden by my wife, won the Owner's Equipment, Open Equipment, and is the only mare to date to win the Pope Cup. She was shaping as a brilliant Camp Horse, having been placed in her first three starts. She has a grey colt foal at foot by RAPID HOUR at the moment and should be one to watch.

J.K. Mackay

Sire - CAVALARY	by CARBINE	Sire MUSKET
		Dam MERSEY
Dam - PIASROOT	by PIASTRE	Sire POSITANO
Dam was Arroroot [Imp]		Dam CHAND BEE BEE

Page 7

Cairo also sired TERLINGS SILVERTIP (dam of Terlings Gold Finger and TERLINGS TREMBLE) and CINCINATTI AZIZA, dam of the mare Blue. Blue, the dam of Ellerston Cavalier, become famous throughout the polo world when played by 10 goaler Horacio Heguy. She was then purchased by *Ellerston* and played by Kerry Packer for many years. She produced many top horses including Sheltie, Heeler, Corgi, Coyote, Irish and Husky.)

Cincinatti Aziza was a good mare for polocrosse player John Thrower, producing the sire THROWERS STUD WIZARD OF OZ and the mare WITCH OF OZ.

Kerry Packer on Blue

Cairo did leave the sire TERLINGS MUSKET (1965), from the Thorough-bred mare Santa Lucia (Friars Fancy x Lady Lucia). Though his breeding is not recorded on the ASH online studbook, this information was provided to me from the Hill family records. Musket was in turn the broodmare sire of GLENUGIE GUNDY (by LITTLEWOOD MONTEGO), which sired BYDAND IGUACA.

Terlings Gold Finger

Should have been recorded in the ASH studbook as Terlings Goldfinger
(Terlings Mountbatten x Terlings Silvertip) 2004 ch h 15.2h.

Terlings Gold Finger at Glen Devon

Hugh MacLachlan regarded Terlings Gold Finger as one of his best polo ponies. "He was 15.2h, very much a Thoroughbred type and stood over a lot of ground. Hugh called him 'the complete package' – a top pony, very quiet and a top sire.

"I bought him because I wanted the Panzer blood, and he carried two crosses. I had previously tried to purchase the Panzer colt Tinagroo Rommel from Bob Mackay and offered him $7000 back around 1977, but approximately 4 weeks later I received a letter saying he couldn't sell him.

"So I was thrilled when I was able to buy Goldfinger. He won a lot of champion pony prizes, usually playing 2 chukkas, later alongside his own progeny. He played till he was 15yrs old. When I retired from polo, I sent some progeny to *Retreat* Station on the Barcoo River, others to *Hampshire*.

"I kept some very old Gold Finger mares, one of whom I rode myself, namely Kiss who was foaled in 1998. Spangle, foaled in 1994 was with my daughter,

Islay, and Saffron, foaled in 1991, was with my daughter, Brooke.

"I kept the bay 15.1h stallion Glen Devon Kelso, out of my best mare Kintra (Romantic Gentleman (TB) ex Glen Devon Faith). Romantic Gentleman was by Romantic and Faith by GLEN DEVON BELLVUE STAR by Hawa. Faith was also the dam of WREN, by Rannock (See p176). Both Romantic and Hawa stood at Lindsay Park, SA. Glen Devon Bellvue Star was a great sire for me in those early years, siring some very fast horses. Kelso played very well and has a kid's horse temperament."

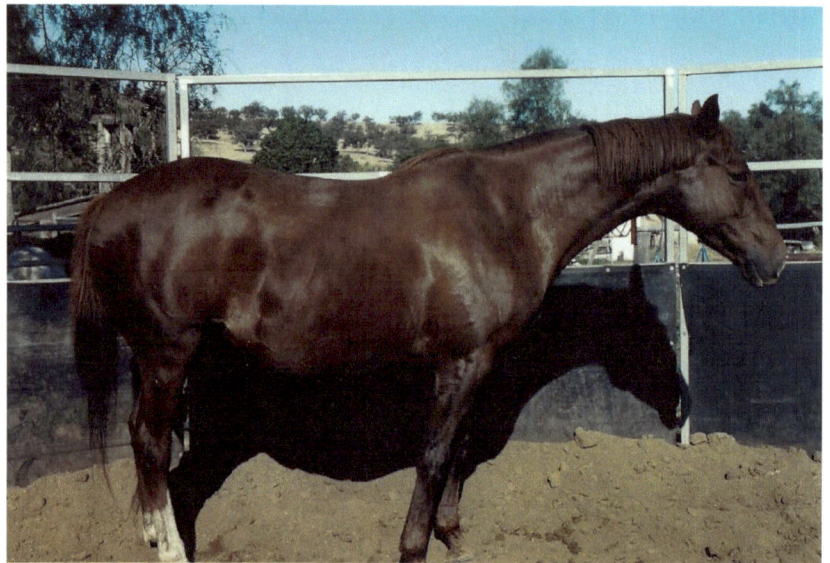

Lady Jayne 04, ex Rosa 02 by Terlings Gold Finger, typical of the Witch-etty-Terlings Gold Finger cross station mares bred on Hampshire. This puts "Panzer" in her pedigree about 5 times.

Andrew Gray has a Terlings Gold Finger mare Contessa. Says Andrew "She was so easy to play, a kid's pony, and was my best mare. She is now a brood-mare."

Gold Finger left the sire WONDABY SHARKA, a 1991 black stallion bred by John (Patto) Patterson of Wondaby, Victoria. John rode/played him and stood him at stud before eventually selling him in 2003 to Joe Curran in NSW and thereafter he was known as 'Patto'. Bred over TB mares, he produced some excellent polo ponies. John still has a stallion son of Sharka, and two grandsons out of NZ thoroughbred mares.

Kelso, shown here with Rosie Ross doing endurance.

Kelso's only registered progeny is MYARRA LEO who has had a successful showing career in working events. He was Reserve Champion Novice Hack, ASH Nationals 2012 and has been a great kid's horse for Dave and Rachael Neale, of South Australia.

Myarra Leo with Rachael Neale

Rugged high country of the Liverpool Range, NSW.

Chapter 10

Witchetty Progeny

"Until 2020, we were still using 4 Witchetty mares so the bloodline is very strong through our horses. The stallion we have been using for the past 20 years is SIMMARON who is by STAR BLACK MINSTRIL. He has bred great horses for us, not only from Witchetty mares but we are now also retaining daughters of Simmaron. All 3 of our children play polocrosse, Sam, Grace, and Jack.

Raindrops ex Rainbow, b m.

Raindrops with Sam Halsted circa 2005

"Raindrops was played by our eldest son Sam. This photo was taken when he was representing Hunter Valley zone at the ASH Nationals in about 2005. She was used for station work by staff till she was five or six. I took her to the Merriwa campdraft just after we arrived. It was the first time she had ever been off the place and ran a fifth in the maiden from 110 starters. She has never had to do station work since. This mare played good polocrosse, was very cowy, and was one of our best brood mares. We have used several Raindrops foals and we still have 5 of them.

Halsteds Black Rain (Simmaron x Raindrops) – Matt Devereaux (NT).

Meg, ex Lady Bosca (TB)

"Meg is by Witchetty from a straight blood mare, Lady Bosca, we played years ago. She has bred some very good horses for us, including HALSTEDS MANOLITO, by Simmaron. Grace played him in the NSW senior women's team at the NSW

Halsteds Marilyn (Simmaron x Raindrops) - Josie Wilson riding.

Nationals 2016. Tom Trisley rides Manolito mostly and has won a lot of player awards on him. Manalito is a lovely gentle giant, an absolute pleasure to have around.

Manalito played by Tom Trisley, at Warwick.

Manalito

Jacky ex Dolly, b m

"Jacky is by Witchetty from Dolly (a station mare bred in SA). Like Raindrops, Jacky spent her early years doing station work until we arrived and used her for the kids, polocrosse, and local shows. She also didn't have to do any station work after that.

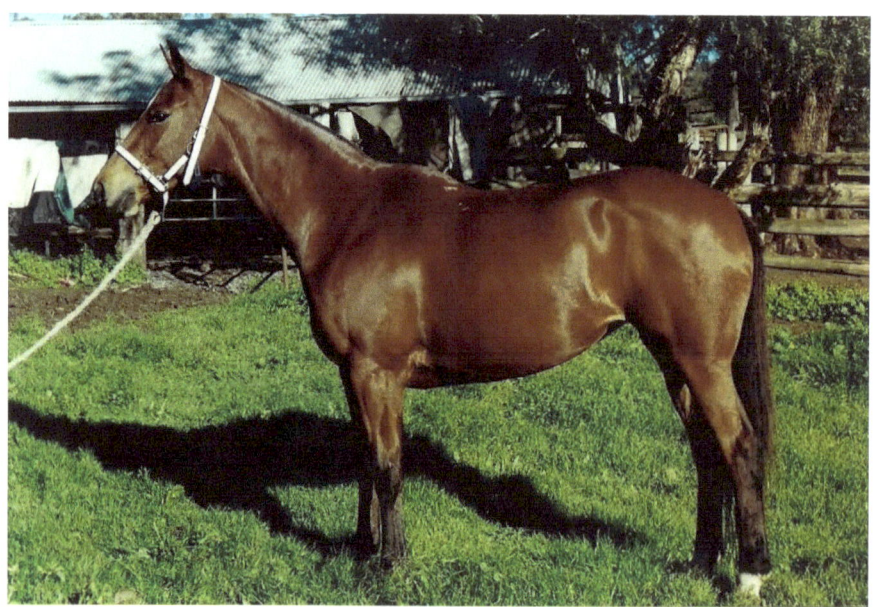

Jacky

Jemima, ex Rosa 02 Ch m

"Jemima is the last by Witchetty born at Hampshire, foaled 2001. She was played by our second son Jack for a number of years. Jack played her at the 2012 Australian National Polocrosse Championships at Warwick in Queensland. Their team won their division which was the Under 21's, with Jack awarded best Number 2. She is one of three full sisters, Jemima, Monica, and Blondy.

Monica and Blondy

"I played Monica for a season. She was the easiest horse I think I have ever played. We have some nice horses from her by Simmaron. Blondy was an aged mare when we arrived so was never used for anything other than station work. She bred 5 very nice foals. One daughter is now a brood mare here after playing good polocrosse for 10 years.

Frances (Witchetty x Bonny) br m

"Frances was bred at *Gunbar* and about 8 or 9 when we arrived at *Hampshire*. She was by Witchetty from Bonny. We went to a polocrosse carnival and took her for Sam to play as his horse was injured. She had never been off the place and won Champion Junior's Horse at that carnival. She is the dam of HALSTEDS FAITH, owned by the Leggetts of WA" – John Halsted.

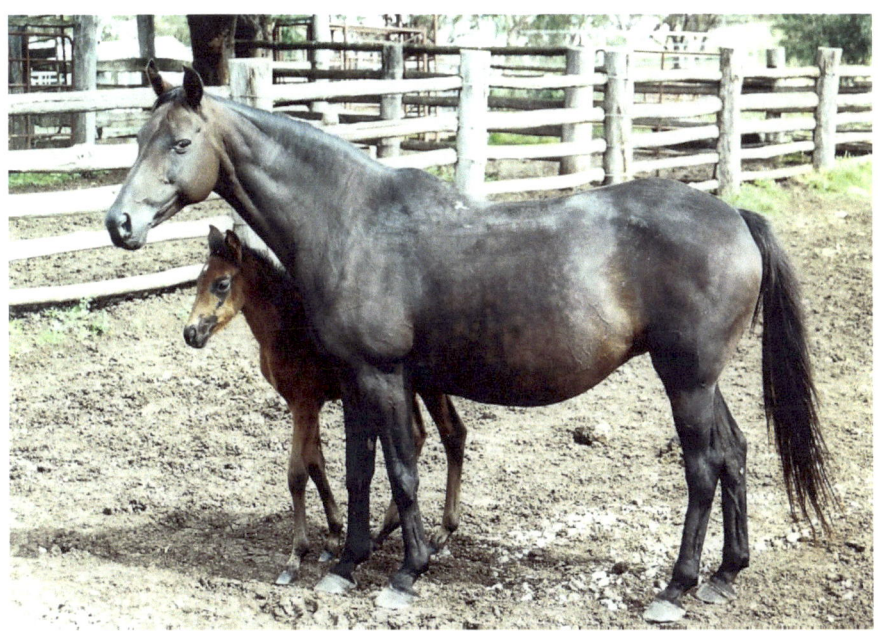

Frances

Jack Halstead on Monica, mid 2000s.

Jack and Jemima.

Blondy

Throughout these pages, when looking at the pedigrees of the best perfoming horses, it is evident how much the families valued the use of Thoroughbred blood. Thoroughbred blood is to the fore in any good horse. Even more so in Australian Stock Horses where speed and stamina combined is required. We *must* keep infusing Thoroughbred into the ASH if we are not to lose the type of horses proven to be 'the breed for every need'.

It is no excuse to state that Thoroughbreds aren't 'like they used to be.' That is a cop-out! Great Thoroughbreds are still to be found as breeding stock, especially in Australia, where the Off-The-Track system of re-education is well accepted, proving them in multiple disciplines. The ideal ASH in the breed standard is a horse between 15h-15.2h. Without some level of Thoroughbred blood, many lines become way too small and quality is lost.

Author's note: I am indebted to John Halsted, Hugh MacLachlan, and the Hill Family for their dedication to the record-keeping of their horses, and assistance with this section of the book. Even though I had recorded as much information of the Rannock descendants as I could, this entire line was unknown to me, since Witchetty was only foal recorded as "unnamed" in the ASH studbook until he was adult registered as a 19 year old. To find this line, even though well known in local circles, was exciting to me. I wanted to bring the line back to South Australia and in 2017, I was thrilled to be offered the mare Halsteds Gidget by John Halsted.

HALSTEDS GIDGET   (Simmaron x Lady Jayne) 2001 ch m 16h.

Purchased as a 16 year old with filly foal at foot by PEPPINS YOUNG IVORY and in foal to him again, it was a dream come true to bring the line back to South Australia, for *Chalani*.

John said "Gidget was bomb-proof from the day she was broken in. She did station work up until she had her first foal and was always the 'go to' horse for inexperienced riders we had working here. She was 100% bomb proof. She was my main mustering horse for 10 years and never missed a day off sick. You can carry a sheep on her and do anything you want. She has great 'stock sense'. She even watches lambs."

In 2020, after seven years off as a broodmare, Gidget was ridden at *Chalani* for the first time. Taken straight from the paddock she never missed a beat. She has also been used for a season in the *Leading Change Experiences* adult and child workshops of Jess Keenan. Her foals for us are SECRET, SURPRISE, COVERT AFFAIRS, MYSTERY and INTRIGUE, and at the time of writing, she is currently in foal again to CHALANI SUNSTREAM.

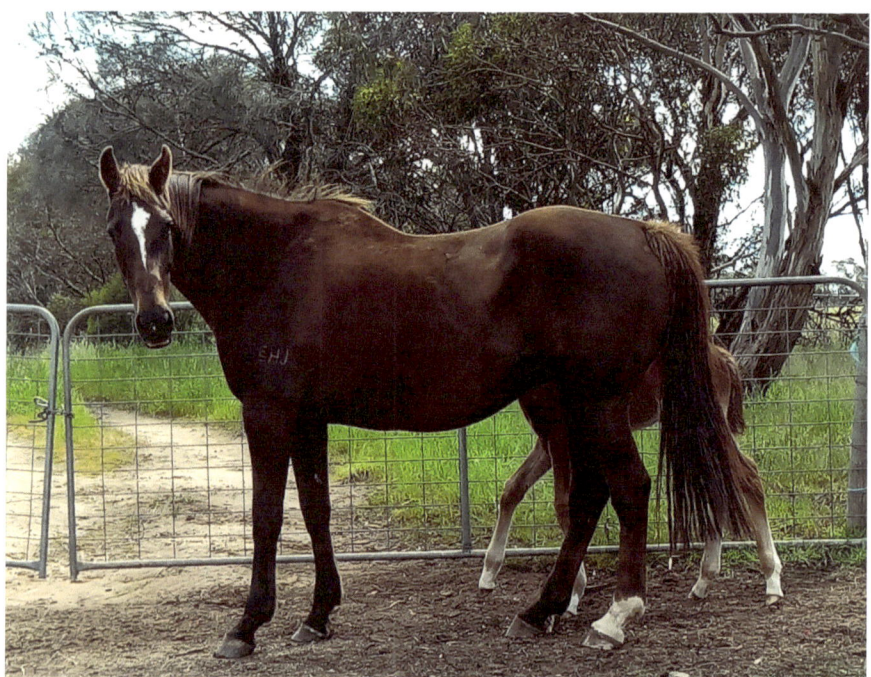

Halsteds Gidget at Chalani, at age 20.

Even more exciting, this mare carries Terlings Gold Finger on her dam's side, and is a direct descendant of the taproot mare Terlings Jewess. Her pedigree is a combination of some of the best blood available in the polo / polocrosse world.

LEFT: Sinclair Hill on Lady Jane. RIGHT: Peter

During the recent Quirindi Polo Carnival, it was brought to our notice that among the 16 teams competing, 35 of the horses played were bred at "Terlings", Moree, by Sinclair Hill and his family — 24 of these in A Grade.

Angel (out of Bambi by Wayside Inn), trained and played by Peter Cudmore was the Champion Polo Pony, his fifth such award. Angel's dam, Bambi, had 15 foals, of which 11 have played polo and 4 of these (Jan, Angel, Bangle and Rainbow) have won Champion Polo Pony awards. Her grand-daughter Twinkle has won three awards.

At Scone Carnival this year Sinclair won the Polo Pony with Jessica, who he considers the best pony he has ever ridden. Jessica is by Cairo out of Jewess, one of Sinclair's original ponies. Jewess had 7 foals, and of these seven, 4 were playing in Sydney at Easter time — Jessica, Lady Jane, High Noon and Lear (chestnut mare played by Hugh MacLachlan). Sheba is at the Stud and two have not yet seen the polo field.

Hoofs and Horns clipping which mentions Jessica, the pony Sinclair Hill considered the best pony he had ever ridden at that time. Jessica is out of Jewess, one of Sinclair's original ponies. Juliet had yet to play when this was written.

LADY JAYNE

Ch m

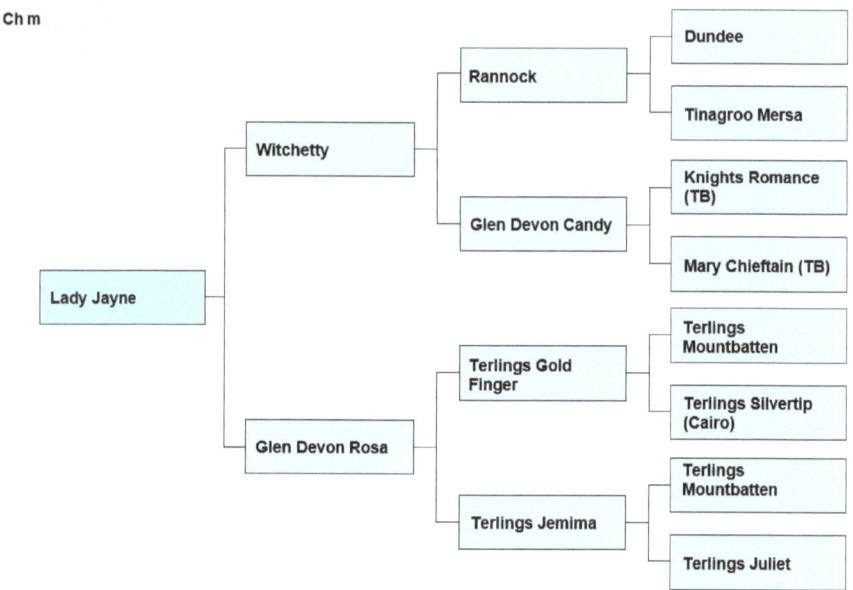

Lady Jayne
- Witchetty
  - Rannock
    - Dundee
    - Tinagroo Mersa
  - Glen Devon Candy
    - Knights Romance (TB)
    - Mary Chieftain (TB)
- Glen Devon Rosa
  - Terlings Gold Finger
    - Terlings Mountbatten
    - Terlings Silvertip (Cairo)
  - Terlings Jemima
    - Terlings Mountbatten
    - Terlings Juliet

CHALANI SURPRISE (Peppins Young Ivory x Halsteds Gidget) 2018 b m 15.3h, has been an exceptional mare for us, outstandingly quiet, placing at ASH Nationals as a 2yo and winning the SA ASH State Futurity. Now leased by 13 yr old Avah Bowen, she is already winning Championships in the show ring and honing her jumping skills.

Chalani Surprise, Macclesfield Show 2024, SRS Imagery.

Chalani Surprise with Avah Bowen, 2024, Roger Foster photo.

Chalani Surprise, Roger Foster photo, 2024.

SIMMARON

(Star Black Minstril x Julie Wirth) 1997 blk h 15.3h

John Halsted says: "We purchased Simmaron from Les Frazer in Warwick Qld as a weanling when we were living out at Warren. We brought him with us to Hampshire in 1998 as a yearling. His mother was by SAGE KING and was played by Les for several years. She also played for Australia ridden by Ross Sheppard.

"We rang several people who knew what a good horse was (Terry Blake, Joy Poole, Darrell Smith) and got the same answer from each, that was she was 'tough.' Sage King was a very successful campdrafter. He was known as a 'horseman's horse' and his daughters have bred on very well.

Sage King

Star Black Minstril

"Simmaron is still going strong aged 25. He won led and working events including the Nationals and Hunter Branch Shows 2003 and placed in drafts. As we play polocrosse, he didn't compete much. We used Simmaron over the station mares in exchange for the use of a few Witchetty mares. Lady Jayne was one of these mares.

"Simmaron has bred a lot of very good horses, 15.1 to 16h, which have done Eventing to Polocrosse, Campdrafting and Pony club. They are very easy to break in, have great minds and are very easy to teach. They can handle pressure at an early age and are very 'cowy'.

"The first of these was HALSTEDS XENA. She was unbeaten in sporting events at Pony Club. She won the NSW State Pony Club Campdraft Championships ridden by our son. She took our daughter Grace to every National Polocrosse Championship from Junior (under 16) to Senior (>21) over a period of 10 years, and won every Pony Prize along the way. Grace would have won more junior player prizes than any player in Australia on her.

We refused an offer of $50,000 for her. She is retired now.

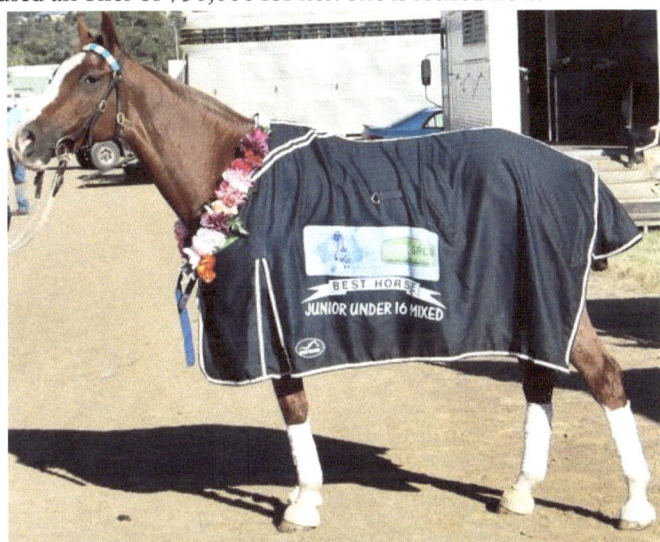

Halsteds Xena

"One daughter is HALSTEDS GABRIELLE, by our next sire Peppins Young Ivory, winner of multiple awards in Tasmania, and which sold at the 2022 Berragoon Sale for $18k."

Simmaron. Below, 2018 Advert.

Chapter 11

Narrangullen Anakin

An incredible partnership

(Witchetty x Narrangullen Tikka), 2006 b h, 16h.

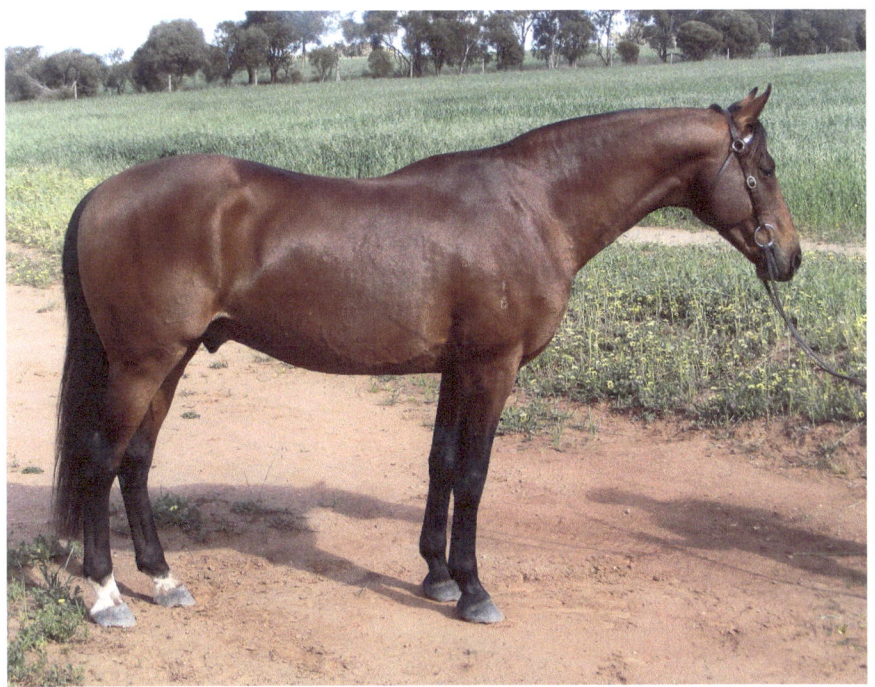

Anakin in 2018.

The story of Rannock has taken many twists and turns. Witchetty was a line that had remained undiscovered for a few years, due to him being foal recorded as 'no name.' Sheer coincidence led to the discovery of NARRANGULLEN

ANAKIN, when it was reported to the author that there was a 'Rannock stallion' winning around Victoria, and that he was an 'amazing horse'. This had come from several sources before I was able to track him down.

This then, is his story, starting with the message from Von Mitchell that got my attention:

"Watching that horse (Anakin) compete for a few years now, especially in the brumby catches, is mesmerizing. This is the stallion that gets 'top ten' most years at the Snowy River Festival. He is incredible to watch chase and catch the brumbies. Michael Green, his jockey sits there so still and at ease. The stallion is a big boy too, and he just scoots around easily and is awesome to watch. He just gets his head in front of the brumby and lightly nudges them around in circles to turn. When they're caught, he is amazing too. He can just sit on a dime, loose rein, and whip around the brumby. He is just amazing, so calm and not aggressive towards them like a stallion could be. A wonderful partnership to watch."

From Kimberley McCallum - "a friend has some progeny which are very quiet and correct. He's a lovely big stallion which does very well in Challenges. Michael has always been known to have good horses. Anakin's breeding is quite unique."

From photographer Sarah Martin – "I took a photo for the ASH Journal in 2013. This horse was sensational to watch. I am so pleased to see him getting some recognition. What a partnership!"

Witchetty sired Anakin at age 26. Incredibly, this makes the span to Rannock in direct sire line a mere three generations away, with Anakin at the time of writing, 18 years old! The valuable heritage genetics also includes that of his dam, NARRANGULLEN TIKKA, herself a good mare under saddle. She was 20 years old when she produced Anakin. She is the dam of multiple good horses, including NARRANGULLEN VODKA, for Lauren Vest. Vodka, by Carey's Wee Jasper, was a successful all-round sporting horse, Pony Club mount and eventer for her, and later Rhiannon Philby.

Narrangullen Tikka is by Darth Vader from the Cairo mare NARRAN-GULLEN FIDDLESTICKS. In turn, she is out of an Enry Iggins mare, a TB which sired some useful polocrosse ponies, including the sire KIMLOCK, for John Thrower. (*I note that several of the Narrangullen horses ended up with progeny with the Thrower prefix in the ASH studbook*).

Thus, Panzer appears in Anakin's pedigree three times. It is a testament to the quality of the Panzer line and the astute dedication of breeders of the past that no inherent faults have been found; the perfect formula for the making of top sires and consistency of breed attributes.

Michael Green takes up the story:

"I picked Anakin up as an untouched weanling off his mother with a view to using him later for polocrosse and drafting. I spent 10 minutes or so halter breaking

Narrangullen Anakin

Foaled 2006
Bay Stallion
16.1h.

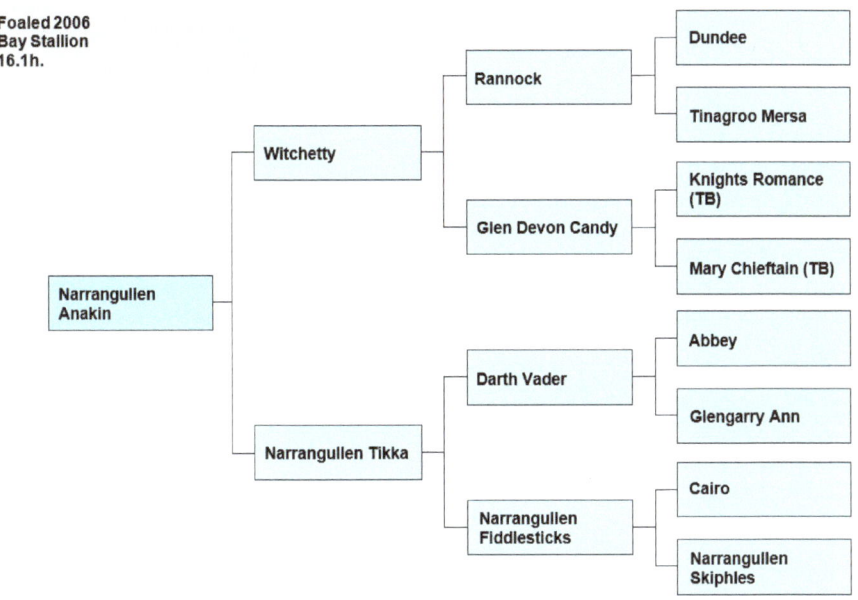

Narrangullen Anakin	Witchetty	Rannock	Dundee
			Tinagroo Mersa
		Glen Devon Candy	Knights Romance (TB)
			Mary Chieftain (TB)
	Narrangullen Tikka	Darth Vader	Abbey
			Glengarry Ann
		Narrangullen Fiddlesticks	Cairo
			Narrangullen Skiphles

Narrangullen Vodka with Lauren Vest

him, and he loaded like a trained horse. I broke him in as a 2-year-old when I lived in the Hawkesbury area. He spent some time turned out at my parent's place, Moruya, New South Wales, and then I moved him up to Braidwood, Queensland, as a 3-year-old.

"I had intentions to put him into training but work and life kept him almost untouched for most of his third year. He ran in a bush block at the back of Braidwood with little to share it with but cows. I would get up there to see he was ok most weeks but riding him was a once or twice every-few-months thing. One thing I knew, he was always pleased to see me whether he was hungry or mud fat, and he was both at times. He was also always willing, a pleasure to ride and train, so much so that I never considered gelding him, though it wasn't my plan to have a colt when I bought him.

Michael Green on Anakin at Comet.

"As he got close to four years old, I got properly fed up with my work/life situation. I had gone to Man from Snowy River Challenge (Corryong) on a little black mare in April 2011. There I met Charles Mckinley from Comet in Central Queensland who offered me a job on his property. So, by late May 2011, I was on my way to Queensland with three horses including Anakin. I stayed and worked up there at Comet until about October that year. With horse work almost every day, it was the makings of the young colt. He spent a lot of time covering big paddocks gathering stock and then walking mobs back to the yards. We would also draft off the 'tops' to go for export, in a holding paddock beside one set of yards. The main thing was the long miles travelled walking mobs to and from yards.

"I would practice movements on him at the walk on the track, lead departures, front leg crossover, pushing hind quarter in, just building on it slowly. I took him to Home Hill Draft in which he came fifth in the maiden. I went back to Braidwood with a 4yo colt on a very solid foundation. He was relaxed, soft and supple in the bridle and off the leg through the front, ribcage, and hind quarters.

"April 2012 came around and I had entered in Man From Snowy River Challenge 2012. I scraped into the final ten, but with some good fortune and an exceptional performance by Anakin, we finished second that year. I must confess before going into the brumby catch, I had no idea what to expect from the young stallion. I pictured him running sideways out of control in the main arena in front of thousands of people.

"What happened was breathtaking... when that brum ran into the arena Ani seemed to know exactly what I wanted to do, where he needed to be. Being a rooky myself in this event, I couldn't handle a head collar and the reins, so I dropped the reins on his neck and let him go. In under 30 seconds he had me right on top of the brum and allowed me to drop the headcollar straight on with ease, then continue to work right where I needed him to control the brum effortlessly.

"I returned to Queensland the following 2 years between June and September, with 3 horses each time, but always with Anakin, working for Charles. I travelled to a few drafts as far as Home Hill near Townsville and did miles at a mate's place around the canefields near Mackay; just an adventure really.

"We returned to Man From Snowy River 2013. We didn't do quite as well, placing fifth overall (through no fault of Ani's I might add.) I am notorious for being a terrible whip-cracker; lucky I've got a good horse for the other events. But we got what he really deserved, a win in the Brumby Catch, again making my job so simple. The brum was caught in about 15 seconds at full speed!

"That same year we also went to an Invitational Challenge at Sydney Equitana, placing fourth.

"We finalled again at Battle of the Bidgee (BOTB) in 2015 but he had knocked his knee on the cross country and although not lame, I wasn't risking him and withdrew. BOTB was cancelled in 2016 due to rain.

"At 2015 MFSR we came sixth. We caught quickly but having drawn a very tough, fast brumby which wasn't slowing up in the headcollar, I hazed him into the fence. In a second the brumby was behind me, around me and I was wrapped up in the rope. As the brumby bolted away, I was strung-up and about to be dragged clean off Ani's back. I grabbed for the saddle to cling a few more seconds and Ani turned and went after the brum. What seemed like minutes at the time was mere seconds, but in that moment without any control by me, Ani had turned and matched pace with the brum, allowing the pressure from the rope dragging me to the ground to be released, long enough for me to untangle myself and get back in the saddle!   He probably saved my life!

Winning Brumby Catch, Man from Snowy River Challenge, 2012.

Brumby Catch, photos Sarah Martin.

Promotional pic on the side of the Man from Snowy River ute, with Anakin.

Winner of the Brumby Catch, Michael Green on NARRANGULLEN ANAKIN

"We made the final at MFSR again in 2017, placing eighth. Again, Ani didn't let me down, though I let him down fouling my own attempts to catch the brumby. With new rules allowing only two attempts, our campaign ended quicker than it should have. But we did convincingly win the Bareback Obstacle and Freestyle sections, finishing with flying changes on a straight line with a string around his neck!

"We finished BOTB 2017, and 2019, top ten again. My highlight at the BOTB competitions is the dry pattern. Basically, it's a working stock horse pattern. He has consistently been one of the top half dozen horses in this event over many years, three of them consecutive second places, each year pipped by a different horse. I haven't shown him much but when he has been shown, he has rarely been beaten in working ASH classes and makes a fair hack as well.

2014 took Michael to the final in The Battle On The Bidgee for an overall third.

"In 2019 and 21 (2020 not held due to covid) and 2022, they placed in Top Ten MFSR again. The partnership has now placed in the finals no less than eight times!

"We have been to the Lower Lakes Challenge (Strathalbyn SA) four times, coming away with a fourth and three thirds. He is impressive to watch on a cross country, very bold. Consequently, he has quite a fan club in SA. He has made appearances on Performance Horse Magazine, the ASH Magazine, Horses and People Magazine 2013, Horseland Diary 2014 and his picture has appeared on the cover of Australian Horseman Magazine. Anakin is without doubt the best horse I have ever owned. He is 16h and just such a lovely type of horse in every way."

Being ridden without a bridle or neckstrap in Man From Snowy River Challenge,
2012, photo Sarah Martin.

Author's note: In 2017, I fulfilled a long-held dream to travel to Man From
Snowy River Stockman's Challenge, Corryong, to see Michael and Anakin perform,
in front of an estimated crowd of 30,000. The partnership of horse and rider
is spell-binding. This horse is courageous across country, easily taking the hardest
options for more points and earned an almost perfect score in the Bareback Obstacle.
The atmosphere leading up into the finals was electric. Michael and Anakin were
one of only two horses to complete the Brumby Catch!

I decided I must breed a mare to him, which was arranged when Michael came to
a Lower Lakes Challenge SA, in 2018.

"He did go top ten at King of the Ranges again in late 2019, but with Covid, buying a small acreage at Wandandian, NSW, family commitments, and breaking in some progeny, Anakin has had limited opportunity at stud.

"I have two very promising, very smart daughters, one out of a DOGWOOD COMET mare, Comets Haley. We have named her Valkyrie, and another, Hella, from a CATTLE KING mare. This one was pulled straight out of the paddock and placed in 2023 King of the Ranges Working Cow Horse, placed 3rd in a novice draft, and second in a Novice Working Horse Challenge. Hella also won the 2022 Inaugural Terry Bennett trophy at Nowra Show for Flag Racing with me. She is now being ridden by a 10yo girl. Others are getting brilliant feedback on temperament and ability.

"I have a gelding Loki, ex ELLIOTTS CREEK CADET mare, which is the best horse I've ever campdrafted. He won his first Novice last year, also placed in several (and we don't draft much). Ali, my wife, made her first Open Campdraft final on him at Corryong MFSR last year. Loki and I also won a horse float in a Team Sorting Series at K Ranch." – Michael Green.

Photo Sarah Martin.

STOP PRESS: Ali and Anakin took 2nd place (Ladies) Man from Snowy River Challenge 2024.

Photo gallery of Narrangullen Anakin progeny.

Loki, Goulbourn Campdraft, 2018. Jensol Photography.

TOMAR PARK SPECIAL EDITION, ex RAYMA CHINA GIRL (2016) has won numerous Champion Hack and Working events for Jenni Afflick, including Reserve Ch Junior Novice Hack at the 2021 ASH Nationals.

Hella, at King of The Ranges, Working Cow Horse 2023. She was pulled straight out of the paddock and placed. Kristy Butler photo.

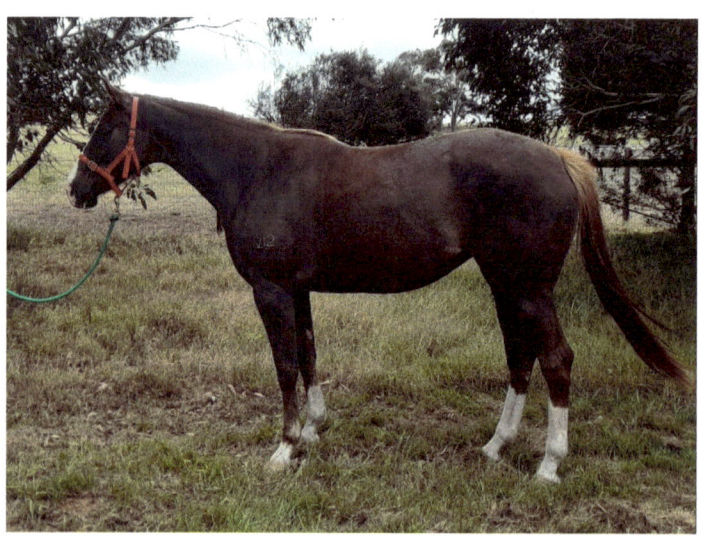

CHALANI SKYWALK (2019) a beautiful-natured filly by Anakin, from CHALANI SKYLARK (a full sister to Chalani Tempo) who goes back to the Rannock mare, Chalani Skelter on the dam's side. Retained for breeding by Chalani.

Chapter 12

Littlewood Montego

So easy to play

(Rannock x Gamma) 1983 b h 15.1½h.

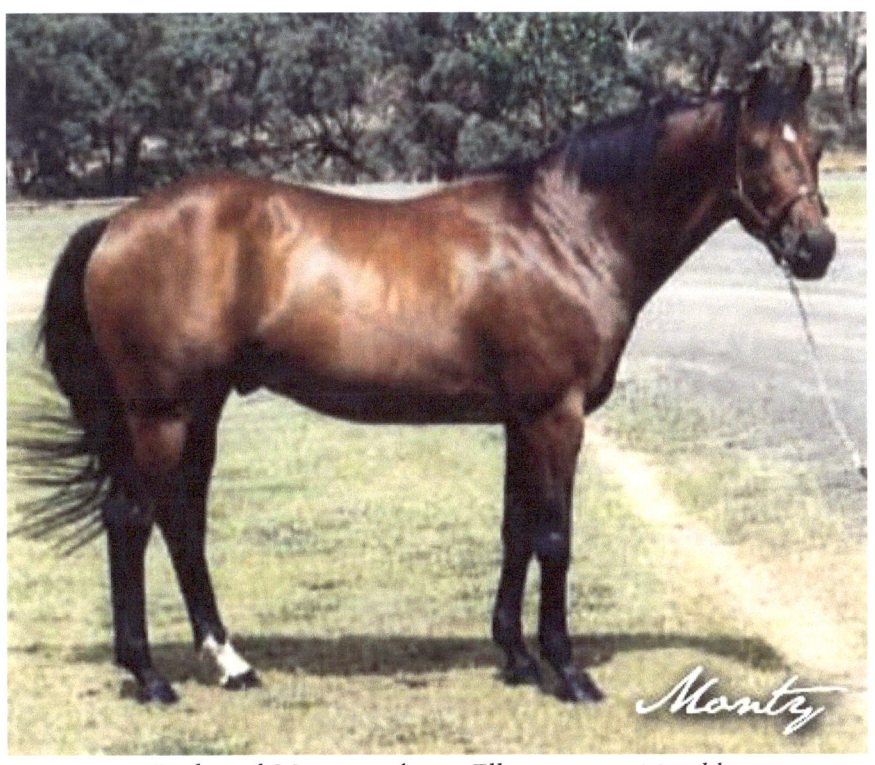

Littlewood Montego, taken at Ellerston, circa 16yr old.

The influence of **LITTLEWOOD MONTEGO** on the polo world, both in Australia and internationally is huge, particularly incredible, if one considers the relatively short period in which he stood at stud. Despite this success, few registered lines have made their way into the Australian Stock Horse Society.

After a good career as a polo pony, Littlewood Montego, better known as 'Monty', stood at *Ellerston* for some nine years on lease from his owner-breeder Andrew Gray. He was a classic-fronted, true to type polo pony, the image of his famous ancestor Panzer, with his sire Rannock's excellent head. He sired multiple International ponies, and has made a name for himself as a sire of sires. Many consider him one of the greatest sires of polo ponies of his era, certainly remarkable, since Monty's stud opportunities were limited until after he retired from playing, at around 12 years of age.

In the late 1970s, Andrew Gray at Littlehampton, SA, bought three full sisters by HILL to play polo, which he named Alpha, Beta and the youngest, Gamma (1977).

Says Andrew Gray - "I always liked the Hill horses, so I asked Michael and Rosie Vincent who stood Hill at *Wombena*, Naracoorte, SA if they had anything. Michael told me of a shearer who had these three for sale. (There was also an older broken gelding which I didn't buy as he had more money on him. I heard later he was a successful campdraft horse.)

"Alpha turned out to be a particularly talented playing pony, my best horse for years. I sold her to Angus McLachlan for $3000 when I was short on cash, which was good money in those days, and she became his equal best pony. Gillon McLachlan also played her for years after Angus retired, but she never had a foal.

"Beta was a promising pony but unfortunately, she dropped dead in her first chukka from an aneurism.

"Gamma broke her pelvis around the time I was breaking her in and I really didn't expect her to come good, even to breed from. Two years later we decided to try her, and I led her round to the Gowers to be bred to Rannock. In fact, her hip was displaced a good three inches so we knew there was a chance she'd never be able to deliver a foal. But she punched it out.

"Monty was her first and Anto (by Gyprock), a very talented pony, came next. He played 15 years of polo brilliantly, some really tough polo. Hughie and Zeta, were also by Gyprock. We mostly hunted Hughie, but Zeta only played polo. We reckon Gamma had fifteen foals in the end, as we gave her to Sylvia McLachlan who bred on with her for some years."

When Jeanette and Peter Gower saw Monty at about 8 weeks old, their impression was of a somewhat non-descript foal, but he certainly lived up to the promise of his breeding as he matured. Andrew had already decided to keep him a colt as he really liked him. "I just really liked that blood, the Rannock blood I already had in Gyprock, and the other Hill horses I knew. I didn't think I could go wrong."

Unfortunately, Andrew didn't have the breeding of Gamma at the time Littlewood Montego was registered. Stud records of the Vincents reveal she was out of GISSA, a 15.1h grey mare owned by John Hood. As Hill played polo in 1976, Gissa was the only mare he served that year.

The author rang John Hood, who confirmed this information. He advised me of the following: "I bought Gissa off her breeder Jack Gysbers, for polocrosse, so I registered her ASH as Gissa, a shortening of Gysbers. Gissa was the fastest horse I ever rode, until her son Jimmie came along. She was very good but she was very fine skinned, so I had to have a fleece-lined girth. Robert Seymour, who owned Hill at the time, (and was Rosie Vincent's brother), gave me a service for helping him out on the property. In all, I bred 7 foals, only one of which wasn't by Hill. The first three I named after family members.

Minka with Jack Gysbers (Snr) (circa 1967)

"Jimmie was a top level pony. I never wore a spur as he was so fast. I played him Number 1 in A grade for many years. When you got on Jimmie it was like stepping off a mini-moke onto an E-type Jag! He was quite big, around 16 hands, with much speed and stamina. You could whistle him up from the paddock after 6 months, and play a tournament on him.

But like most of the Hill horses, he could really buck. I broke him in with the overhead check and an underhead check at 18 months. One day during breaking I rode him out 27 miles and on the way home he still wanted to buck, so I put him in a 500 acre paddock and rode him around for another hour. He never ever tried to buck again, but I was always careful to lunge him when I saddled up.

"When I married, I had to sell some of my horses. Jimmie went to my brother, who played him in the finals at the Nationals one year. Music was another top pony from Gissa, played by the Berken brothers for many years and won many tournament prizes."

The ASH has Gissa listed as being by Matador ex Minka. Minka was a much loved, finely built TB around 15.0hh, who though small, was very fast. Jack Gysbers (Snr) bought her as a 6 year old off trainer Roy Lowe, after winning a few races in the lower South East of SA and Western Vic over the shorter distances. His son, Jeff Lowe had played a little polocrosse on her. Jack says, "We played her A grade with Mt Gambier Club for 5 or so years (with a foal in between) and had success with her in a few picnic races. She always looked a picture as her coat was so fine. She had great cow sense and good temper. She would be there almost before the cow turned. She was a good mare for us."

Unfortunately, Minka cannot be found in the ASB. It is likely she raced under another or similar name. There is a black mare registered as Minker, (1968) by Basalt from Patharu, but dates of her studbook foals reveal this cannot be the same horse.

HILL

(Terlings Deo Juvante (TB) imp x Terlings Action) 1970 blk 16h.

Named after his breeder, Sinclair Hill, he was selected in the 1971 *Terlings* sale and bought for $650 as a yearling by Robert Seymour, while Hugh MacLachlan bought Terlings Gold Finger, both on the recommendation of Bob Osborne, who they took with them. Robert stood him at his property at South Killanoola (near Naracoorte). Hill earned a Best First Season Pony award for Penola Club, but Robert only played a few years himself. He also found the handling of the visiting mares didn't fit into his programme so he gave Hill to his sister, Rosemary Vincent and husband Michael.

Michael only drafted him during one season and then only on limited occasions. Notably in Western Vic, on only his second weekend, he won the Maiden, and the Novice, and came fourth in the Open.

The Vincents also found it difficult managing visiting mares, so after a number of years, when a client wanted to send multiple mares, he was sent there to serve and collect semen. Unfortunately, in an accident, he broke his leg and had to be put down.

HILL

Foaled 1970
Blk Stallion
15.3h.

		Djebel
	Targui	
		Palencia
Terlings Deo Juvante (TB)		
		Tehran
	Ambar	
		Pasqua
Hill		
		Fairway
	Wayside Inn (TB)	
		Sundae
Terlings Action		
		Royal Commission
	Lady Lucia (TB)	
		Ruth Rivoli

Michael campaigned Hill's progeny almost exclusively at campdrafting with much success, while others played polo to a fairly high standard for various members of the Adelaide Polo Club. Other progeny became good showjumpers in the South East.

Michael says: "It has to be said that many of his progeny weren't easily managed. Like their sire, they were athletic, strong and intelligent, but had to be convinced that their rider was worth performing for."

Hill was a double cross of Carbine, and was a combination of the three great Terlings Thoroughbred sires, Deo Juvante, Wayside Inn and Royal

Commission. Hill is a full sister to the mare TERLINGS TWIST, possibly Sinclair's top pony at that time. She became the dam of ROSEBANK SUPERMAN (by Super Alton), sire of many good polo ponies for Ian and Sylvia McLachlan, *Rosebank*, Mt Pleasant SA.

Their dam, TERLINGS ACTION, is a half-sister to Georgie, who won 4 individual polo pony awards touring New Zealand, Woodbine, and Cupie, and closely related to Joker and Golightly. In the pedigree above, Lady Lucia is also the granddam of Terlings Musket, mentioned under Cairo.

Sinclair Hill considered Deo Juvante to be the most celebrated and successful sire in the history of Australian polo, siring the likes of Martini, Lady Jan, Jewel, Remembrance, Mushroom, Mary Jane, Century, Joker, Stormy, Geronimo, Siesta, to name a few, and the sires TERLINGS SMOKEY JOHN, SUPREME, and JACMAN (which went to WA), all with the Terlings prefix.

Deo Juvante - his full story was written up in an article for the ASH Magazine in Sept-Oct 2005, and may be found on the ASH website.

Minka only ever went to three stallions, the Thoroughbred Glen View, a Green Valley pony stallion of Max Baker's, and an Arab stallion lent to Max Baker for a couple of years from Roy (Toppy) Topperwein, of Millicent. The pony sired a black gelding Monaro, which played A Grade polocrosse for about 15 years for Mary Dewit, Jack's daughter. The grey filly (Gissa) which was sold to John Hood, followed a few years later. Jack (Snr) described the Arab as "the most magnificent white horse I ever saw in my life!"

Despite an exhaustive search, the author can find no trace of a horse called Matador, either part or pure, nor information regarding Mr Topperwein having owned a horse called Matador. Those who knew Max Baker insist he never had an Arab, only ponies and some thoroughbreds. The author has confirmed with Mary Dewit and Jack Gysbers (Jnr) that the Arabian stallion was Mataranka (1958) by the great Riffayal, owned by Roy Topperwein.

Gamma

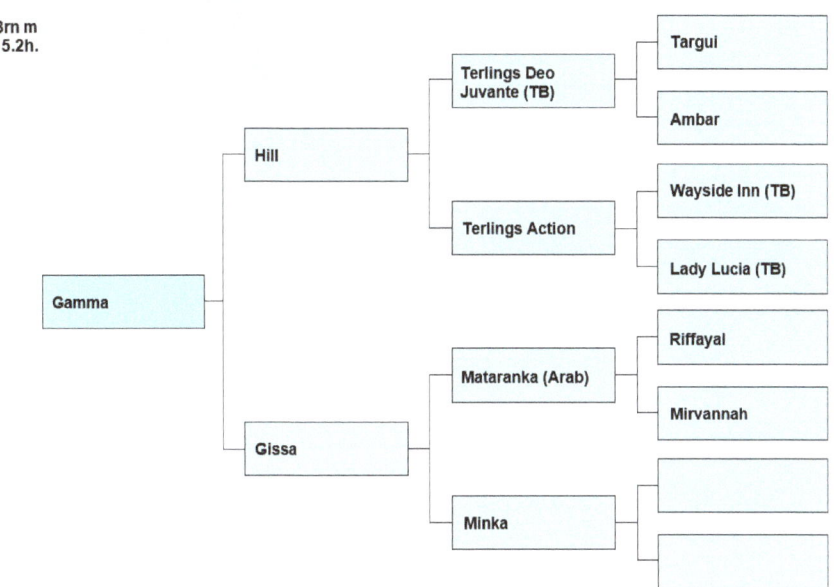

Andrew Gray first rode Littlewood Montego as a three year old.

"I started him when I was working for Francis Nelson and he bucked so much that it took me an extra week to break him in. In the end I lunged him in the sand yard and then the round yard until he could barely stand up and then got on. Two days later I rode him round the paddock and could open and close a gate. That was it. He just went on from there, green, but a natural horse. He went to polo green as hell, but just did it. Those really good horses, you don't have to spend two years training them, or three months cantering around the back so they're not scared of sticks and horses. You just pace them and keep them fit. Gyprock was the same, willing to learn right from the start. Lots of naturals can be hot, or angry before you can get them to think properly, or get them settled. These just played.

"I first played him as a 4 year old, and he proved a very quiet, talented pony to play, winning a B-grade pony prize at Hexam in 1990, his first tournament. Yet he and Chalani Gyprock were opposites. Monty would be keen at exercise, and super calm at polo. Gyprock would find exercise boring and spark right up for a game. They were my two best ever horses, with Monty ahead by a whisker, because he had the reach, being that bit taller, around 15.1h. I played them together for some five years on my team, retiring only because I got married. I never bred from him at all, since the only broodmare I had was his mother. Neville Sprod, my neighbour, sent a mare one year, and that was the only foal I think, during the time I had him. (*That foal was Veloce Nel, see in progeny gallery.*)

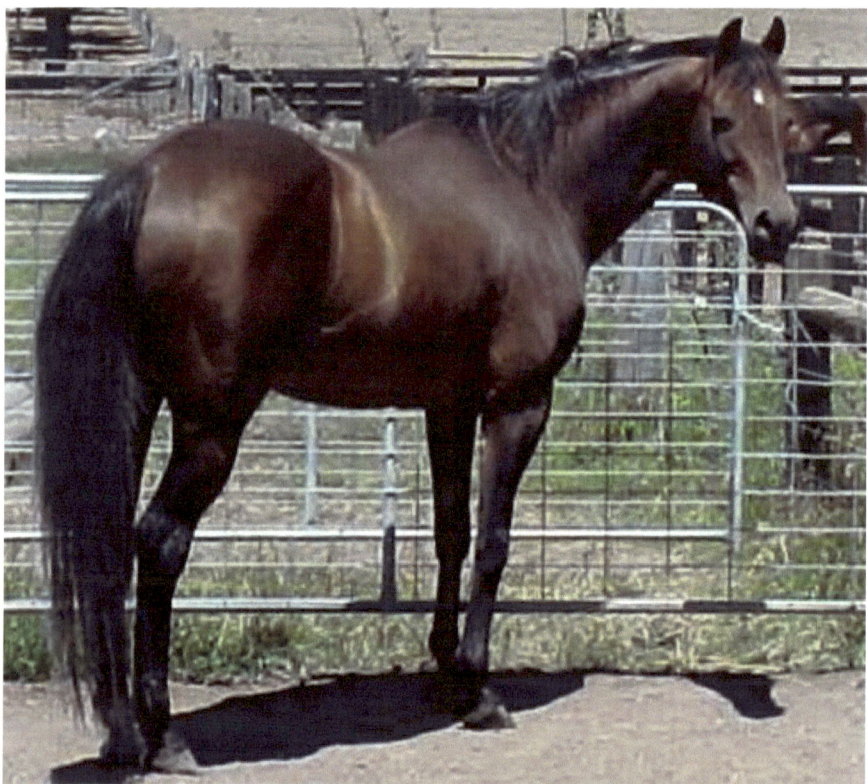

Littlewood Montego at Geelong Vet clinic, approx 2004.

Andrew Gray continues: "In 1992, I lent Monty to Jock MacLachlan to play in a couple of tournaments, in which he excelled. Jock's father, Hugh MacLachlan, who was good friends with Kerry Packer, rang Kerry one day and said "you have to have this horse!" Hugh described him as "a top pony, very talented". Not long after that, I received a phone call from Jim Gilmore, manager, and a deal was struck for a three year lease with *Ellerston*. I photocopied the cheque!"

Monty left for Ellerston, and was there for approximately 9 years, where he served some 80 mares a year, then finishing up in the hands of polo player James Vanner of Geelong Vet Clinic (Vic) and Anthony Baillieu, retired player.

Anthony Baillieu recalls: "I watched Monty on numerous occasions and was in awe. He had the most wonderful stop. He was never any trouble and was so easy for Andrew to play. Had he been in the hands of a high goal player, he would have been one of the top 3 or 4 playing ponies in the country."

Many of the Ellerston progeny were sold overseas as going ponies, some for $70k and most >$40k. Some were taken to England by Ruki Baillieu, 7 goal playing son of Anthony, and sold there. The reference of pace in the dam's line supports the fact that the likes of his daughters Claret and Music have done so well in the Argentine Open, where speed is just paramount.

As a sire, Littlewood Montego's record is incredible. Ultimately he has been recognized as one of those rare horses to become a sire of sires.

Littlewood Montego has only 13 progeny registered with the ASH. This is a tragedy. It means that the Society is missing out on valuable promotion on the international stage, and is losing one of its most valuable and versatile lines available today. Indeed, without the foresight of members such as the Hodges and Haydons, the Society could lose this line forever.

"One thing we've found over the years, looking at sires and their progeny, both in Australia and oversees, is a lot of people talk about having a good stallion. I see now, that Australians should have made more effort, and paid more emphasis on breeding better horses, because those great polo families were already doing it in the 1940s to 1980s with the finest of Thoroughbred blood.

"But there are not a lot left who are really making that effort, or with the knowledge and bloodlines to do it well. Australia is in danger of losing its good proven lines, the genetics of which are still highly valuable. When you lose proven lines, you virtually have to start all over again." - Anthony Baillieu.

Littlewood Montego (circa 1990) with owner-breeder Andrew Gray.

Chapter 13

Littlewood Montego progeny

The following information was taken from the 2015 Reduction Sale Catalogue of *Ellerston*, the famous stud of former polo player, Kerry Packer, which acquired and produced some of the best playing horses in the world.

"A staggering 113 ponies offered have the Littlewood Montego bloodline. Monty has produced numerous outstanding polo ponies."

Mares by Littlewood Montego

Music, ex Tango:

An outstanding polo pony for Ellerston before being shipped to Argentina for Ellerstina to play the Open. She went on to become one of the greatest open mares of the last decade. Blessed with speed, power and great handling ability. Music instantly became a champion in all levels of polo. She was shipped to the UK in 2007 to play High Goal with Facundo Pieres for Ellerston, before returning to Argentina to continue her open career. Her oldest progeny are now playing the Argentine Open and High Goal polo in the UK.

Casa, ex Borracasa:

A brilliant mare for Ellerston before being shipped to the UK to play High Goal for Ellerston. Winner of many champion pony prizes. Casa was then shipped to Argentina to play the Open for Gonzalito Peires. After 2 seasons of the Open, Casa continued her career in the UK to play High Goal for Gonzalito Pieres. Her superb handling ability was much more suited to High Goal in the UK. Casa then retired to stud in Argentina. This bloodline is very dominant with her oldest progeny being very similar in ability to her, being much sought after throughout the polo world.

Claret, ex Touch of Pink (TB) better known as Pinky):

In Jim Gilmore's opinion, Claret was the greatest mare ever bred by Ellerston. A truly great mare at all levels of polo. Her amazing career began at Ellerston in 2004. She was shippped to Argentina for Ellerstina in 2005 and played amazing polo in her first season of the Open, before being shipped to the UK for Ellerston in 2006. In her first season she was awarded Best Playing Pony in the Gold Cup final for Gonzalito Pieres in both the UK and Argentina.

A magnificent type, with superb action and handling ability, this great mare is now one of the worlds most valuable broodmares. Her progeny include Argentina stallions Clarion, Clark, Cabernet, Classify, and Clarify, Clariet (Spain), and Clarry (Australia). She has daughters Clarity (Aust), Clarita (Argentina), Clarinet (Argentina) and many more for Ellerston.

Other remarkable polo ponies by Monty were Champagne, Jamaica, Actress, Armanda, Retail, Jackpot, Punch, Disco, Burgundy, Canoe, Ferry, Samoa, Nana, Saint, Soprano, Polka.

In polocrosse, ROTHWELL SECOND CHANCE, played by Islay Young, was 2016 Champion Horse, Rose Bowl Carnival, Warwick QLD.

Veloce Nel, ex Chrisy, 1989 b m 15.2h.

Jill Bourton says "Veloce Nel was a big bay mare bred by Neville Sprod's daughter from her hunting mare, a part Arab containing WENCESLAS and Stefan bloodlines. Since her paternal grandsire was Rannock, I knew when I bought her she would have stamina. and along with the Wenceslas/Stefan influence I knew I couldn't go wrong!

"She was rising 8 and virtually unhandled when I got her. Roslyn Day broke her in for me in December 1996. She completed her first 80 km ride in April 1997. That year she easily clocked up 800 kms, placing 3rd in the Kuitpo 200, which was her first ride out of Novice. The following month she Won and got Best Conditioned at Sandy Creek 120 km. I had plenty of success with her in Endurance including 2 x 160km SA State Championships and my first SA Quilty buckle after 2 previous attempts. I had many wins and Best Conditioned awards with this horse. I sold her overseas at the end of 1998. She performed well in Dubai, breaking a leg speed record at the time, in a youth event of about 98kms or so."

Veloce Nel

Sire sons of Littlewood Montego include Ellerston Revenue, TIMORPOLO PATON (1993), ELLERSTON CHURCHILL (1999), Ellerston Cuba, Ellerston Saint, CANGON GILETTE (2001), Spartacus (2004), Cullen (ex a NZ TB mare) and Glenugie Gundy to name but a few.

Space prohibits going into more detail on these horses. Of necessity, the rest of this chapter will concentrate on those *sire line* descendants which have had Australian Stock Horse registration or influence.

BALWYN CAVA, (Ellerston Revenue x Ellerston Fiji) 2004, brn h 15.1h.

BALWYN CAVA

Brown Stallion, 15.1hh
DOB :   28/11/04
Brands :   KP, 24/4
Service Fee :$1,000 plus GST
Owner :   Balwyn Equestrian Services Pty Ltd
             C/- Adrian Lester, 0419 937 037

Littlewood Montego (Monty) – (ASH#73540)

Sire : Ellerston Revenue

Glenugie Sold

Wickerwork (USA TB 1977)

Dam : Ellerston Fiji

Ellerston Suva (NZ TB)

Note :

1. In 2005, Ellerston sent 6 mares to Argentina to play at the Argentine Open in the Ellerstina team. Ellerstina were defeated in extra time by La Dolfina. The mares were : Numea (out of Suva), Music (by Monty), Claret (by Monty), Cuddles (by Wickerwork), Martini, Jacquie. Cava is related to 4 of the 6 mares.
2. A condition of service – Balwyn Equestrian Services has a first right of refusal to purchase the progeny if the progeny owner decides to sell.
3. People who've already sent mares to Cava :

BJ Thomas	Nikki Cant
Rob Sibley	Greg Johnson
Wayne & Pip Crook	Matt Welsh
Clinton Wheatley	Twynam Cunningham
Phil & Catherine Crabb	

Old advert. Note on Balwyn Cava pedigree above – Wickerwork is by Tom Rolfe ex Royal Picnic. Ellerston Suva is by Palm Beach from Tropical. Glenugie Sold is by NABINABAH CHALLENGER from Glenugie Gypsy.

Writes Adrian Lester - "I purchased Cava from Ellerston in 2005 as a foal, not long after weaning, and soon moved him to WA. He played very good polo here in WA, fast, strong and very soft to handle.

He has 29 registered progeny, most of whom were bred by us at *Balwyn*, predominantly playing polo or polocrosse. My son James is a professional 4 goal polo player and they form the basis of his playing string. He plays 4 – 16 goal and was in the Australian Team at the World Cup in 2017.

James has won Champion Pony and Champion String of Ponies with BALWYN USAIN, BALWYN EVANGELINE, BALWYN WIGWAM, and BALWYN UNO in 2017. BALWYN EDNA played in the Mens Open final at Barastoc Tournament at Warwick Qld (April 2018). BALWYN CORVETTE is by Cava and from the HAYDON DRAWN mare, HAYDON EVETTE.

Unfortunately Balwyn Cava died prematurely in 2012 from complications with laminitis.

GILGANNON STAR PANAMA, (Ellerston Cuba x Gilgannon Mystic) 2006 b h.

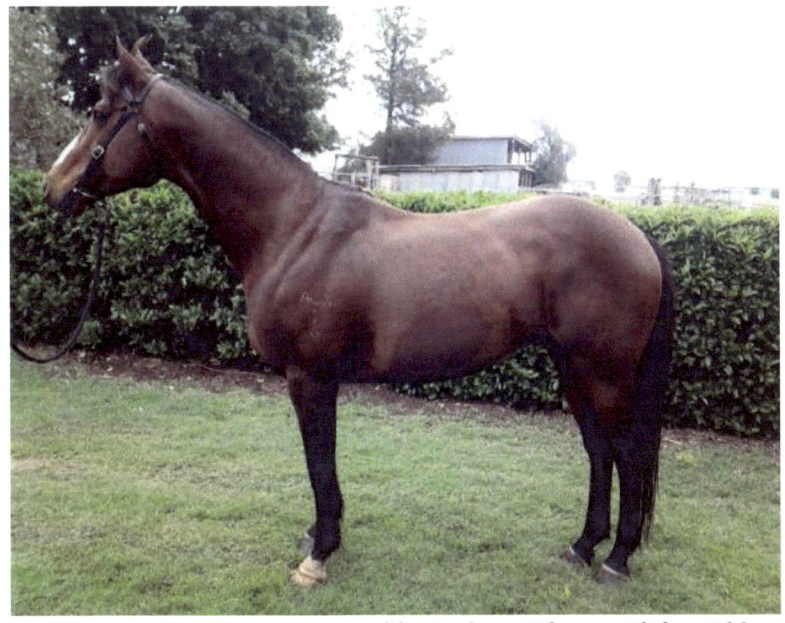

Gilgannon Star Panama, owned by Andrew Gilmore, Clifton Qld.

Ellerston Revenue (Littlewood Montego ex Glenugie Sold) br h.

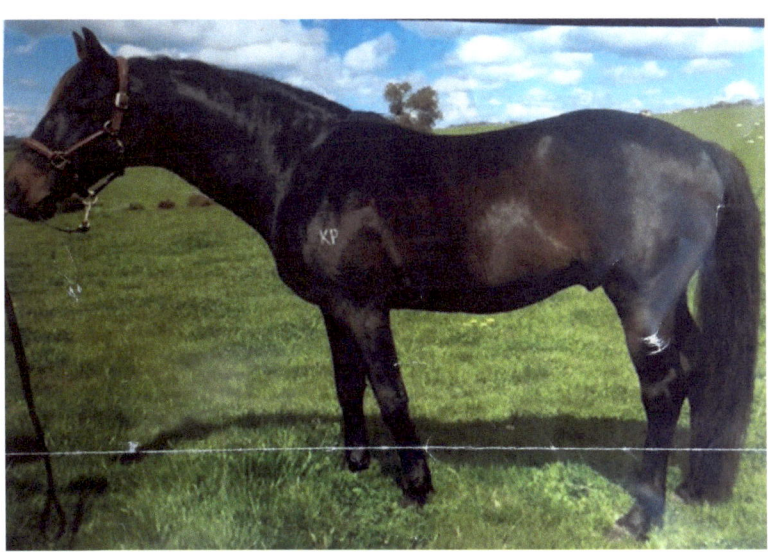

Ellerston Revenue

Once again from the 2015 sale catalogue. "Born at Ellerston and the second most prominent sire in the catalogue, Revenue has produced some outstanding polo ponies for Ellerston, including the sire Hermitage and a number of playing ponies overseas, such as Impress, Casanove, Lisa, and Surprise.

Sire Sons of Revenue.
Ellerston states:

Hermitage ex Touch of Pink, encompasses all of Ellerston's finest bloodlines. His progeny include Mistral, Mambo, Elegant (Champion Novice Pony at Goodiwindi as a 4yr old).

Mambo ex Tango, is beautifully bred and is our next up and coming sire. His oldest foals were born in 2012.

Focus ex Clarity. "Focus is one of the nicest looking stallions you will find. He has an impeccable temperament and is a lovely mover."

Spartacus (Littlewood Montego ex Spank (TB)) 2004, br h 15h.

Spartacus is perhaps the youngest of only a handful of horses alive, who can claim Panzer in their fourth generation. Bred by Anthony Baillieu, he was later given to Anto White *Belltrees* Scone, to use privately over their mares. Spank which produced Spartacus, was a thoroughbred mare, which then went with Ruki Baillieu the following year to play in England and America, proving to be a very good polo pony. Anto described him as "a lovely type, kind natured and passing this onto his progeny. Spartacus has been a good sire. His progeny are very nice but are horseman's horses. They are very athletic but will buck.

"His first foal, Jaffa is perhaps one of the best polo mares we have bred. Four mares by Spartacus played in the 8 goal at Ellerston recently, three with Alec White and one with Jack Archibald. He sired Alec's best young mare Perfection. Alec has taken two embryos out of her."

Unfortunately, no photos were available at the time of publication.

Timorpolo Patton *Spelt on the ASH website as* **TIMORPOLO PATON.**

(Littlewood Montego x Mirawala II) 1993 br h 15.1h.

Timorpolo Paton photo taken 2014 at 22 yrs of age

TIMORPOLO PATON is out of the top NEVER IN DOUBT (TB) mare Mirawala II, who played all levels right through to the Ellerston 40 Goal. when played by Gonzalo Pieres, the world's top 10 goal player at the time. Mirawala was only started as an older mare and unbelievably won her first BPP award six months later. She also became a very successful broodmare.

Patton has proven a sire of many good polo horses and is a genuine sire of sires, which doesn't happen all that often. These are Maximus, PINKDIAMOND BELLAGIO, TIMORPOLO AUGUSTUS, TIMORPOLO JULIUS, the taffy TIMORPOLO ROCKSTAR, and Mr Timor. Sadly, he only has 10 registered ASH progeny.

Patton is the sire of top Ellerston overseas mares Tweetie, dam of Best Polo Pony (BPP) at Ellerston, Canary, and Posh, played by Charlie Hanbury in the Queens Cup 2009-2012, Gold Cup 2009-2011, Deauville Gold Cup 2010 and then the 2013 US Open. Tweetie has produced many playing progeny for the Hanburys.

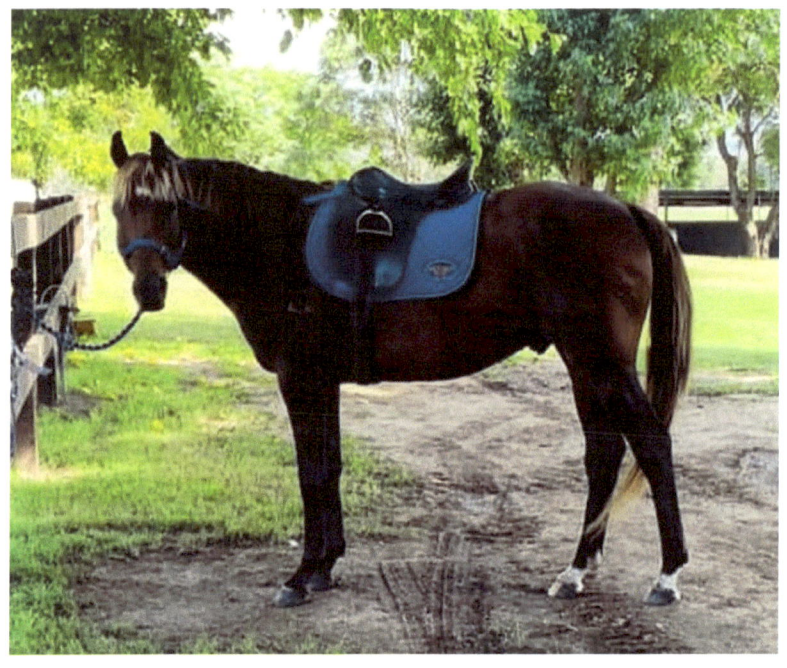

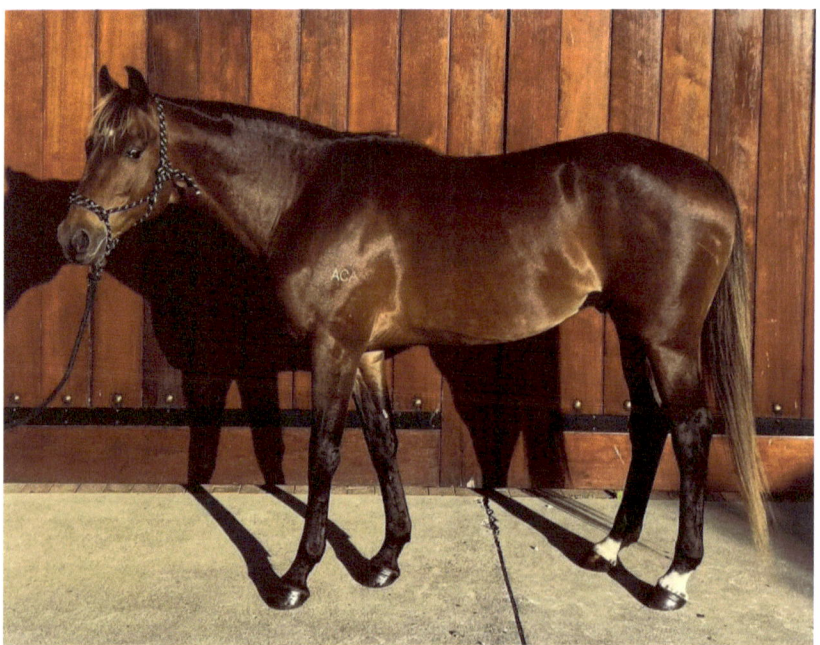

TIMORPOLO ROCKSTAR, ex TIMORPOLO HOLLYWOOD 2010, taf.

In 1997 Patton produced at Ellerston the very good horses Limbo, Oak, Pimms, Spider, Jillian, Pine, Henry, Rely, Halo, Snip, Messenger, China, Padre, JD, Kenny and Suzerain.

At Timor, he sired a multitude of very good horses including; Naomi won a BPP winning the Hector King, Vegas a BBP winner, Julia BPP at Alsace 2017, Tutu, General, Charlize, Hawaii, Carrera, Elle, Verona.

Mr Timor.

Maximus   (Timorpolo Patton x U2) 2005 brn h 15.1h.

Timorpolo Patton was in turn the sire of Maximus, which stood at *Haydon Horse Stud* in 2015. Full details of this horse are available on their website, and I quote:

"Maximus was started at polo proving a lovely horse to ride, stick & ball and play. However, he got kicked during chukkas and was retired. His full sister Stella won BPP at the 2017 Queensland Silver Cup. Another full sister Tutu played very well, won a BPP, was in the winning 2015 Hector King Team and is Fiola's best horse. His full brother General and his half-brother, the stallion Gold Dust, played very well overseas. Cole Aguirre selected General when he was given the pick of the horses for his 21st birthday and he was his best horse to play overseas.

"Maximus dam was the highly rated Thoroughbred international polo mare U2, who started playing in Australia before excelling in England and Spain. She was a compact chestnut Thoroughbred mare 15.1 hh with a star and small strip. She had a lovely head and took to polo as a real natural. High goal Los Tamaro's patron, Bob Aguirre, rated her as one of his best ever. It was decided her feats playing overseas warranted her return to Australia to be used as a broodmare. She was a good type, a natural and just so easy to play.

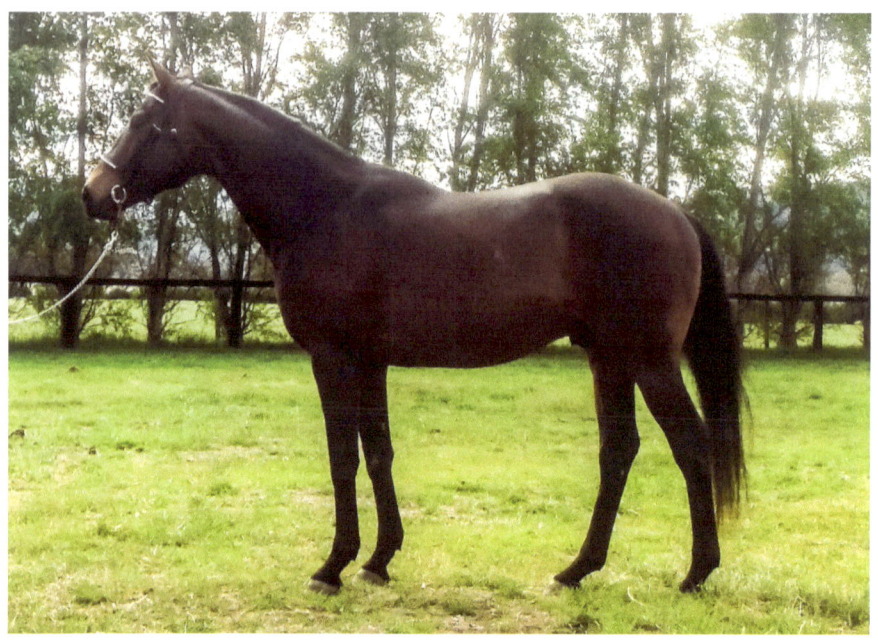

Maximus on the Haydon property, 2015

Maximus progeny:

Maximus's first foals were born in 2016. Haydon Horse Stud has 16 weanlings by him to register. 10 are brown fillies with light muzzles reminding us so much of the Never Doubt/Never In Doubt progeny. These fillies are like "peas in a pod", great types with great temperaments. At least 3 colts show sire potential.

They have all handled up very well to lead, tie up, load, lie down, been sat on, had their feet done, drenched and vaccinated.

Ten fillies by Maximus like "peas in a pod" tied up at weaning time waiting to be filmed by Landline

"We have kept the stallion **Haydon Spartacus,** ex HAYDON TOURMALINE, by him. He has some progeny shaping up to be good prospects. Spartacus has a very good temperament, ability and trainability traits. He is like his siblings with natural ability, cool on a loose rein, naturally picks up his leads, has an inbuilt rate, works off his hind legs and has a great mouth. He displayed all these traits during young horse chukkas in 2018, following and hitting a ball in his first month of riding with no hands on the reins.

Haydon Tourmaline is a full sister to Adolfo Cambiaso's international, Hall of Fame mare, HAYDON ANGEL JEWEL who won every major polo tournament in the world. His siblings include HAYDON VICTORIANA, who played the Argentine Open, HAYDON ORACLE, a sire in the UK, DUNKIRK, played polocrosse at the top levels, and top polo mares SKY JEWEL, PANDORA, CRYSTALLINE and ARGYLE. Tourmaline has had 13 registered foals.

Such a natural. Haydon Spartacus, (2016) ch h 15.1h, 2 years old, stick and balling without reins.

Stella, full sister to Maximus, taken at 2017 Qld Silver Cup.

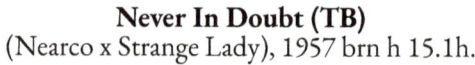

Never In Doubt (TB)
(Nearco x Strange Lady), 1957 brn h 15.1h.

This photo of Never In Doubt was taken by renowned Bloodstock journalist Brian Russell when Never In Doubt stood at Wagga. It was seen by Scone breeder Jack Johnston, who ran the Tyrone Stud, who said, "I just had to have that horse." He stood him at Tyrone for the rest of his life.

Foaled in 1957, Never In Doubt was imported to Australia after two wins in England. It is amazing from the few he produced how remarkable they were, such as Mirawala (mentioned previously). NABINABAH KYLIE was rated in the top few ever at Ellerston, producing the stallion ELLERSTON CHURCHILL and a string of top overseas horses.

The renowned Impact Mare NABINABAH EASY GOING won Champion at Test level. Zanzalee was ABCRA Novice horse of the year and won top campdrafts for Ken MacCallum. Never In Doubt's son, HAYDON NEVER DOUBT, has left a lasting legacy, including being the dam's sire of ASH Hall of Fame mare Haydon Angel Jewel.

Haydon Horse Stud has reintroduced his blood through the sires Churchill and Patton. The whole Never In Doubt story revolved around this one photograph! – Peter Haydon.

ELLERSTON CHURCHILL ex Nabinabah Kylie, 1999 Ch h 15.1h.

It is not widely known that the all-time great campdraft mare NABINABAH BREEZETTE and her full siblings, were great polo ponies. Breezette won polo prizes before conquering the campdraft world with her 6 wins in Sydney, 2 Warwick Gold Cups, 2 Horse of the Year awards and an Australian Championship win.

Some of these siblings and their descendants were bred to polo pony sires of the likes of Littlewood Montego, and the lines continue to this day in the hands of well-known players, albeit unfortunately mostly unregistered.

One of these is the grand horse Ellerston Churchill, which stood at *Haydon Horse Stud* and I quote from their website:

Ellerston Churchill at 18 yrs at Haydon Horse Stud.

"Churchill is from one of the all-time great Ellerston mares, NABINABAH KYLIE, by renowned sire Never in Doubt and from legendary mare Breezette's full sister NABINABAH BREEZE. He has three crosses Panzer.

Breeze performed right to the top level in polo before drafting with Bob Palmer. She produced the stallion NABINABAH CARIBOU, ISIS BLUE BREEZE, ISIS SOFT BREEZE, ISIS PURDETTE, NABINABAH GUNNADILLY, NABINABAH DUNDEE and Churchill's dam Nabinabah Kylie. She was a standout mare for Ellerston, both on the field and as a great producer of 11 foals. Rated in the all time top few at Ellerston.

This is one of the most celebrated female families in the ASH stud book. Other siblings include BELLTREES MUSKET, NABINABAH COOL GUN, COOL CHANGE, COOL BREEZE, CALM II, GUNNER, TOP GUN, HERALD, SHOGUN, SOLO, ZEPHYR, all from the Foundation Mare NABINABAH COMMA, who produced 16 registered foals in all.

Says Peter Haydon "Churchill was great moving horse, light on his feet and athletic, with his progeny being the same; good types, athletic and easy to play. He was a horse with a huge overtrack, an uphill walk, great bone and depth of girth. One of the things I really liked about him was his soft, athletic tread, nearly creepy-going, and the stock around by him are proving very good.

Churchill at 18 years old.

"He was ridden at Ellerston and named by them after the Monty war/leader connection. They swapped him for a playing mare and his owners finally got to the stage where they only had mares by him and could not use him any more.

Peter continues "Though sparingly used, Churchill had two playing in the 2017 Polo World Cup, Rosco and Miyo. Churchill has produced the stallions Phoenix used by Chris Anderson and a young stallion owned by Bruce Gavin. Bruce Gavin is playing four by him, rating them very highly, including the lovely mare Glitter. Garangula bred a good overseas mare and Lach McGuiness is playing ones by him."

Glitter played by Captain of Australia, Glen Gilmore, was part of the Winning Australian Team against NZ at the Sydney RAH Easter International 2019. In the same tournament, Marigold and Pamela (both by Churchill out of WANSEY LEON mares) were part of the Champion Team of Ponies for player Lachie Gilmore.

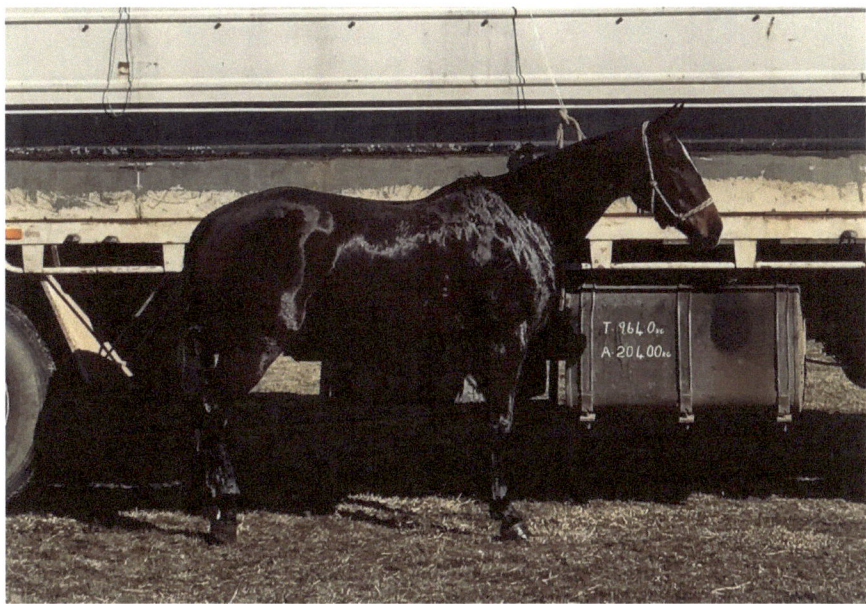

Bruce Gavin's Glitter

Churchill's first foals for the Haydons were foaled in 2017 and reflected the quality and ability one came to expect from this celebrated line. Unfortunately, the stud had to put him down in 2019, as he developed a growth on his penis.

Churchill's first progeny at Haydon Horse Stud were born in 2017 including:

Haydon Blenheim ex Haydon Celestial

Haydon Charmette ex Haydon Saffron Jewel

Some of his stock bred in that time included Chanel, a good type which has started her polo career well, similarly HAYDON LUNETTE, Rafa, Nightbird and Blenheim. HAYDON KARA was a nice colt that went over to WA, and the Pilmore's have a colt out of HAYDON MAYLIGHT.

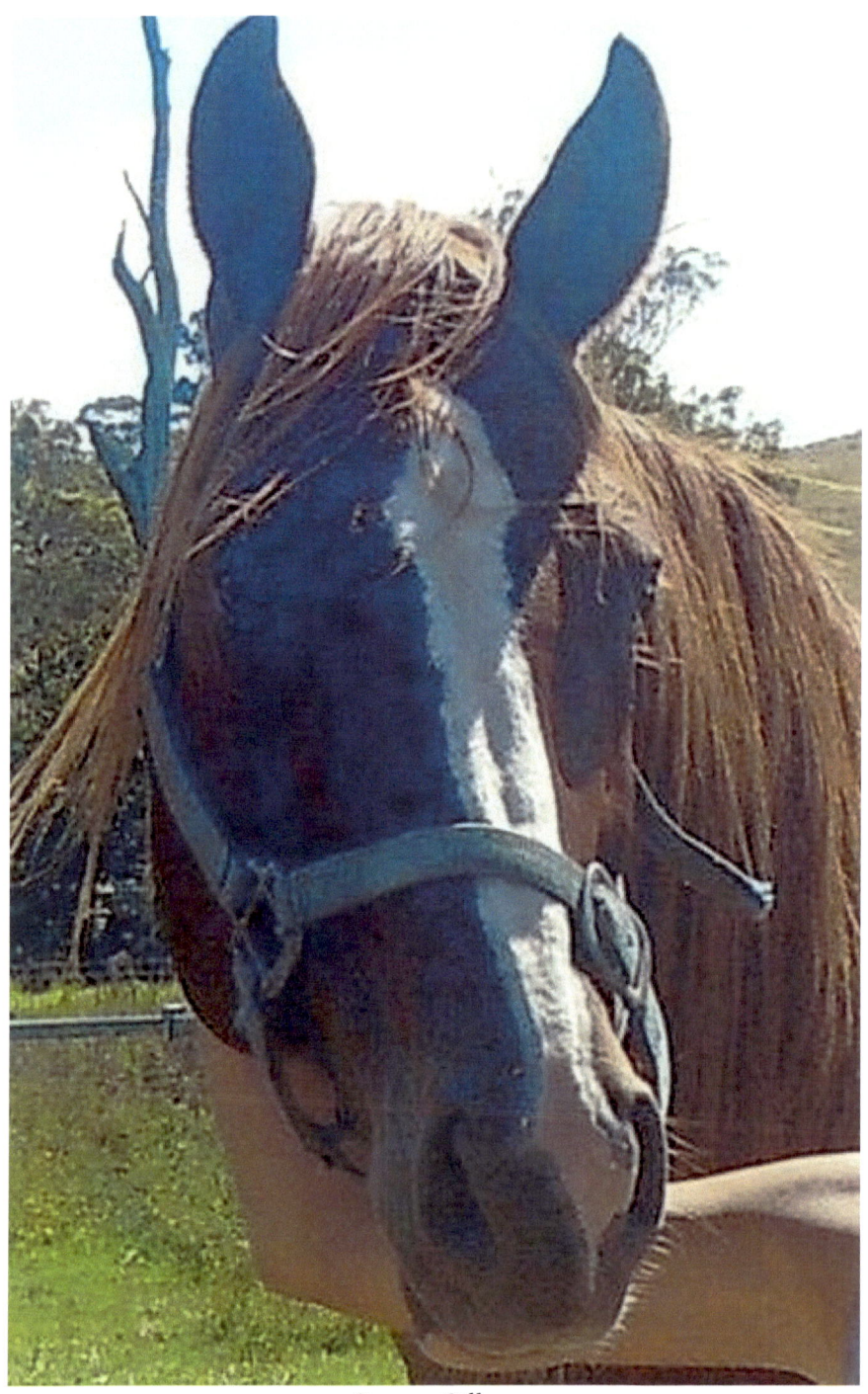

Cangon Gillette

Chapter 14

Cangon Gillette

(Littlewood Montego x Pretty Woman) 2001, ch h 15.1h.

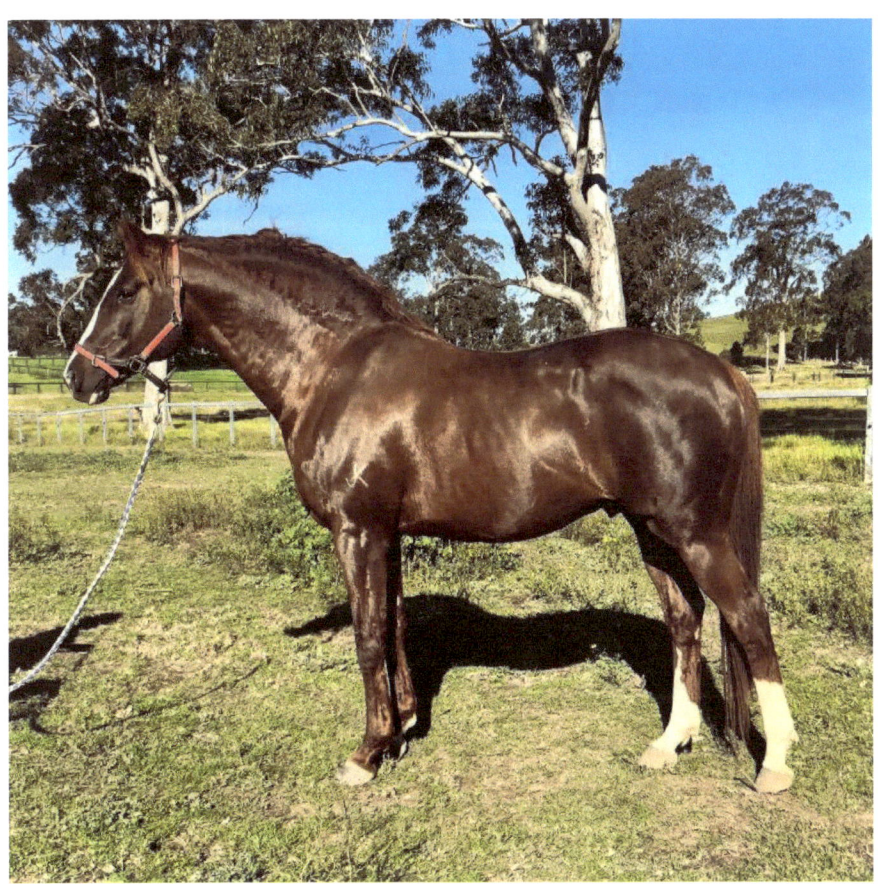

Cangon Gillette

CANGON GILLETTE was bred by the late Jaime MacKay, at *Cangon*, Dungog, and following his father's death, Jock returned from playing in England, to manage the stud. Jock describes Gillette as an outstanding individual, combining temperament, conformation and natural athletic ability.

Cangon Gillette with Jaime McKay

Gillette's dam, PRETTY WOMAN was as an extremely good polo pony played by Jaime. She played at the highest level of polo in Australia, many international test matches and won many polo pony prizes right across the country. She was a real eye catcher being liver chestnut with her white blaze and four white socks. One couldn't miss her! She died at the age of 29. Her full sister, Lucida, was equally as good. She played in the 40 goal tournament hosted at Ellerston and also won many pony prizes. Pretty Woman won Best Mare of a carnival at Ellerston 2000, where she won the free service to Monty, which got Gillette.

Pretty Woman was by MOSCOW (TB/reg ASH) from Boonerai by RAPID HOUR, which was a grey Thoroughbred horse raced by the Mackays. He was by Sunny Hour (Fr) which was imported after a successful racing career to breed polo ponies. This was another good line of polo ponies. Pretty Woman's dam has a double cross of Sunny Hour. Jock says "Gillette is the most balanced horse I have ever sat on. He did everything with ease. Unfortunately he didn't get to make it to the polo field as he was too valuable fulfilling his stud duties.

Moscow

(Sweet Moss x Lady Winalot) 1969 br h 15.2h.

Old advert

Moscow, was a beautiful led class thoroughbred horse. He was best TB exhibit at Sydney Royal several times and won Champion ASH 3 years running at Sydney Royal. He stood at *Cangon* in his later years on loan from owner Diane Cheetham, and sired some very useful horses that went overseas.

Others included BLACK BISTRO, Stylish Moss, SA polo player Nick Simpson's sire ELDORADO, and Heath Harris's black beauty Moscow's Legend. Lady Winalot was by Pipe of Peace. The Pipe of Peace (TB) line figures in many good polo ponies of that era and is still present in today's lines through the likes of ROMANDA, SPLASHDANCE and HAYDON DRAWN.

Moscow (TB) reg ASH.

Progeny of Cangon Gillette:

HVIRFS LONDON (see overleaf) 2012 g.g. 16h

"London is a lot of fun to ride and has brought me a lot of pleasure since owning him. He plays all positions but excels as 3. He is an impressive animal, a proper athlete and true professional in every respect! He is one of the most renowned geldings in the country, winning many Best Overall prizes and Best ASH at carnivals and State Championships. The big grey has had a stellar year; his majestic style and striking near white appearance have made him a fan favorite wherever he goes. He has been ridden by a number of top players in recent times but his pairing with Anderson has been a match made in heaven" – Ike Murray.

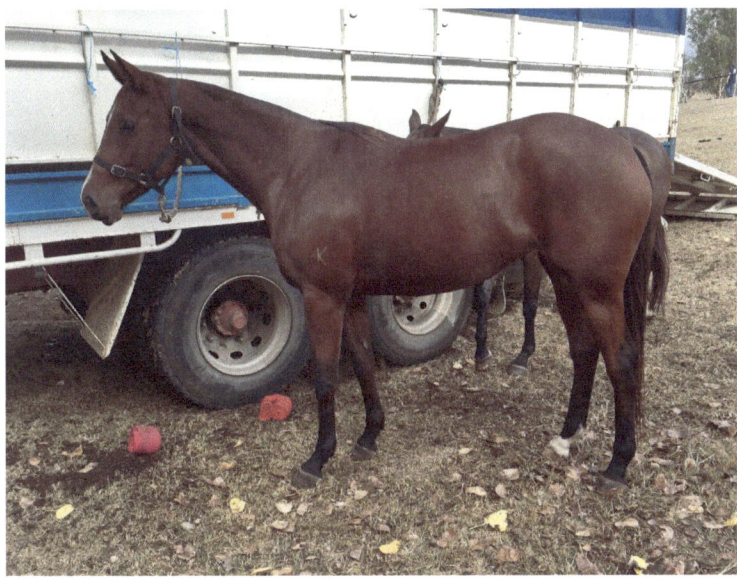

Chewy - "My A string of polo ponies are made up nearly entirely of Gillette's stock and his progeny continue to win a number of pony prizes. Two of these, Chewy and Precision, are out of outstanding polo mares by WYNASTRA (TB/reg ASH) and they would be my best playing mares at the moment. Gillette's progeny have definitely been blessed with his looks, brains and action." – Jaime McKay."

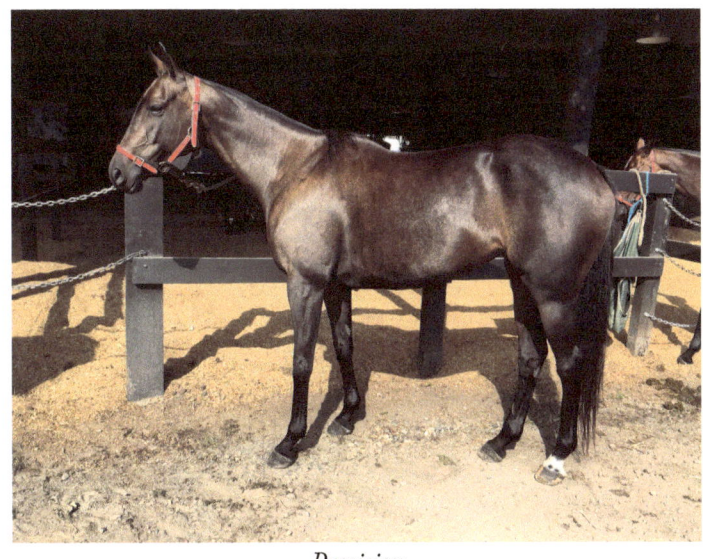

Precision

Hvirfs London

Foaled 2012
Grey Gelding

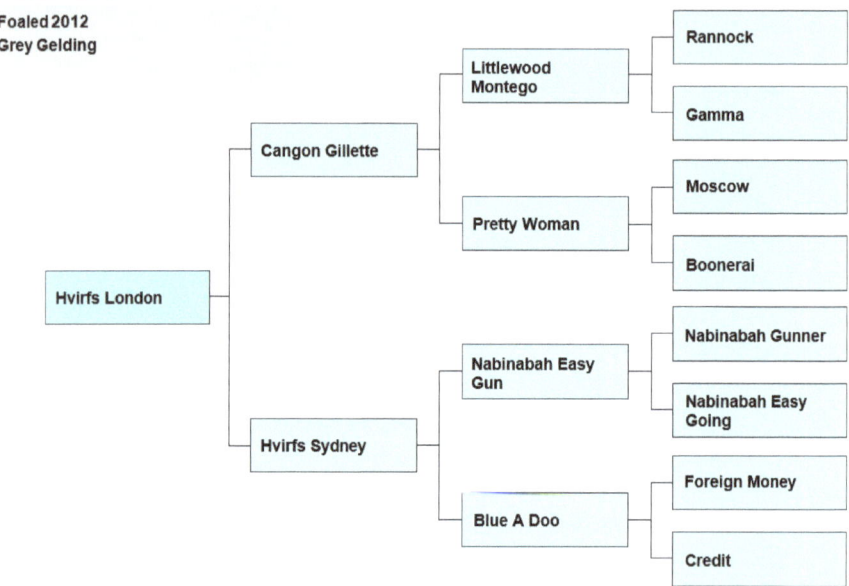

- Hvirfs London
  - Cangon Gillette
    - Littlewood Montego
      - Rannock
      - Gamma
    - Pretty Woman
      - Moscow
      - Boonerai
  - Hvirfs Sydney
    - Nabinabah Easy Gun
      - Nabinabah Gunner
      - Nabinabah Easy Going
    - Blue A Doo
      - Foreign Money
      - Credit

Hvirfs London with Lance Anderson, owner Ike Murray, photo Justine Wake.

ARAKOOLA TRADITION

(Cangon Gillette x Fintona Rhythm) 2007 ch h 15.2½h.

Arakoola Tradition, with Erin George.

From owner-breeder Brian Hodges of *Arakoola* Stud:

"**Arakoola Tradition** was from the most beautiful mare we had, a mare I had sought to own for many years; a lovely bay mare with no white, of heritage breeding. We think she is a very special mare. While she didn't compete, she was considered to be the best horse on the property by people who would know what they were talking about. Her sire COOPLA MING, owned by Doug Knapton, left a lot of very good station horses in the top of the Hunter, and the mare herself could have been a serious led class contender in her day. She has the classic CHAN front which I wanted to maintain in my horses.

"On her dam's side is two crosses to the famous YANDOOYA SOVEREIGN of Peter Tindal, which left very good quality horses in the New England Tablelands area. Sovereign was all Haydon breeding and obtained as a colt foal when the mare was purchased by Ventry McLennon, a famous breeder of the time.

"Tradition hasn't arrived here by chance. I was in need of a stallion to join to my Nabinabah Easy Gun mares, but didn't want to lose the Panzer top line, which had given us the athleticism and good temperament, while seeking to add more quality and speed. I wanted to have another Panzer-line horse but a different line. I had been an admirer of Rannock and Littlewood Montego for a long time, so Gillette, with his strong dam line looked ideal.

Fintona Rhythm, (2007), b m.

Erin George with Arakoola Tradition.

Erin George with Arakoola Tradition, photo Janet Hodges.

"When on loan to Kim Peterson, Tradition was a favourite mount. Her passion is Dressage and now Working Equitation. She instructs and judges in the discipline. He has excelled in these events but equally Tradition could have played polo or campdrafted. He has done well in ASH events, both led and ridden with my daughter Erin George. They say he is like riding a cloud. I have been pleased, even surprised, that the progeny have such beautiful temperaments. They are athletic, smooth-riding and very quick to learn."

Kim Peterson spoke of her time with him:

"Arakoola Tradition (Tiger) was my best mate. When I appeared at his gate he headed straight up to be caught. He enjoyed his training sessions. Tiger had a great work ethic and trainability. He was a super dressage mount for both myself and my two daughters, always placing in the top of the field. For the last few years we competed in Working Equitation. With his amazing movement he was rarely out of first place in the Dressage Phase. His calm nature and ability to collect, helped him breeze through the Ease of Handling Phase, which is an obstacle course ridden with finesse.

"It is judged on quality of execution and harmony between horse and rider. The third phase of Working Equitation is the speed phase. Tiger was happy to open his back and run, then come back and sit and wait. It took us a while to master the speed phase as I had to learn to ride a horse at speed. Poor Tiger had to wait for me to catch up!

"He placed or won at all of his Working Equitation starts. He is the ultimate all rounder, with paces to die for in the dressage arena, whilst maintaining a calm attitude in the speed round. Not only was the boy a great competition mount, he was also safe as houses with my grandchildren on board. He was quiet to ride down a busy road or bring the cows in on the farm."

Kim Peterson with 'Tiger' - no bridle.

Cody Wilson (Kim Peterson's daughter) with 'Tiger.'

Kim Peterson with "Tiger"

Photo gallery of Arakoola Tradition progeny.

CHALANI TRADITION, ex CARALTA PARIS, won SA Maturity, 2018. Shown here Peter Comiskey clinic, 2017.

ARAKOOLA JACK, ex ARAKOOLA MELODY, ridden by Leena Pfluger, SA. Winner at Lockington 2017.

ARAKOOLA MATILDA, ex ARAKOOLA NIKKI,
with Simon George.

ARAKOOLA HANNAH, ex CANNINGVALE HANNA, S.A
. Davidge.

ARAKOOLA HANNAH

Foaled 2012
B m
15.2h.

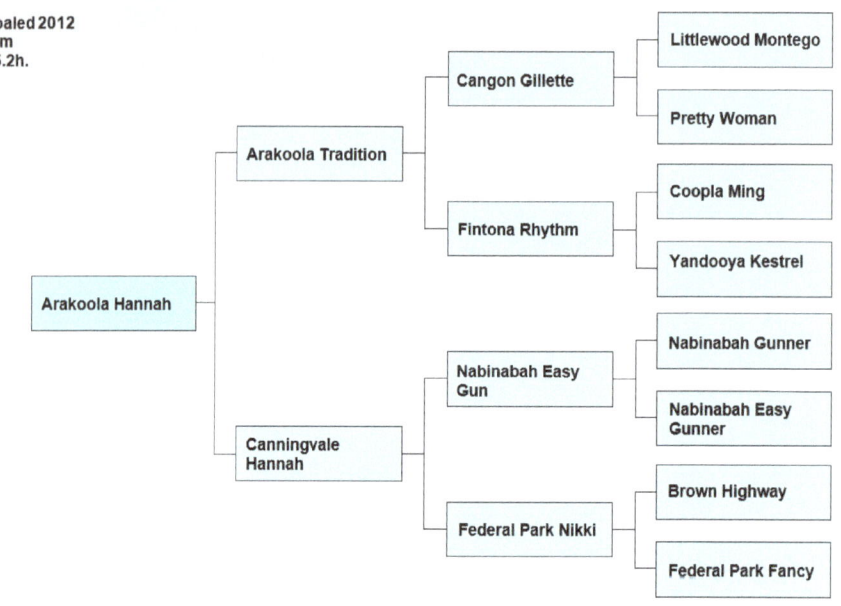

Arakoola Hannah

- Arakoola Tradition
  - Cangon Gillette
    - Littlewood Montego
    - Pretty Woman
  - Fintona Rhythm
    - Coopla Ming
    - Yandooya Kestrel
- Canningvale Hannah
  - Nabinabah Easy Gun
    - Nabinabah Gunner
    - Nabinabah Easy Gunner
  - Federal Park Nikki
    - Brown Highway
    - Federal Park Fancy

*Zelper El Macho, (Palmers El Condo x Canningvale Hannah) 2019,
colt owned by Sally Esdaile, NSW, combines the great mares Romance,
Breezette and Easy Going. He also has the Panzer sire, Nabinabah The
Gun, on both sides of his pedigree.*

Modern day efforts to preserve valuable bloodlines

At the Ellerston 2015 sale, Arakoola purchased one ridden mare, Ellerston Fuchsia, and an embryo, which is the black mare Arakoola Ella. Apart from both going back to Littlewood Montego, they were purchased to add the Norman Pentaquad (TB) blood, while keeping Panzer as well. "Fuchsia was bigger than most on the day, and I really liked the additional Nabinabah breeding in the embryo mare. They proved quiet to ride and were bred to ARAKOOLA JAZZMAN for two fillies foaled in 2023.

"Only a day or so afterwards, we lost Fuchsia and fostered her foal on another mare. We think the foals are close to the best we have bred, and as Jazzman is now 22, we bred Ella straight back. – Brian Hodges."

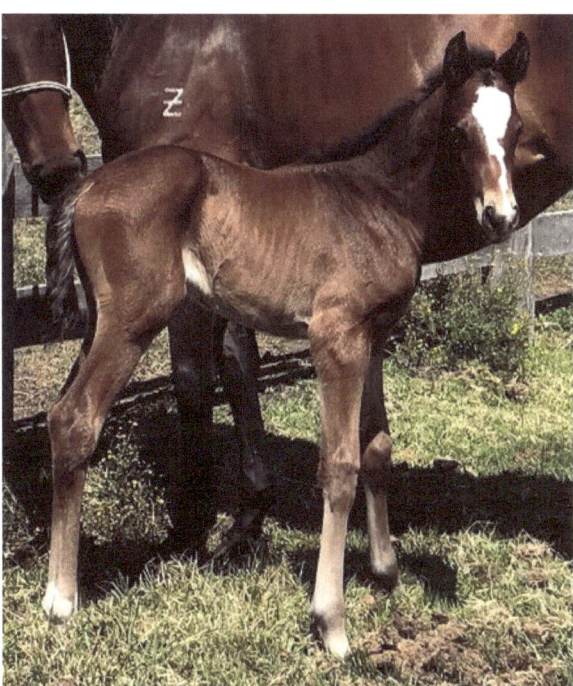

Arakoola Magenta, 2023 filly from Ellerston Fuchsia, carrying valuable genetics.

Author's Note – Arakoola are to be congratulated for their foresight and long-term planning, to keep the traditional Heritage horse alive in the breeding of modern day Australian Stock Horses. As I explained in my book, The Thinking Horse Breeder, a stud's most valuable genetics are its female lines.

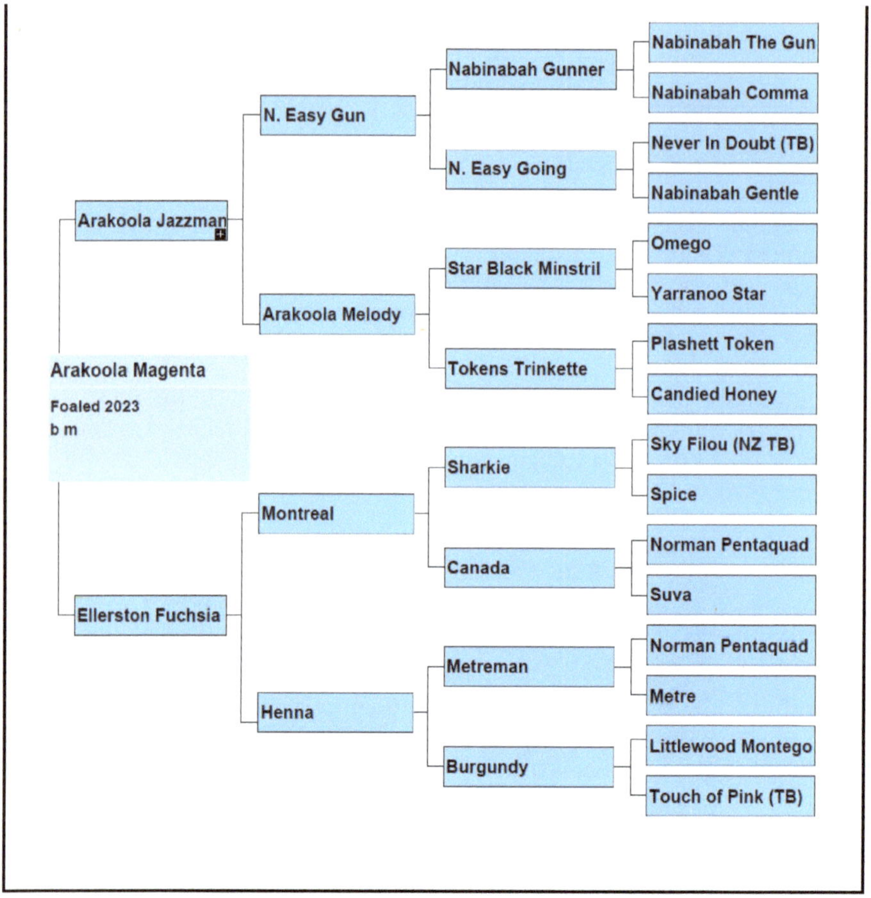

			Nabinabah The Gun
		Nabinabah Gunner	
	N. Easy Gun		Nabinabah Comma
			Never In Doubt (TB)
		N. Easy Going	
Arakoola Jazzman			Nabinabah Gentle
			Omego
		Star Black Minstril	
	Arakoola Melody		Yarranoo Star
			Plashett Token
		Tokens Trinkette	
			Candied Honey

Arakoola Magenta

Foaled 2023
b m

			Sky Filou (NZ TB)
		Sharkie	
	Montreal		Spice
			Norman Pentaquad
		Canada	
			Suva
Ellerston Fuchsia			Norman Pentaquad
		Metreman	
	Henna		Metre
			Littlewood Montego
		Burgundy	
			Touch of Pink (TB)

*ARAKOOLA ELEGANCE, ex CANNING-
VALE HANNA with Simon George. First
polocrosse carnival, 2017.*

Chapter 15

Master Herbert

The quiet achiever

(Rannock x Yooroona Gidget) 1984 br h 15.2h.

Master Herbert at Chalani, 6yo, 1990.

This truly top horse never got the opportunities he deserved, being in the sheep and grain-growing region of the Mid-North of South Australia, yet despite this, he left some really good progeny whose records have largely gone unnoticed. Without doubt, Master Herbert has been the 'quiet achiever.'

I well remember when the mare YOOROONA GIDGET (Captain Stand x Patsy) owned by Peter and Chris Roberts of *Narrioota*, Spalding, SA, came to

Rannock, as she was all quality. Upon Rannock's untimely death, I rang and suggested that should Gidget foal a colt, Chris should consider keeping it entire. MASTER HERBERT was bred with no plans of breeding a line of horses, but as he was of good quality and easily managed, he was kept a colt.

Yooroona Gidget, circa 1975.

Gidget was brought from Queensland by JY (John) Maitland, a well-regarded horseman of the area, who stood the grand horse Charble (TB), sire of two Olympic horses and many other successful SA polo ponies and quality performers. (He called her 'Gidgeon'). She played for ten seasons, remaining sound throughout, before retiring to stud for the Roberts. Gidget was a calm mare and always reliable. She was a smooth-actioned, athletic type and played an active part in Clare polo teams in the 1970's. Gidget won a polo pony prize at the Hexham tournament in 1979 in the twilight of her career, and was admired by many.

In a letter by Philip Fitchner to Jeanette Gower dated 28th June 1985, he said:

"Captain Stan was a Thoroughbred horse by Captain Fox (by Nearco) ex Cinnafast, who traces to Carbine. He was bred by the Jenning family of "*Alma Vale* Stud" Greenmount where Captain Fox was standing. [*From research by Peter Gower, the horse's correct name was Captain Stand, brn 1956, though I have not been able to find out anything more about this horse.*]

"He was handled but unbroken, as he was hurt as a yearling and never raced. This is how my uncle Ron Fitchner happened to get him. He used him as a paddock stallion in a rough mountain paddock. Unfortunately, my uncle only had him for a few seasons when he was found dead from a stake. He was about 15.3h and most of his progeny were used as local stock horses. Gidget was one of his last foals. Ken Telford broke her in and reported she was very calm to break in and ride and never put a foot wrong.

MASTER HERBERT

Foaled 1984
Br H
15.2h.

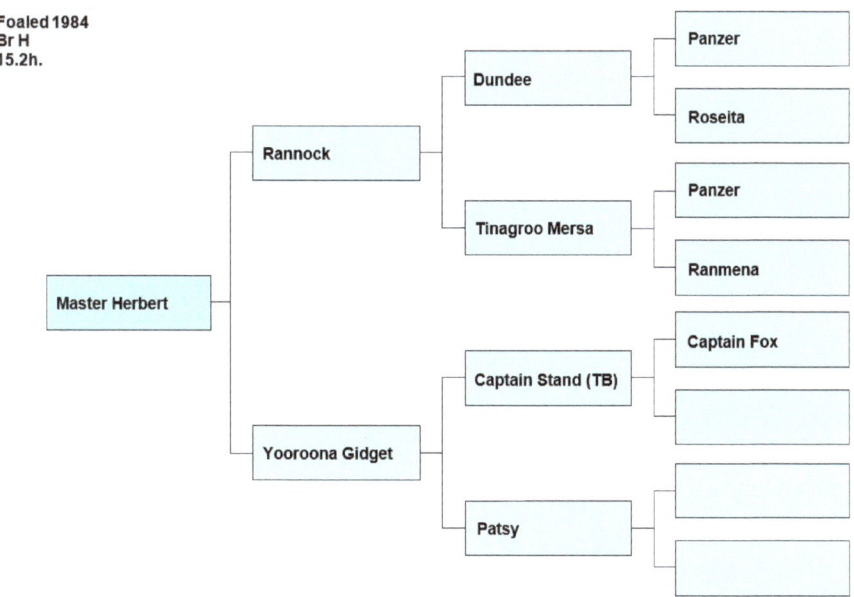

In a 1991 letter, Chris Roberts wrote: "Herbie's temperament is great as he can be a quiet farm horse and then put in an athletic performance under pressure. Last weekend we had an endurance ride here and Herbie has become an endurance horse. He did the 40k section easily after having spent nearly 3hrs out the day before marking sections of the course which were too rugged to drive over. He has great stride and strength for the long rides and hill work being a real pleasure to ride. Quite a few people have commented on him, especially in the vetting ring. Regular riders say we provided the toughest SA course this season.

"There were a lot of novice riders which made it tough for the first 15ks, as people on mares travelled very close to Herbie's nose generally giving him no respect. He handled it all very well, actually better than any of my previous geldings."

Herbie mustering, circa 1995.

Master Herbert

"I can remember writing in the 1990's that I hoped Master Herbert would make a worthwhile contribution to the horse industry in South Australia, but it has continued beyond that time. I think ASH breeding has progressed in the last 20 years with more horses of better temperament and ability and that our Master Herbert progeny have been part of that development.

"We have not run a commercial stud and been proud to offer our horse and his progeny locally and see them being used and enjoyed by South Australians. I consider that each Australian state is different and that each should make its own identity while within the framework of the Australian Stock Horse Society. We do not have large cattle numbers or many big country centres in South Australia, so it is hard to specialise in any discipline because travelling long distances is not always practical. To get best usage of our horses they need to be multi-disciplined, requiring good temperament and athletic ability.

"I believe that Master Herbert progeny have been able to meet that need." – Chris Roberts.

Chapter 16

Master Herbert progeny

There being few registered ASH mares available, the Roberts set about acquiring some well-bred Thoroughbred mares. The first of these was YOOROONA SALUKI, by Follow Me out of a Charble mare. She produced 6 registered full siblings. Her youngest progeny YOOROONA SCHWEPPES and SAMSON were an important part of their son, Scott's, polo team.

Schweppes was an Adelaide Royal Show Champion Led ASH mare and Res Champ Ridden 2002 ASH SA Show Series winner. She performed well in Challenges and placed in a campdraft. She had a foal by Mr Fitzjester (TB) which played good A-grade polo for Guy Cunningham. Ten years later, Schweppes won a polo pony prize. In between she foaled, did pony club, campdrafted, trail riding, then had 2 more filly foals after her ridden retirement.

A full brother YOOROONA SHIRPA had a similar career, being ridden by Scott for many years and then going into the TV industry as an all-rounder, used regularly in *McLeod's Daughters*. He then taught a family to ride and started them in campdrafting.

It is hard to say which were the best offspring of Herbie. Schweppes, Pacemaker, Shirpa were all well performed over a long time in many disciplines. Nine played polo: Samson, Tinka, Schweppes, Pacemaker, Scamp, Pancho, Pebbles, Matrix, Rapids.

YOOROONA PACEMAKER (ex Pep em Up) a champion Royal Show performer, also placed in the Nationals at Narrabri 2004. He campdrafted, did polo then dressage. Full siblings Pacemaker, Pebbles and Pancho were in our polo string. There is a full sister, YOOROONA PIP, unfortunately injured as a yearling and used only for breeding.

The Sunny Coronation (TB) mare WIRREANDA COMIC of Grant Waterman from Melrose, bred some talented progeny in a variety of fields, from dressage to pony club and polo. YOOROONA COSMOS with Jo Cullen, YOOROONA COSMIC with Hayley Crommellin. Guy Cunningham played grade polo with Comic and Hattie in 08-09 season, with Comic regularly playing double chukkas.

Yooroona Schweppes, shown here ridden by Scott Roberts. Photo Joe McInally.

Most of Master Herbert's early progeny stayed in the Mid-North of South Australia and were not registered. In 1990, he was leased for a season to the Gowers at Echunga. CHALANI GISELLE was the best performed of the progeny bred from that season, and she is the dam of CHALANI NIGHTDANCE.

Samson, Schweppes, Pacemaker 1998 at Narrioota. Three of a kind!

CHALANI GISELLE ex Chalani Cat Ballou, 1991 blk m 15.2h.
A top-class mare in anyone's language, Giselle was the last filly retained of her famous dam, Chalani Cat Ballou, which is on the Society's Wall of Renown, alongside Rannock.

Chalani Giselle

Giselle has an ASH Soc. All Round Supreme Award, only the fifth in SA, achieving this in 1997 as a five-year-old. She is one of the few horses to win the three major SA ASH events, namely the 1993 Yearling Futurity, 1995 Ridden Futurity, and 1996 ridden Maturity, both times ridden by Jeanette Gower.

She won High Point Performance Horse at leading ASH Shows, led and ridden Championships, working, and even barrel races. She qualified for Adelaide Royal as a hack under the Gower's (then junior) daughter, Kim. Giselle was a natural showjumper, with the ability to remain cool under pressure and handle all types of going. She was loaned to beginner and novice riders to learn on and retired at *Birdrise* Stud.

Giselle has made an amazing contribution to the ASH through her 11 progeny, which have had excellent careers. They include the multi-award-winning sire CHALANI NIGHTDANCE, (sire in turn of Chalani Tempo), CHALANI PLAYWRIGHT, (sire for the Henzen family, then gelded), the beautiful CHALANI DANCE, winner of many Championships in SA, led and under saddle, BALLET and OPERA, both dressage and open hack winners, and ACTOR, dressage, and show jumping winner. These are all full siblings by Splashdance.

L: Chalani Opera (Belinda Battersby) and R: Chalani Minerva (Jeanette Gower) Res Champ and Champ Led ASH Mares, Adelaide Royal 2013. Photo by Kangra.

The beautiful Chalani Dance with Kim Gower, 2010 winner SA Four Year Old Maturity, photo by Kangra.

Chalani Playwright, Melbourne Summer Royal, 2011, with Kelleigh Henzen.

PRECIOUS HOPE, ex Coal Miners Daughter, 1999 ch m.

Precious Hope

Tom Dodd bred three lovely types by Master Herbert out of his well performed COAL MINERS DAUGHTER. The first, Precious Hope, competed successfully quite regularly with Tom in ASH events, and later at the 2007 Nationals with Chari-Lee Hoad, placing third overall in the under 18 Junior. The second, TAYLORS BROOKE competed in six drafts with Tom, for three wins. The third, TOMALI MASTER RANNOCK (Bucky), has been a regular stewards horse at Adelaide Royal, before joining Chari-Lee's school horses.

Precious Hope is now with the Zanker (nee Hoad) family, with progeny kept as schoolmaster horses for Chari-Lee's students to ride. One of her foals WILLIAMPARK KOKODA (by VANCOUVER PARK WATCH MY DUCO) placed in the 2013 National Futurity with Dan Steers riding, and is now drafting for Tom.

Long time Quarter Horse breeder, Merrie Elliot of Booberowie, says: "Matt Donoghue's stewards horse, Dollar, is by our Great Stuff (QH) and out of a Master Herbert mare. He does a top job, and he is just an all-round cowboy type work horse. We have his full sister Yooroona Cruise in the mare band and it's a real pleasure to have her. She is a wonderfully strong mare with no coarseness, of a beautiful rabicano coloring.

"Dollar and Cruise are out of Yooroona Pip. The dam of Pip was a well-bred running mare Pep Em Up. Matt is husband of well-known horse-woman Leanne. He has had two fabulous fillies out of Yooroona Cruise, by Winning Deck (QH)."

Dollar (Matt Donaghue) and Bucky (Kate Growden) sterward's horses at Ade-laide Royal Show 2017, Horizons photography.

YOOROONA RAPIDS, ex Expressa (TB) 2005 ch m 15.1h.

Yooroona Rapids with Scott Roberts, photos Chris Roberts.

Yooroona Rapids was an excellent stock horse type, very classy, out of the Thoroughbred mare EXPRESSA, by Green Line Express. Kim Ide leased her from

Chris Roberts with a view to hacking her, but her own pregnancy meant a change of plans. She bred one foal from Rapids, which resulted in the palomino stallion Chalani Sunstream, now an influential sire.

Yooroona Rapids with Scott Roberts

Rapids returned to Scott Roberts' team of A grade polo ponies. Speaking of her (first) season, Chris Roberts said "Rapids had a great polo season and finished fit and strong and mentally good. Her first week off from polo she had a lovely trail ride around the roads. It was well worth not hurrying her. She has plenty of everything needed. Scott's season varied from A to C grade which is also hard on horses and she coped well with the changes. Scott says she is light to play and gallops smoothly over the ground."

Rapids played four seasons of polo and has been used as a lead horse for Chris's breakers. She has since produced two bay fillies YOOROONA RIVAH by CAWDELL'S SAMSON sold to Penny Maynard following the retirement of the Roberts from breeding horses, and Ripple. Says Chris, "Ripple is an amazing filly by ALERT II (TB/reg ASH). She looks like an Argentine polo pony with a long wither good for keeping a saddle in place. She is very athletic, quick and has nice movement."

In 2008, Expressa foaled an exceptional, full brother to Rapids, which the Roberts planned to keep as a replacement for his sire, but a paddock injury meant that wasn't to be. However, the future of Master Herbert's line in SA is secure through his daughters producing the notable sires Chalani Sunstream and Chalani Nightdance. *(Their stories to follow).*

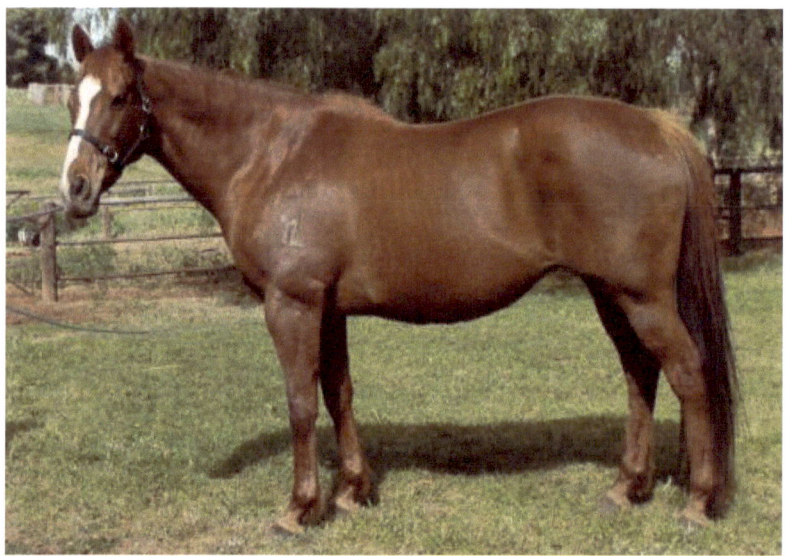

Expressa (TB) and Greenline Express below.

CHALANI MINERVA, ex Chalani Aurora, 2008 brn m15.2h.

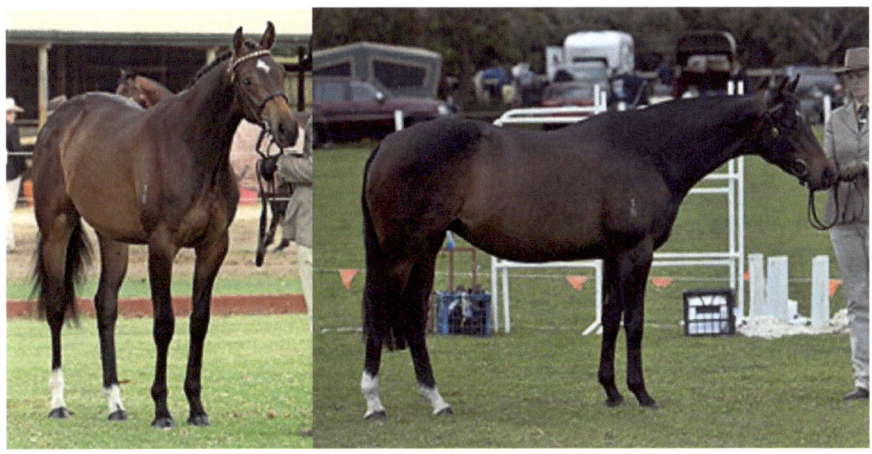

Chalani Minerva, considered by many to be the ideal type of ASH. Left, Yearling Futurity 2010, winner, right, Supreme Led All Breeds Fleurieu Extravaganza, 2013.

Chalani Minerva is probably the most successful of Master Herbert's progeny, and a leading SA mare for both her record and versatility at the highest levels. At 15 years of age, she is the youngest horse alive today with Rannock as a grandsire. She is a top-quality type, very much in the mould of her sire.

CHALANI MINERVA

Foaled 2008
B m
15.1½h.

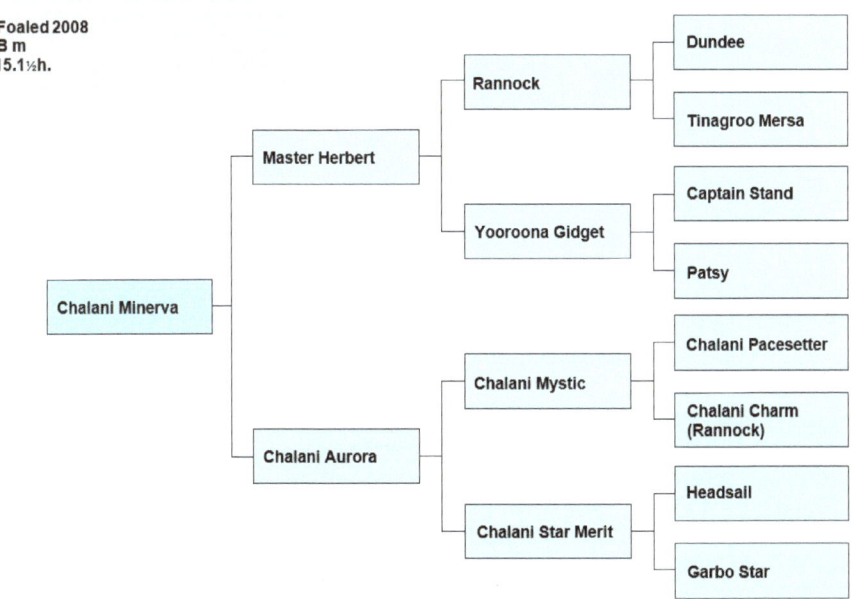

Chalani Minerva won multiple Supremes.

Minerva has a lovely disposition and is calm and sensible in varied situations. She is an athletic horse in working events, has been admired by many in the show ring, and rates a cow very well. She is the ideal type and quality of horse *Chalani* wish to breed. As a foal she was obviously well balanced in conformation and never seemed to go through an awkward looking growth stage. She was the horse that owner/breeder Kim Ide used to return to riding after having twin boys in 2013.\

Shown successfully from a weanling, Minerva won many led, hack and working champions as well as Supreme Led and Ridden awards in ASH, often beating mature horses when only a youngster. She was an All-breeds Supreme winner, as well as ASH Futurity wins, Challenge places and an Open Hack ring winner at Show Horse Council shows.

As a 3yo at the ASHS National Show in Tamworth, in huge classes, she was 1st Hack in English attire, 4 years and under and placed 4th Led filly 3 years, 3rd Pleasure Hack 3 years, and placed in 4 other working and ridden events.

Minerva was Champion Led ASH mare at the 2013 Adelaide Royal Autumn Breeds show. She was a winner at the Melbourne Royal Show (2014) in the Hack Mare over 15hh class and the Time Trial. She also achieved placings in ASHLA, Working ASH mare and the Station Horse.

Minerva drafting with Kim Ide, Fleurieu Campdraft, 2014,
Shadows Farm Photography.

At her first ever campdraft, Minerva won the Encourage at Keith, Oct 2014 with Kim. Minerva had only ever seen cattle once before this event, at a Pete Comiskey clinic and Kim had only started doing a few campdrafts herself on Minerva's half-sister, CHALANI TRIVIA. Minerva displayed a natural ability to 'rate' cattle and steady off so as to not run past the cow when outside. She made several maiden and novice finals. Kim credits Minerva as the horse that enabled her to 'get the hang' of working cattle. has been lead horse for the kids' children's ponies and horses being broken in. Minerva has also been loaned to encouragement and youth riders at campdrafts and shows.

For several years Kim attempted to get a foal from Minerva, which was unsuccessful for no apparent reason. In 2017 Minerva went to Goulburn Valley Equine Hospital in Victoria for keyhole surgery to unblock her oviducts, this being the assumed diagnosis for her lack of conception. Vet Angus McKinnon suggested that an embryo transfer be done, which fortunately was successful. A quality brown ET filly named CHALANI ARIEL, by Chalani Tempo, in 2018 was the result, a Supreme Led ASH winner at her only show 2023 to date.

Next Minerva foaled a 2019 chestnut filly, CHALANI NOVA, by GAMBER-LEE JAGUAR (by DOGWOOD COMET).

Chalani Nova, with Kim Ide, Adelaide Royal 2022. Photo Lisa Gordon.

Xander Ide and Chalani Nova At Wannon River 24.

As a youngster Nova won her ASH State Two Year Old Futurity, and was Reserve Champion Led and Champion Ridden ASH, Adelaide Royal 2022 (at only 3yrs of age). Nova is proving to be very cowy and exceptionally steady. Her first draft win was with 10yo Xander in the Junior at Wannon 2024, as a 4year old!

CHALANI GALAXY was her next foal, an outstanding colt by Chalani Sunstream, which has been Supreme ASH Exhibit at each of his Led shows in 2023. He has been retained for the stud (see p 290) and carries a double cross of Master Herbert.

Minerva followed this with a top quality buckskin full sister, DELTA, in 2023.

Minerva, with Jeanette Gower, Champion ASH mare, Adelaide Summer Royal
2013. Photo by Kangra.

Minerva with Kim Ide.

Minerva, Time Trial, ASH Nationals, Tamworth, 2013, Narelle Wockner photography.

Minerva in dressage, ASH Nationals 2013, Narelle Wockner photography.

Part III - The next generations

Significant sires of the Rannock bloodline

"My beautiful Chalani Gamboller (Chalani Gyprock x Chalani Skelter) was a double cross of Rannock. He lived to be over 30 years. I miss him every day." – Anna Booth.

"I have a mare by Memphis Park Memory. I bred her mother, but never registered her or her mum, as life and disciplines changed. Her dam is by Thorlindah Royal Mint (by Crown Law) out of an ASB Gielgud mare. Magnificent temperaments both of them. Memory gave her her looks. Her mum was structurally lovely, but plain. I think Rannock's influence is evident in her." – Kathy Brown

"Looking forward to the next instalment and wondering how I could mention that if I had met Rannock before becoming enamoured of Quarter Horses, I would probably have gone down the Stock Horse route! The improvement in all things stock horse, as gathered from the Journals, has been astonishing I reckon." – Merrie Elliott, July 2019, following on from an article in the ASH magazine.

Rannock descendants often came First, Second, Third in classes. L-R Belinda Battersby, Chalani Opera; Cathy Beer, Chalani Auster; Kim Ide, Chalani Minerva.

Chapter 17

Chalani Pacesetter

An easy, bold horse

(Hill x Chalani Skelter) 1983 ch h 15.3h.

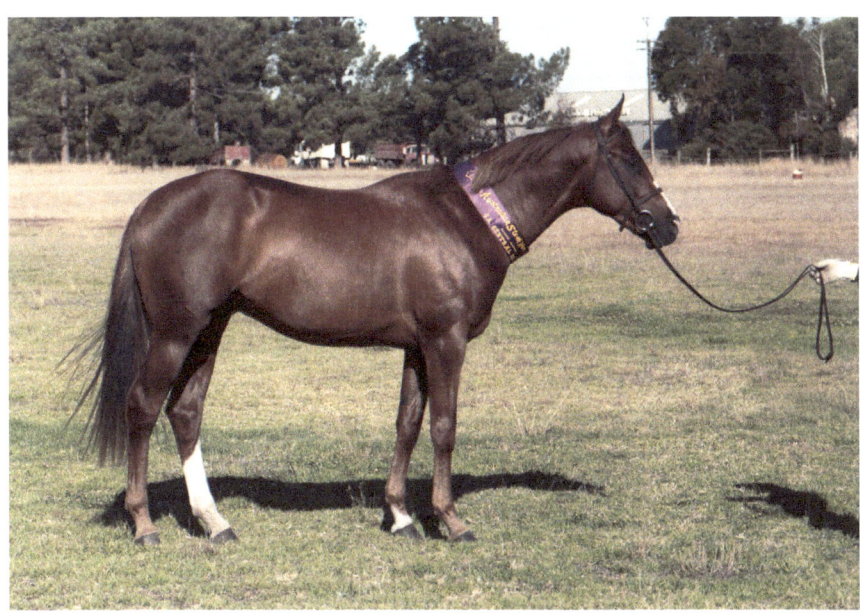

Chalani Pacesetter as a three year old.

With the untimely death of Rannock in 1983, Chalani sought to reappraise its breeding plans. A small and progressive stud, a few Rannock daughters had been retained, with the intention of performing them before breeding them out to other well-performed polo lines. Fortuitously, they took a look at their current crop of foals and decided to run on one rather leggy, well proportioned youngster who would come up in the paddock and allow himself to be caught; the kind of horse you'd be proud to ride as a top-notch gelding, a work horse or show hack. We thought 'A good stallion must always make a good gelding! Why not?' This handsome fellow was **CHALANI PACESETTER**, named after the 'movement' theme of his dam.

Chalani Skelter with Jeanette Gower.

Skelter was a 'do anything' mare. She was from the first crop of Rannock for the Gowers and had performed creditably in open western events at a time when there were no working stock horse classes available in SA. She was the winner of the huge Expo 80 Trail class, defeated only once in a two year career in trail classes. She gained an ASH Award of Merit in Working events, including Reining, often runner-up to her stablemate Chalani Galena (see p 28-30). Skelter produced progeny which competed with success from dressage to eventing to ASH competition. Her daughter CHALANI PIVOT was retained by the stud and went on to produce multiple first-class progeny, including sire son, Chalani Tempo, Chalani Skylark and Chalani Ripple, both broodmares at Chalani.

We had wanted to breed a Hill horse, based on Hill's record as a sire of polo ponies and his breeding. But we knew his reputation and plainness, so we thought carefully as to which mare to select. Chalani Skelter was chosen because of her sweet nature, ridden performance, and quality. She was out of our foundation mare PARADIS, a versatile mare off Cordillo Downs station, of Anglo Arab breeding. Disappointingly, when we picked Skelter up from the Vincents, the vet said she wasn't pregnant. In those days it was a 45 day manual examination. A few months later, we realized he was wrong!

Chalani Pacesetter proved an easy horse to break in by Jeanette. He showed great overtrack and tremendous balance for a young horse and was calm and focussed on his work. He won many awards in SA ASH competition from limited outings, including 1985 Yearling Colt Futurity, Supreme Champion Led Exhibit 1986 ASH Show Strathalbyn, Champion Led Junior ASH 1986 at Salisbury All-Breeds Show, Champion Led and Ridden ASH at Murray Bridge Ag Show in 1987.

The highlight was receiving Champion 1986 Adelaide Royal ASH Entire at 3 years old, no mean feat from a field of 15 other stallions! It is still the biggest field of ASH stallions shown at any Adelaide Royal. Pacesetter was a horse with outstanding movement, an effortless ground-covering trot, even bold temperament and strong hooves.

Pacesetter was sold to Michael and Pauline Heffernan of *Yagoona*, Eudunda SA, in 1987 for polo and endurance, with the aim of retaining his son, CHALANI MYSTIC. This purchase was subject to a vet check, upon which the vet declared Pacesetter had the best resting heart rate he had ever seen on a young colt. Friend Paula Mathews remembers "Pacesetter was a lovely eye-catching horse with a remarkable temperament and a lovely mover, attributes he passed on to his progeny." He was later sold to Dennis Sugars, Naracourte SA, who continued to breed endurance progeny with him under the *Devious* (DVS) prefix. Pacesetter was leased back to Chalani in 1999 upon the untimely death of Chalani Mystic, but unfortunately broke a leg in a paddock accident, shortly after his return.

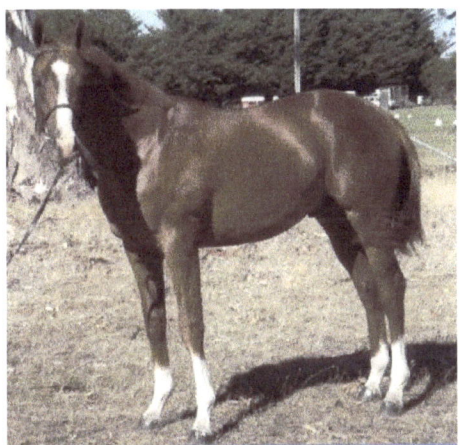

Memphis Park Memory, (Chalani Toy Soldier x She's Ideal (TB/reg ASH) 2013, owned by Crystal Ballard.

Chalani Pacesetter, did leave two sire sons, Chalani Mystic and CHALANI TOY SOLDIER, which sired MEMPHIS PARK MEMORY, the latter two both being gelded after siring foals, due to their owner's circumstances.

Chalani Pacesetter sires Quilty winner!

The prestige Endurance ride, the Tom Quilty Gold Cup, held in Queensland 2008 was won by China Doll and Meg Wade. They also won the Pat Slater cup for the Best Conditioned, and the teams event. China Doll was previously 4th in the European Championships of 2005.

China Doll, ex Warrondi Pearl, 1985 gr m.

One of Australia's greatest endurance horses, was the mare China Doll. She was a household name in endurance circles and her story has been featured in several magazines.

China Doll built one of the most impressive records of all time for an Australian endurance horse, ridden mainly by owner Meg Wade of *Castlebar* Arabians. She always displayed guts, determination and the ability to mow down the competition, no matter how far in front of her they might be, making them a formidable team.

China Doll began her career in 2001, completing her novice rides in SA. She competed 33 rides with only 2 non-completions, and to 2008 had managed a total successful mileage of 3233ks.

She successfully completed eight out of nine 160km rides with the impressive results of five 1st placings, three Best Conditioned (BC) awards, 4th in the European Championships, 8th and 13th achieved in the United Arab Emirates President's

Cup, as well as being the highest placed foreign horse at that event (2007). Twenty three times she completed in the top five, winning 11 of these and taking out the coveted Best Conditioned award eight times.

China Doll knew her job and wanted to get out there and compete. Her recoveries were phenomenal and she was known on many occasions to present in the time it took to get the saddle and bridle off and walk into the vet ring.

Her recovery on the day after a big ride was also nothing short of amazing, where she would present looking like a show horse, displaying no effects from the big effort of the day before by completing her workouts effortlessly and very fluidly.

Photography by Matt Bennet

At home, China Doll was treated royally, being given the best paddocks, spoilt by all the staff at *Castlebar* and generally pampered like a princess. She was bred by Michael and Pauline Heffernan, in SA and was out of a WERRONDI WENCESLAS (Arab Imp UK) mare, registered in ASH stud book as WERRONDI PEARL. China Doll produced five geldings for Castlebar and one filly, all by Arabians.

Author's note: I remember seeing Wenceslas as a 2yo when he was paraded at Werrondi shortly after his arrival from England to South Australia. A lovely kind, sensible, well balanced horse, of the old type one rarely sees nowadays. Arabian blood is still present in the third and fourth generations of many Australian Stock Horses, and there are several studs bringing good types of Arabian blood back into their first and second crosses. Time will tell if there is longstanding influence.

China Doll

CHINA DOLL

Foaled 1985
G m

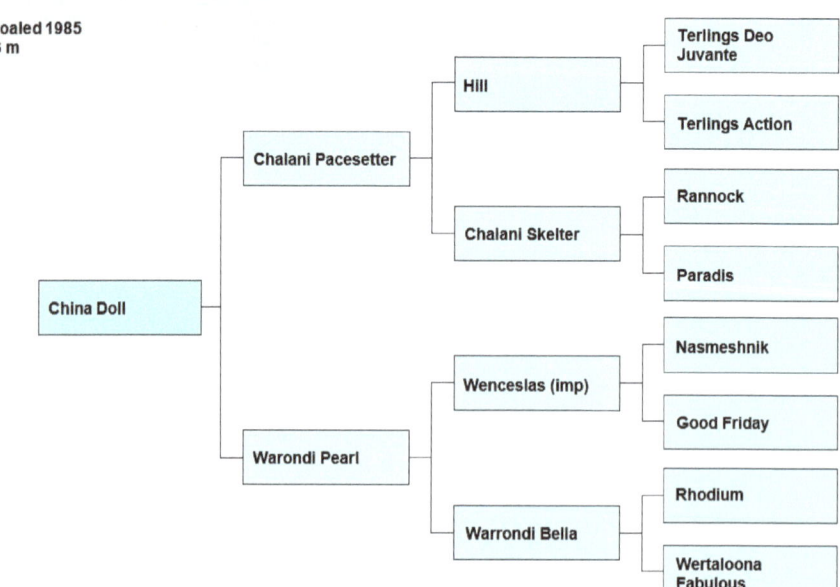

			Terlings Deo Juvante
		Hill	
	Chalani Pacesetter		Terlings Action
			Rannock
		Chalani Skelter	
China Doll			Paradis
			Nasmeshnik
		Wenceslas (imp)	
	Warondi Pearl		Good Friday
			Rhodium
		Warrondi Bella	
			Wertaloona Fabulous

Chalani Pacesetter progeny gallery.

Heffer, ex Warrondi Kate, b m.

This Pacesetter mare was purchased off Michael Heffernan and is dam of the *Magic Glenn* endurance horses of Sheik Mohammed. She is out of a Wenceslas mare.

L-Heffer R-Magic Glenn Heaftie, ex Heffer.

Magic Glenn Honey Bee (2010), a daughter of Heffer, bred by Shelly Cowan, is now a successful endurance horse. She started her endurance career at four years old and proved to be very talented. In 2019 she completed the Tom Quilty in SA and then she won her first 80km ride in a time of 4.55 hours.

From, Debbie Grull, Tasmania: "We've had some magnificent endurance horses from the Pacesetter line. I have loved every minute riding them. And they are real characters!!! The line is still going strong here. They were all so good. Many we didnt have for long as they went overseas. At the time of writing, Highland View Pearl (still early in her career) has 2 x 100 mile completions, a Tom Quilty buckle, and a Tasmanian State Championship. We have two full sisters to China Doll which are broodmares, Cricket and Holly."

DVS Cricket
She produced quite a few nice horses: DVS Jimminy DVS Bradman, DVS Bellara, DVS Sunsilk, to name a few. DVS Sunsilk has 2 x Tom Quilty buckles, 1 MW win and some good placings.

DVS Holly Her foals were: Highland View Steel, Highland View Crystal, Highland View Platinum, Highland View Pearl, and a few as yet unnamed coming through.

YAGOONA MICHAELA and **DEVIOUS REBECCA** are other full sisters, both owned by Dennis Sugars.

Yagoona Ben Buckinara, bred by the Heffernans, completed both Shazada (400kms) and Quilty endurance rides in the same year,1999, finishing in top 10 fittest horses. Another gelding sold in 2000 for $30,000 to Dubai for endurance.

Pacesetter proved a consistent sire of performance horses which played polo, evented and show-jumped. They include:

CHALANI ENCORE ex She's Ideal TB/reg ASH, 2000 c m. 16h.

Encore with Junior rider, Chloe Matthews, circa 2006.

Reynella Horse Trials 2006, photos Jenny Barnes.

Bush Orphan - Outstanding eventer in SA during 2000 and 2001 seasons, successful up to Novice level. Ruth Roberts rode him mostly as an eventer, but sometimes her son David did. Ruth described him as "a wonderful, versatile horse, who thought he was a human. He was such a character and very quiet and honest. He did Pony Club and sidesaddle too. We bought him off his breeder Rose Ross of *Glen Gillian* Mt Pleasant, SA, who hand raised him as an orphan. When she sent him to us to be broken in, we bought him. We just fell in love with him. He was a good 16h."

Bush Orphan with Ruth Roberts.

CHALANI LARK, (Pacesetter ex Wren) 1988, was a regular competitor in Tentpegging throughout Agricultural shows and at Royals (shown here RAS 2005) with owner Phil Roberts. He also hunted for many seasons.

Wren, (Rannock x Glen Devon Faith) 1979, ch m, Adelaide Royal 1988.

INDIANAS LARAKIN

(Anncrouye Indiana x Fossil Downs Skylark) 2020 b h.

Indianas Larakin with Scott Heidke, winner many Championships including Brisbane Royal Champion Junior ASH 2023.

In 1990, we sold 5 horses including the Rannock mare Wren, to Robert Holmes-a-Court, Western Australia, to commence his breeding programme of Australian Stock Horses. Jane Stone inspected the horses, and took Wren's daughter CHALANI DOVE (by MARKITA DOWNS MARKSMAN) as well. Dove produced MT SANFORD PIGEON, which in turn produced FOSSIL DOWNS SKYLARK by Dogwood Comet (which Jane and Paul Stone owned).

So Indianas Larakin, traces in direct female line to Wren, a most beautiful, elegant mare, out of the Glen Devon Bellvue Star mare, Glen Devon Faith, (dam also of Kintra). Following the death of Mr Holmes-a-Court, she was sent to *Mt Sanford* Station, Northern Territory, where she lived out the rest of her days with 'special treatment in the front paddock'.

Indianas Larakin has been highly successful in a very short career both in Led and Ridden ASH classes, as a 2-3 year old. Bred by Scott Heidke, he also owned and was successful with Larakin's sire, Indiana, which traces to Panzer in the fifth generation through his sire, PALMERS NAVAHO.

CHALANI SHEOAK, ex Chalani Aspen, 1988 b m15.1h.

An attractive, successful mare, very much of the Panzer mould, Sheoak was leased to a number of people to ride (including inexperienced and junior riders), who all reported how lovely her temperament was. Among her ASH performances were winner 1992 ASH Ridden Futurity, Maturity winner 1993, top Riding Club mount and High Point Interclub Horse 1993. She proved a bold eventer, basically unflappable, with Kim Gower riding!

Sheoak was certainly one of the favorite mares at Chalani. She produced seven top quality progeny but sadly, no fillies were retained. Her sire son CHALANI CHAPARRAL (by FINTONA ARTIST) was later leased back from Jenny Schiller, Waikerie, in the latter part of his career, in an effort to return her bloodline to the stud. Sheoak was retired as a riding horse to *Birdrise* Stud.

Chalani Sheoak

Jeanette Gower with Chalani Sheoak and Chalani Chaparral as a foal, 1995.

CHALANI CHAPARRAL, ex Chalani Sheoak, 1995 br h 15.3h.

Chaparral. This is the same cross, but upside down, as Arakoola Tradition, see p133.

CHALANI CHAPARRAL

Foaled 2010
b/brn
15.3½h.

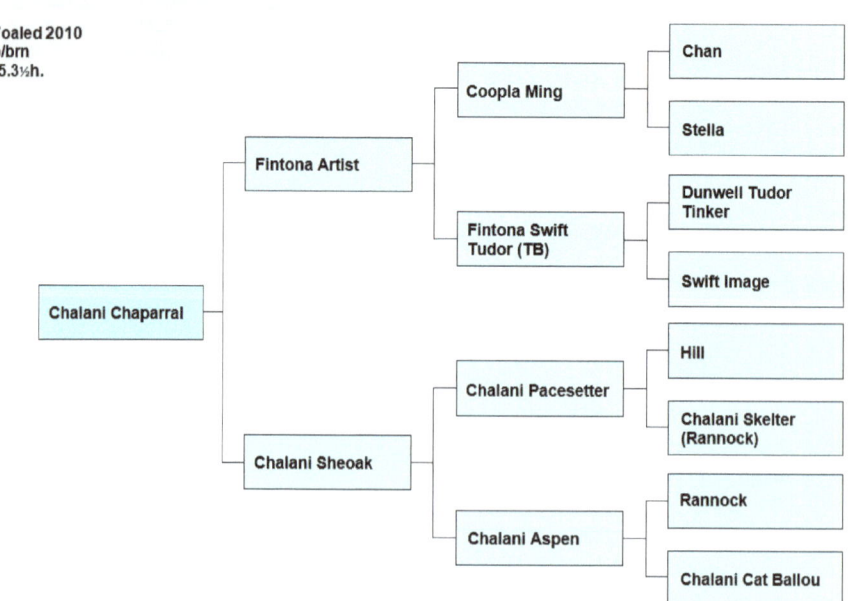

Progeny of Chalani Chaparral

HILLBRO ARAMAC, ex SUNNYRIDGE BRIDGET, 2000 b g,
at Adelaide Horse Trials, 2013, and below 2014.

HILLBRO REYN MAN, ex IR Hollywood Ruler QH, (2010) br g,
with Lucy Boseley.

MEMPHIS PARK ROYALTY, ex SHE's IDEAL (TB/reg ASH),
2007 br m, with Crystal Ballard. Photo Jenny Scheepers.

Fintona Artist
(Coopla Ming x Dunwell Swift Tudor) 1988, b/br h 15.3h.

*Fintona Artist, approx 1992, at Chalani, before being sold to Col
Byron. Below: Old advert 1999, featuring Col Byron.*

CHALANI PAPER LACE, ex Chalani Paper Tiger, 1990 Ch m 15.3h.

A well-known, versatile mare, multi-champion led and under saddle, Chalani Paper Lace was noted for her outstanding extended trot. Paper Lace's dam was the renowned CHALANI PAPER TIGER, a well known QH sprinter raced by the Gowers. Her performances included a second in the All-Australian Futurity, Canberra 1980.

In 1995, Paper Lace won Led ASH mare at Adelaide Royal as well as competed in four ridden events in which she won or placed, ridden by the Gower's daughter Kim. She was one of the few horses in the SA Central ASH Branch history to have won all three major events, namely the Yearling Futurity 1992, Ridden Futurity 1994, and Ridden Maturity 1995.

Under Kim she represented her Pony Club at State Championship level on four occasions, winning Teams on the Flat in 2000 and 1st, 2nd and 3rd in Team and Individual showjumping in 1996 and 2000. She won Monarto Horse and Rider of the Year at Zone Eliminations, twice won Teams on the Flat and in the Mounted Games, placed 2nd overall in 2000.

Chalani Paper Lace with foal CHALANI CHIFFON, 2011, by Splashdance, Horizons photography.

In 1996, Paper Lace received an ASH Directors Trophy for High Point Eventer of Australia, completing her career with an ASH All-Round versatility award (1000 Points).

Paper Lace was best known as a successful eventer in Pony Club circles, very sure-footed, safe and bold across country. In 1997 she was pointed into

Chalani Paper Lace with Kim Ide (nee Gower).

Grade 1 eventing following a win at Monarto ODE. Ironically, bemused spectators watched with incredulity that same year during the Adelaide Royal ASH Time Trial, when Paper Lace lined up the gate and jumped it, resulting in elimination!

After being retired to stud, this much admired mare produced 10 foals for Chalani. Her daughters have been sold throughout Australia, for polocrosse to showjumping, with her last, CHALANI CHIFFON, now in the hands of Kelsey Stafford of Rockhampton, Qld, which has proven to be an exceptional mustering horse. Another CHALANI SATIN, has been a wonderful broodmare for Kimberley McCallum, at Viewhill Farm, near Nathalia, Vic, and later Sal Esdaile, Zelper Stud, NSW. CHALANI TWEED, a gelding, is a winning dressage and showjumping horse for the Bradshaw Family in SA. These are all sired by Splashdance.

Chalani Paper Lace won many awards at Adelaide Royal,
over several years.

Chalani Tweed, 2012, b g with Brianna Bradshaw.

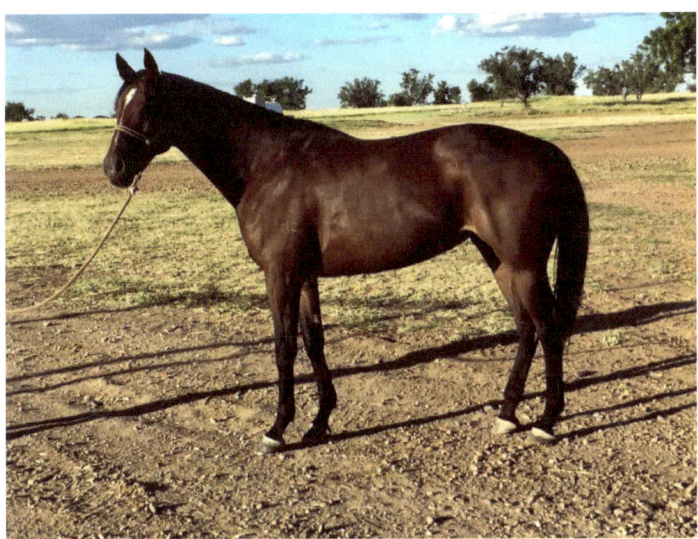

Chalani Chiffon, 2011, b m, is a "beautiful natured mare who is easy to do anything with. She is one of the best horses I've ever ridden mustering, with a huge walk and ground-eating stride. She is super cowy and loves working cattle. She did some showing in 2016 and won Champion Led ASH at Katherine Show 2016 amongst others." - Kelsey Stafford.

CHALANI CHIPPER ex Chalani Pivot, 2000, Ch m 15.1h.

Chipper was a half brother x half sister mating. She was Champion Led ASH mare and first Station Horse at 2006 Adelaide Royal Show. Her son CHALANI CAVALIER (by Fintona Artist) played polocrosse and daughter MERRIBANK FLICKA (by GLEN LEE RIVOLI RESIST) has been highly successful in ASH and Western events. CHALANI SPIRIT (by Chalani Sunsteam) has been successful at everything he has been put to, and was a Steward's horse at Adelaide Royal for several years. Chipper is still breeding foals for Chad and Kate Growden at age 23.

Chipper with Kim Gower, at Adelaide Royal 2006. This is the same gate which Paper Lace jumped over in the Time Trial, (see p 186.)

Progeny of Chalani Chipper

MERRIBANK FLICKA, 2011, b m, by Glen Lee Rivoli Resist, with owner Lisa Halling. This combination have been successful in a variety of Western Events, and Western dressage.

Champion ASH female, Lucindale SA, 2011 with Lisa Halling.

CHALANI SPIRIT, 2013 pal g, with Kate and Chad Growden.
He won in showjumping, and was a favorite at Ranch Sorting.

Chalani Pacesetter as a yearling, with young 3yo Kim Gower. She had just wandered in without our knowledge and we watched on with curiosity. This photo made the front cover of Rider Magazine.

As I have been writing this story of the Rannock Legacy, I have been constantly reminded of the fragility of a line. The way one develops or fades is due entirely to opportunity. Success in one field will make it stand out as a force in that field, oftentimes meaning they aren't tried in another field. If a horse hasn't been tried, or isn't ridden by someone with expertise in that field, it is 'wasted' as to its true potential.

A line can come to a full halt, with the untimely death of one individual, horse or owner. Many never produce foals for a line to continue, due to giving their owners so much pleasure under saddle, or not being in the hands of breeders. For the Rannock line to be successful in so many fields, is exceptional.

Chalani Mystic, by Chalani Pacesetter

Chapter 18

Chalani Mystic

A standout foal

(Chalani Pacesetter x Chalani Charm) 1990 gr h 15.2h.

Chalani Mystic at 8 yrs of age.

When **CHALANI MYSTIC** was born, he was a standout foal, so kept as Chalani's next sire. Mystic's dam CHALANI CHARM was by Rannock, giving Mystic a double cross. She carried the blood of Master Raeburn (TB) noted South Australian showjumping line, and Delray (a prolific old SA hack, hunter and hurdle bloodline). We had a high opinion of Charm, as she was all quality, very much the type that epitomised the 'breed for every need'. She had an outstanding low resting heart rate, and was a very quiet, comfortable ride. I used to lead her out the car window at a trot for about 3ks to take her to the stallion, and she would trot effortlessly without even blowing at 15k/hr, this on a stony track that most horses needed shoes. She had no issues unshod.

I first saw Charm's dam BLUE TIARA when I was a teacher. She was being ridden bareback by a child with only a halter, up a busy road, near the school. She was aged at the time, and although I didn't know her breeding, I bought her on the spot, as she was a good type which I could see would classify with the Society. She had black flea-bites, and a distinctive black 'bloody shoulder.' Only later did I find out she was well bred.

On a hunch, I rang Joyce Robertson, due to remembering Joyce had always shown greys and named them after jewels. Her most famous horse was Marcasite. I discovered Blue Tiara was owned and shown successfully by her at one time. She was able to give me her breeding and background. Blue Tiara was double branded, so what happened to her after she left Joyce is a mystery, until I bought her, though she'd obviously had several foals. Charm was born almost white and was the first of three fillies we bred from Blue Tiara, after which she was retired for riders at *Woodlands* Riding School; so too was Charm in her latter years. Charm lived until she was 31 years old.

Charm, by Rannock, at Chalani, circa 1990.

CHALANI OMEN (Markita Downs Marksman x Chalani Charm) 1989 ch g.

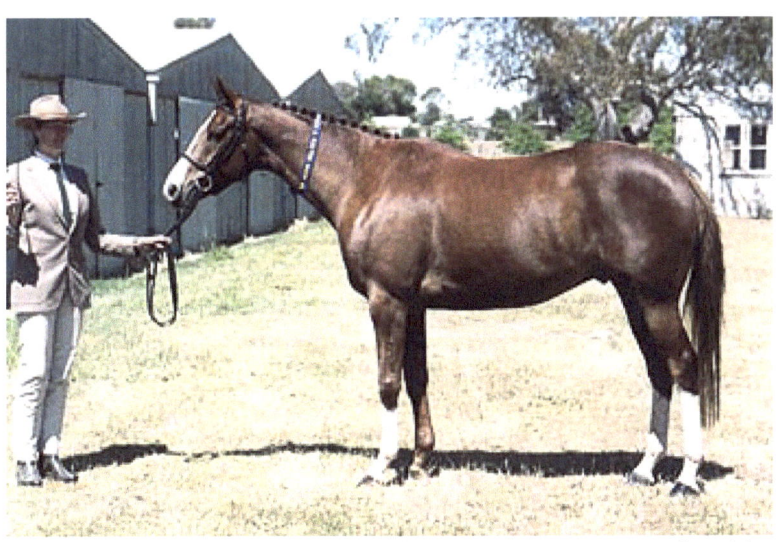

*Chalani Omen, with Belinda Battersby. He won many ASH Led/Ridden
Championships including 1996 Working ASH Adelaide Royal.*

First time out Sidesaddle - Chalani Omen who teamed up with Sue
Marnie to win all their classes.   Port Elliott Show 10 Oct 98

*Omen with Sue Marnie, won many side-saddle hack and open
hack classes, before being retired to Riding for the Disabled.*

CHALANI ILLUSION (a daughter of Charm, by Fintona Artist) was at *Emu Gully* Stud for a number of years, resulting in a son, ANZAC DIGGER (by ROYALLE SCOTSMAN) being used until gelded when the stud was closed. He is now used for Light Horse re-enactments and heritage days.

Chalani Illusion, 1993 b m.

EMUGULLY DIGGER WILLIAMS, by Anzac Digger, 2012 b g.

Chalani Mystic was several times Champion Led as a Yearling. He was the ideal show horse, perfectly behaved, with presence, that all important 'look at me' quality, and an ability to be wonderfully easy on the handler to show. Even as a foal he could out-walk most horses. He had a true four-beat walk with big overtrack and impulsion, stunning extended trot, easy canter and a naturally square stop. Mystic also had a tough set of perfectly shaped white hooves of the right size and slope, a blacksmith's dream, and of course that Rannock trademark, a clean-throated neck and lots of elbow room.

Although broken in by Peter Gower, due to a leg injury, Mystic was never shown under saddle. He stood at Chalani for seven years until his untimely death through colic, at only 9 years of age. As this was in the middle of the stud season, it was immediately arranged with Denis Sugars to lease back Chalani Pacesetter till the end of the season, to honour our outside mare obligations, and hoping to breed a replacement colt. But it was not to be. Charm's colt the following year was stillborn, and the other foals were fillies!

Chalani Mystic, circa 1995. Unlike his dam, he was a striking dappled grey.

Chalani Mystic

Foaled 1990
Gr stallion 15.2h

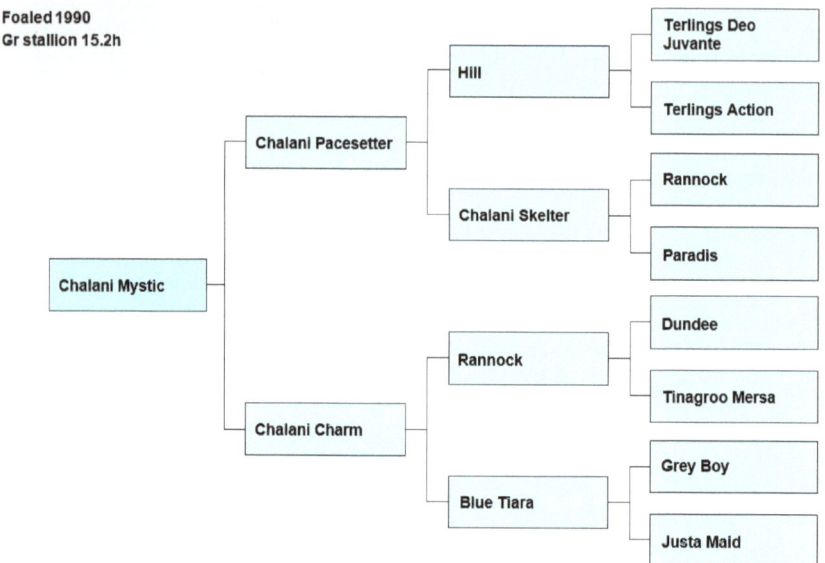

Pedigree chart:

- **Chalani Mystic**
  - **Chalani Pacesetter**
    - **Hill**
      - Terlings Deo Juvante
      - Terlings Action
    - **Chalani Skelter**
      - Rannock
      - Paradis
  - **Chalani Charm**
    - **Rannock**
      - Dundee
      - Tinagroo Mersa
    - **Blue Tiara**
      - Grey Boy
      - Justa Maid

Grey Boy was an Anglo-Arab by Delray from a Master Raeburn (TB) mare, well known SA hurdle and showjumping lines. Justa Maid was a black unraced Standardbred, a show winner in harness classes on the West Coast of SA.

Mystic's ratio of successful, versatile progeny, was extremely high. His progeny won at Royal level in ASH Working, Ridden, Time Trial and Led. Other progeny were successful in Eventing, Dressage and Pony Club activities, being bold, quiet natured and excellent movers. His death proved a big loss.

Chalani Mystic progeny gallery.

CHALANI PAPER NOTE, ex Chalani Paper Tiger, 1994 b m. A half-sister to Chalani Paper Lace, (p184) she was an ASH Yearling Futurity winner 1996, Champion Led ASH and ASH winner under saddle, and well known side-saddle winner. Still going strong with youth riders at age 29.

"Paper Note competed Advanced but was training to all the higher movements, doing 2x changes, piaffe, passage. I did an unofficial Freestyle to Music in side-saddle costume Prix St George with some piaffe added, as her grand finale, before I retired her and the kids started riding her. She won the freestyle comp with highest score of the day. She was so athletic and super trainable. Shows you don't need a big warmblood if you have correct training and accuracy." – Sharyn Edwards.

Chalani Paper Note was used extensively at side-saddle, and also at dressage with great success, shown here with owner Sharyn Edwards.

The Edwards family side-saddle, L Chalani Paper Note at 29 years, and her son, SUMMIT IMPERIAL TOPAZ, (centre). Photo Snafflebit Media.

CHALANI CAVORT, ex Chalani Chipper, 1994 g m, ridden by Sarah Allen, was a successful ASH youth class winner, and Pony Club eventer.

CHALANI THISTLE ex HENRYS BINDY LASS, 1994 g m. 1997 Adelaide Royal Led filly winner, 1998 3yo Futurity winner, Challenge winner, and consistent eventer.

Chalani Thistle at Naracoorte ODE 2014 with owner Ann Parsons. Photo by Julie Wilson.

CHALANI REVIEW ex Roskhill Narrator, 1999, gr g. Winner/placegetter in ASH led, hack, working, time trial and Open Hack events.

Chalani Review, at a Branch clinic, with Matt Holz, circa 1998.

CHALANI LAURA ex MYLOR MISS (TB/reg ASH) 1997, 16.1½hh.

Winner working ASH, Adelaide Royal 2002 with Kim Gower.

Chalani Laura competed over a number of years in ASH, dressage and Pony Club competition, to Royal and National standard, with Kim Ide, (nee Gower).

She started out winning the Branch Yearling Futurity and later the Four Year Old Maturity. She won at Adelaide Royal in Led ASH mare, Working ASH mare and Time Trial events. Laura was part of the winning SA dressage team at the Pony Club National Championships in 2002 as a 5yo, competing at Elementary level. She was also a member of the winning Pony Club Teams of Four on the Flat, in Zone and State Championships, and novelty teams. In 2002, she placed at the Albury ASH National Championships with Kim.

Laura had an outstanding extended trot and was always very willing. Lent to different riders and breeders after her show career, she was dubbed 'Miss Perfect' as she never put a foot wrong, and produced very quiet foals. She even raised 'twins' when she adopted an orphan as her own.

Laura with her 'twins,' CHALANI MAITLAND (br) and TWEED (b)

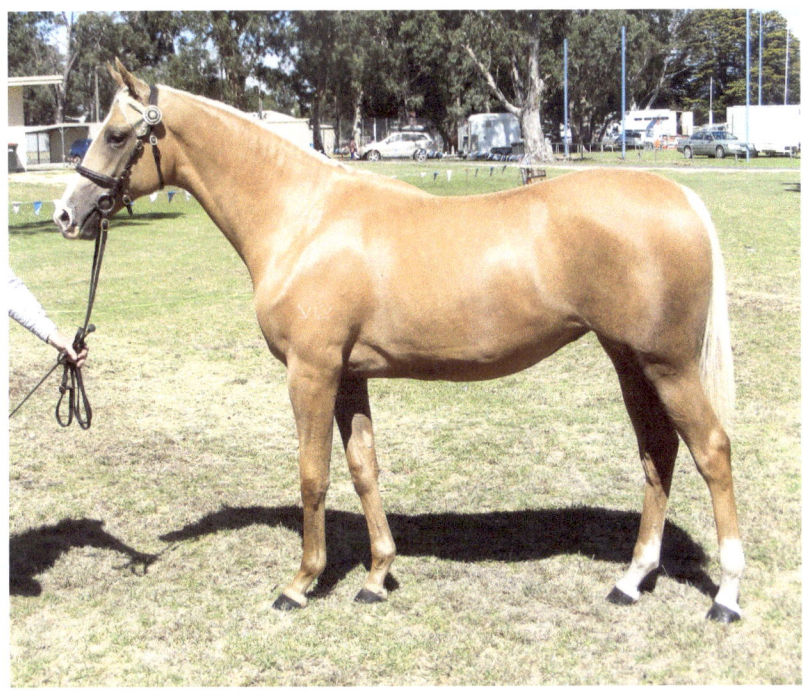

CHALANI TARLEE, ex Chalani Laura, 2019 pal m, SA Yearling Futurity winner, Lucindale 2021, by Chalani Sunstream, retained.

Another of these is **CHALANI MONASH**, just started and going well in Working Equitation, for owner Kate Collins, NSW, and **CHALANI STIRLING** (both by Chalani Sunstream).

Chalani Monash, 2018, pal g, with owner Kate Collins.

Chalani Stirling, 2013 pal g, with Sohpie Rumbold, owned/photo by Jane McDonald, was Dilutes SA High Point Trophy winner for the 2018 season.

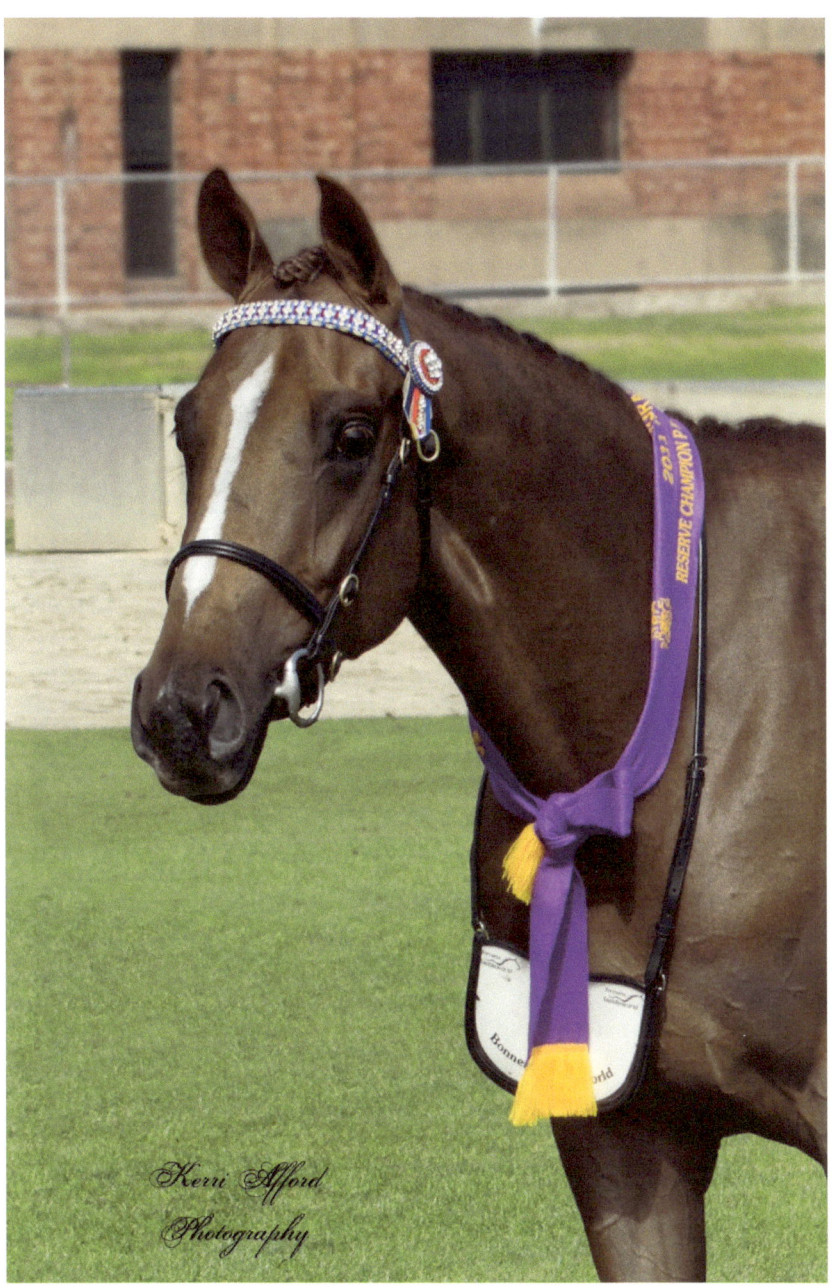

CHALANI CALLANNA, 2008 ch m, by Memphis Park Memory, Res Champion ANSA Mare, Adelaide Royal 2011, owned by Belinda Battersby. Kerri Afford photo.

CHALANI AURORA, ex Chalani Star Merit (TB/reg ASH), 1994 ch m 15.2h.

Chalani Aurora has proven to be a major cornerstone mare for Chalani. Her dam was a nice Thoroughbred with a spectacular swinging trot. She had been used in the *Woodlands* riding school of Mrs Nancy Gower for some years. Her sire was Headsail (TB), a Masthead II horse. She left several foals, one a younger full sister to Aurora, CHALANI GEMINI, was 1997 ASH Yearling Futurity winner, and winner of drafts with Heather Byron and family. She also played polocrosse.

Aurora, Champion ASH mare 1998 Royal Adelaide Show.

Aurora was exceptionally willing, gentle and easy to teach. She was singled out as a favorite by the Gower's young daughter Kim and swapped for another horse. When Kim broke her in, it was just a matter of putting a leg over and riding off. Kim later taught her to bow.

Aurora competed under saddle as a late 3yo. She won numerous Champion led, hacking and working events in ASH competition, including qualifying for the Show Series Finals in all three sections (Led, Hack, Working). In her last season of ASH classes, Aurora won High Point ASH at every show she competed in.

Probably Aurora's best wins were at the 1998 Royal Adelaide Show. She received Champion Led ASH mare, alongside Chalani Pivot filling Reserve. In Ridden, she was 2nd Working mare and 1st Working ASH, plus 1st Time Trial

Star Merit, with Heather Allen, circa 1991.

Headsail, by Masthead II (NZ).

(her first ever Time Trial). She followed this up with a win in the Time Trial the following year (having qualified for and competed in the open hack events during the week).

She was virtually unbeaten in Time Trial and Barrel Races and super handy and bold at Pony Club cushion polo tournaments. She won Champion Hack at Morphett Vale Hack Show 99, and won at various Agricultural shows.

At the Pony Club State Championships 1999, in Whyalla, she won and placed in all the novelty events, was 6th in the C grade showjumping, (approx 40 riders) and 2nd in the 'Teams on the Flat' dressage team of four. On top of this she also received the Reserve Champion Hack. Her versatility was shown not just in the wide variety of events she competed in at this competition, but through the fact she was successful in *every* event she participated in.

At the 2000 ASH Central Branch Futurity and Maturity show, Aurora was rewarded with a win in the 5yo Maturity. She won all 4 sections of this event, with a lead of approx 40 points. Aurora was winner of the Rannock trophy in 1999 and 2000, also receiving other High Point End of Year branch awards.

Always partnered with Kim, Aurora was reliable at even the biggest of Agricultural shows. With her feminine head, lovely big movement, a keen interest in cattle, and demonstrated flair for speed events, she became one of the SA Central Branch's most notable and versatile performers.

Aurora as an older mare, pictured with Kim's novice husband Andy.

After producing 11 foals, Aurora enjoyed retirement as a riding horse. Three of her daughters Maia, Minerva and Trivia were retained. Aurora's progeny proved to be similar in temperament and movement to herself.

Chalani Aurora Champion and Chalani Pivot Reserve, Adelaide Royal with Kim Ide, 1998.

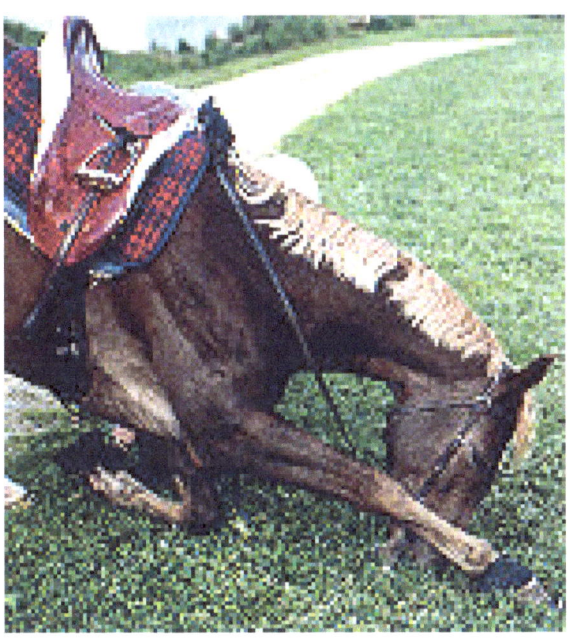

Progeny of Chalani Aurora

CHALANI APOLLO, Mr Cromwell (TB) x Chalani Aurora, 2000 ch g.

Apollo was sold to Chari-lee Hoad as a 3yo when Chari-lee was nearly 10 years old. Together they forged a most successful relationship, winning in ASH competition, eventing, show jumping, dressage and Pony Club, including at National level.

Apollo, Adelaide Royal dressage, 2009 with Chari-Lee Hoad, winner in official Medium Junior dressage.

They also tried their hand at polocrosse training, Australia Day parades and sheep mustering. He was used in a programme by a visiting UK TV team demonstrating the Australian Stock Horse. (This video is on the Chalani Website).

Together they won High Point Youth at the ASH National Show 2007, winning a stock saddle, numerous Champion ASH Hack and Working awards, and Youth High Points ASH. They also won in Pony Club eventing, dressage and jumping competitions. He was perhaps the most versatile gelding in the history of the SA Central Branch.

In Chari-Lee's own words, "Apollo was a character. He was the horse that always opened his gate at night, then open other horses in stalls to have a party. We reached a point where we had to D shackle the gate shut, and found him the next day snoring with his legs up in the air. He had been trying all night to get out and was unsuccessful. I was 9½ yrs old and Apollo was 3½ years old when our lives united. We bonded like no other and the journey began from there.

Chalani Apollo with his junior rider, Chari-lee Hoad.

"He was forgiving, a fast learner and fun. We gave everything a go, starting with Pony Club and Australian Stock Horse competitions. It was a whirlwind of learning and perfecting multiple disciplines. Apollo was the horse we all claim as the ASH All-rounder. Apollo was the horse I could try absolutely *any* discipline, from Pony Club, Showjumping, ASH competitions, Polocrosse, Dressage, including Australia Day parades in Adelaide city centre. What a horse!

"During my time with Apollo I won 100s of awards, winning the Youth ASH National Championships out of 150 kids, competed eventing grade 3, and out-pointed all by the age of 12 years. From all the opportunities Apollo willingly and happily tried, I was able to find my riding career path of Dressage. By the age of 16, I had not only represented South Australia in Interschool and Pony Club Nationals in dressage, achieving top 10 in Australia, but we had also jumped 110cm, and moved our way to Prix St George dressage.

"Apollo was the horse in the paddock you could jump on after school with no gear, canter with full trust and faith to enjoy every moment. At PC Nationals we would sit in our deckchairs watching the mounted games and he would be asleep with his head on your shoulder. He would sleep during the Royal Show line up and you would call his name softly to wake him up, pull off the Station Utility work out, walk back on a loose rein whilst falling back asleep, to then win the class. He couldn't get any more Aussie, hanging with the boys in the truck yard whilst they had a beer to finish off the week, or investigate under the bonnet with the lads.

"Apollo was a horse rarely found, a true ASH, ones written about but never seen. He was a horse you could just think and he would do. A horse that I was blessed to have. He was the pinnacle, the cornerstone of my riding career."

High Point Youth Horse and Rider, winning a saddle! ASH National Show, Camden NSW 2007.

CHALANI TRITON, by Splashdance, 2003, b g,

Winner of his Yearling ASH Futurity. After being broken in by Gill Rolton, his junior rider enjoyed competing in eventing and Pony Club competitions.

Chalani Triton, by Splashdance, with Duncan Chriton

CHALANI TRIVIA, by Splashdance, 2006 br m 15.3½h.

Trivia was a lovely mover, light and responsive to ride with a big extended trot and huge over-tracking walk. She was easy to pull out of the paddock and just hop on. She was a genuine all-rounder, having been used for Tent Pegging, Cattle Work and Polocrosse practices. Trivia attended Adult Riding Club, show jumped and showed ability in novelties. She was the High Point award winner at the Strathalbyn ARC gymkhana 2011, and won and placed in hack and novelties at Police and Emergency Services games, 2012. She qualified for the Adelaide Royal Show in hack classes, won in show hunter and working hunter classes at Ag shows, did combined training events, been Supreme Champion ASH winner led and under saddle.

Trivia went to the ASHS National Show in Tamworth, 2012. She was placed 3rd in the Preliminary Dressage and 4th in the Hack Mare in English Attire, over 5 years. At the 2012 SA State ASH Show, Trivia was 2nd overall in the 5yo Maturity (led, hack, working, time trial) and 2nd in the Open Challenge (Working, Utility, Barrel race, Keyhole race). She was also awarded the Best SA bred Led ASH.

At the SA Central Branch ASH Show, 2013, Trivia won Supreme Champion Led ASH, Champion Hack, Champion Working and Supreme Champion Ridden ASH.

Trivia with Kim Ide, Tanunda Agricultural Show, 2014.

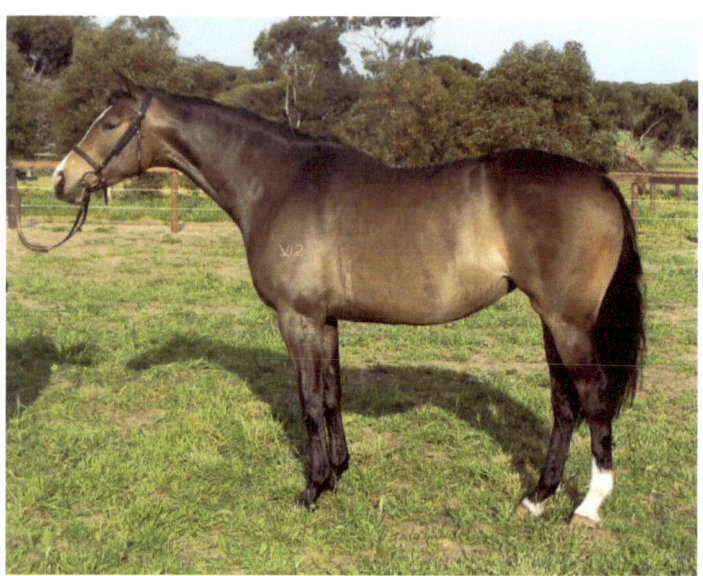

*Chalani Trivia, daughter of Aurora, and the most like her, by
Splashdance, full sibling to Triton.*

Trivia finalled in the Maiden Campdraft at Fleurieu in 2014, then a month later, was Champion Show Hunter at Mt Barker Ag show 2014, also placing in the novelty events. She was Champion Led ASH Mare, Reserve Champion Working ASH and winner ASH Ridden Mare Adelaide Royal Breeds Show in 2014. Her foals have been exceptional.

Chalani Card Tricks (ex Chalani Trivia) in the camp with Kim, Wannon River Campdraft April 2022. (See her story p280). Nicole Cleary photo. She is very cowy and soft to ride.

Trivia with Kim, Fleurieu Campdraft 2015.

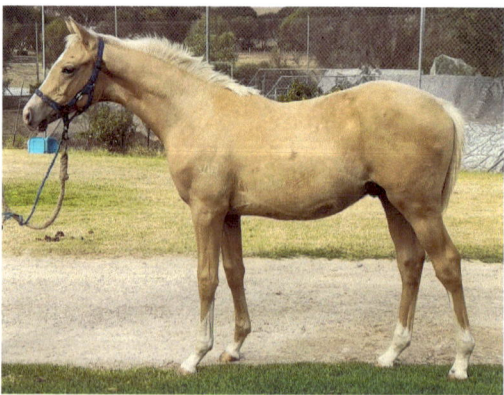

*CHALANI JACKPOT (Chalani Sunstream x
Chalani Trivia) 2023 colt, owned by Shelley
Wells, QLD.*

Chapter 19

Chalani Nightdance

An eye-catching horse

(Splashdance X Chalani Giselle) 2002 Blk h 16h.

Chalani Nightdance in 2013.

In 2002, Paula Talbot-Taylor of Williamstown, SA took a mare to *Chalani*.

"While there, a 2 week old black colt **CHALANI NIGHTDANCE** caught my eye. Thinking about how special I thought this little guy would grow to be, I could not leave without purchasing him.

"I had to wait until he was weaned before I could bring him home to *Ashborn Park*. When it was time, I took a companion pony for the trip home, and as nanny for a while thereafter. I had to laugh. As a weanling, Nightdance (or Bobby as I called him) was already bigger than his nanny.

"Chalani Nightdance would be the most social and inquisitive horse I have owned; his progeny seem to have inherited this quality as well. He has always been best friends with our dogs and cats.

"As a yearling he was shown very successfully in youngstock classes, plus as a young 2-year-old, qualifying and winning the last SA ASH Champion of Champions, out of strong competition of his peers.

"Just before Nightdance was broken in, he cut his hind fetlock very deeply. Once it healed he was sent to Ben Loades to break in. Ben did a wonderful job. When Bobby arrived home, it wasn't like riding a green-broken horse. He was able to do hind-quarter turns, flying changes. I would ride him under the trees to prune the branches. His height of 16h made him very handy for that.

"He re-injured his fetlock requiring more time out, then returned to the show ring to win an array of Champion and Supreme Champion awards including a number of Supreme of All Breeds.

"2006 was his first show under saddle, ridden by Kim Ide (nee Gower). It was located at the old EA grounds in Adelaide, with low flying planes overhead. In those days there was no hot weather policy, with temperatures reaching 40 degrees. To top it off, there was only one way in and out, a fire started blocking us all in, but regardless, he performed admirably.

"2005-2006 Chalani Nightdance won the ASHS High Point Trophy for First Season out. He missed out on the Rannock trophy by a point, as the Supremes weren't counted. The same with the Stallion Trophy.

" In 2007, after starting to compete under saddle, Equine Influenza called a stop to competitions across a large part of Australia. During this time Bobby took on stud duties to a full book of mares, including AI. His stud book didn't slow down once the travel ban had lifted. It is unfortunate that in SA the competition season is the same as the breeding season. I chose to continue his stud duties (live cover) over returning to compete.

"At the end of 2009, after being out of work for some time, on a whim I decided to take him to a show, and came home with Champion Led Australian National Saddle Horse Association (ANSA), Champion Led ASH. Reserve Champion Ridden ANSA.

"Just after his return to the show ring he again injured himself with a large piece of skin being removed from his inner hock joint, on the same leg as his others. Not knowing if he would get full movement back and not wanting to waste such an eye catching and talented horse, I felt he could be seen and show his talents in a different equine circle. So, in 2010 I approached Dan Steers of Double Dan Horsemanship, to see if he would like to work with him for a while.

Nightdance ridden by Pia Steers

"Due to Bobby's nature, he very quickly took to the liberty training, performing with Dan in NSW, QLD, SA, and in Double Dan Horsemanship's early training videos. His daughter, ASHBORNS STYLE AND GRACE, was also in the videos.

"In 2011 Dan took him to the ASHS Nationals, not expecting to place due to his very English look. He surprised me by placing in both his stallion classes. Returning to South Australia, we supported the first Royal Adelaide Autumn Breed Show, winning Champion ANSA and ASHS Stallion classes." – Paula Talbot-Taylor.

Nightdance's progeny show the class and conformation expected of this blood-line. They are ongoing winners in ASH classes, as well as the open hack ring at Royal and Horse of the Year level, and with dressage successes. Nightdance proved to be very popular with mare owners, with limited advertising, due to a messy divorce. As of 2019 he had produced over 70 progeny which are through-out every state of Australia, and at 21 years of age, he was tested to have the semen quality of a much younger horse.

Chalani Nightdance with Dan Steers, 2010.

Relaxing at a Dan Steers clinic.

Nightdance with owner Paula Talbot-Taylor. Photo Kerri Afford.

CHALANI NIGHTDANCE

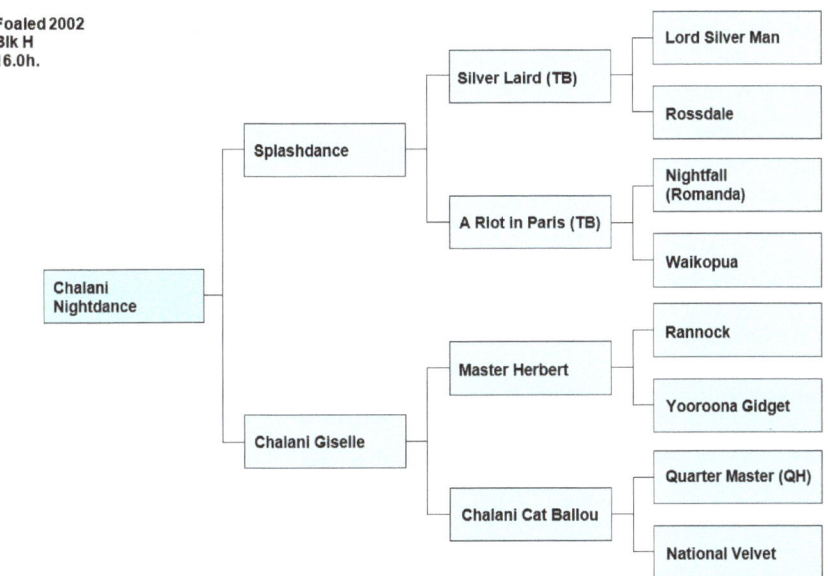

Foaled 2002
Blk H
16.0h.

Chalani Nightdance
- Splashdance
  - Silver Laird (TB)
    - Lord Silver Man
    - Rossdale
  - A Riot in Paris (TB)
    - Nightfall (Romanda)
    - Waikopua
- Chalani Giselle
  - Master Herbert
    - Rannock
    - Yooroona Gidget
  - Chalani Cat Ballou
    - Quarter Master (QH)
    - National Velvet

Splashdance (TB / reg ASH)

(Silver Laird x A Riot in Paris) 1997 blk 16.h.

Splashdance, Champion Ridden ASH at Mt Pleasant Agricultural Show,
2000, as a 3yr old, with Kim Ide (nee Gower).

Splashdance was striking under saddle with natural collection, quality and presence. He had big movement and was athletic, super soft to ride, true snaffle mouth, naturally balanced, easy extensions and outstanding agility, with the kind of canter you want to ride on all day. His breaker John Broadbent described him as a 'Ferrari'.

"He had the balance right from the start. The others of that line I have broken in are exactly the same. They don't hang in around corners, they are correct straight ahead sorts. I galloped him to 3/4 pace and you just ask him up a couple of strides and he stays at that pace until you kick him up some more. And he calms right down and you can throw the reins away.

"It is too easy to forget he is a young horse because everything he does so kindly. He is very comfortable. I have never ridden a young horse with such natural balance. It is like driving a Ferrari - he doesn't lift, he drops behind and drives on. You don't get too many like him." – John Broadbent.

All of this came naturally, indicating a strong genetic heritage which he passed on to progeny. In particular, we bought him because of the successful performances of both his sire and dam in Open, ASH and ANSA competition, and his pedigree, which included Pipe of Peace and Midstream, through ROMANDA (TB/reg ASH), and his successful siblings, the first being the well regarded hack, RIVERDANCE.

Fourth foal "Festival" (by Silver Laird), 1999 Bay filly. (ASH Name "Paris Lilly")

- Supreme Champion Hack Toowoomba Royal Show 2007.
- 1st Open 10 Stone Hack Brisbane Royal 2005
- Supreme Champion Led TB Brisbane Royal 2005.
- Numerous other Royal Show Hack wins and Champion Led awards.
- Read **Horse Deals Tribute to a Champion** on Festival.

Two full sisters to Splashdance, Festival (ASH Paris Lilly) and Ellerslie Vienna, were extremely successful in the hack ring.

Romanda as an old horse.

Midstream blood features in Australia's greatest polocrosse sire EDEN-HOPE SAM, top polo sire HAYDON DRAWN, and many successful campdrafters. Romanda crossed with the Rannock line produced for the Gowers the successful and very attractive ASH and dressage horse CHALANI MIDSPIN (Romanda ex Chalani Skelter) prior to us buying Splashdance.

Splashdance demonstrated a great willingness, a boldness across country, was calm under pressure with a super cool attitude that changed a lot of people's minds about Thoroughbreds. He was a real people horse. He was soft and amazingly supple. He would sometimes be seen reaching across to scratch the opposite side of his spine! At other times, scratching one foreleg with the other foreleg.

MIDSTREAM

THE RACEHORSE
by Brian Russell

It is timely to reflect on the racing ability of the stallions who have written so much of the Australian bloodstock history in the past 50 years and this month commence with some enlightenment on the career on the turf of Midstream*.

Imported to Australia in 1938 for Mr Percy Miller's Kia-Ora Stud, Scone (now the property of Mr John Clift), Midstream proved a high class racehorse from sprint distances to one mile over three seasons of racing.

He started off his career by having three starts in England at two years in 1935 and did so well he was awarded 8.12 on the Free Handicap (13th in the weights).

The juvenile Midstream won his first race the Boscawen Stakes of five furlongs, by three lengths in a field of 13. The effort so impressed that two weeks later he was sent out second favourite to Mahmoud in the major six furlongs race for his age group, the Middle Park Stakes, however, the best he could do was a close fourth.

At the Houghton meeting a few weeks later odds of 13/8 were laid that Midstream would win the Criterion Stakes. He had, however, to divide with Dan Bulger for they dead-heated for first place.

Comment on Midstream's run in the Criterion said that he had a lot of leeway to make up when they came out of the Dip, and would have won outright if the finishing line had been a stride or two further away.

This comment, by the way, was made in the English Bloodstock Breeders' Annual Review. The same report said that it was because Midstream was, in the earlier months of the year, bothered by a small splint under a knee that he did not come to the races until October.

Midstream started eight times as a three-year-old and was undoubtedly one of the leading milers in England though he won only one race, the Wykeham Handicap at York, beating nine others. However, he was second in races of seven furlongs and a mile at Newmarket, including the Autumn Handicap in which he went down by a

head, and third in the Sussex Stakes over the Goodwood mile.

Midstream ran in two English Classics at three and did not disgrace himself in either outing. He helped to delay the Guineas field by restiveness (so did eventual runner-up Mahmoud) but ran well to be near the lead for most of the journey, coming home in ninth place in the field of 19.

Measured at 16.1 prior to his run in the English Derby (also measured at 71 inches girth, 8¼ bone and 42 rein), Midstream was near the lead early but found the one mile and a half, plus five yards too far, finishing 12th in the field of 22.

The winner Mahmoud and runner-up Taj Akbar were both raced by the Aga Khan. Mahmoud was one of the smallest horses in the field, measured at 15.2¼ prior to the race. However, his size did not stop his pounding feet from carving out a new record time for the Derby of 2 min 33-4/5 and scoring by three lengths. The previous time record for the race was 2 min 34 sec made by Hyperion and Windsor Lad in 1933 and 1934.

102   RACETRACK, MAY, 1977

The famous Midstream

From very limited outings, Splashdance was shown successfully. First he was ASH Led Colt, Adelaide Royal 2000. At Mt Pleasant Agricultural Show 2001, judged by Barry Sawyer, he won Led, Junior and Champion ASH

Hack from very strong competition. In the Championship, he was asked to work one-handed with flying changes (amidst the oncoming Grand Parade), scarcely missing a beat - and at only three years of age!

Splashdance spent a stint at *Thornthwaite Station* on lease where he sired a small number of stock due to the outbreak of Equine Influenza, and the shutdown which followed. He subsequently returned to Queensland and was shown in 2008 by his breeder for Champion ANSA Mt Gravatt Show and at Brisbane Royal, all the while demonstrating his calmness and great presence. He later sold to Jack Simms in Far North Qld.

Splashdance at Brisbane Royal with breeder Robyn Unsworth. Photo Narelle Wockner.

Progeny of Splashdance have won at ASH Futurities (led and under saddle), in working classes, ASH and open hack classes, showjumping, and are also successfully competing in eventing, dressage and polo. They have been used for mustering and in feedlots, as well as general leisure and farm work. They have certainly proven to be exceptional riding horses. Chalani have kept three broodmares by him in Chalani Trivia, SANGRIA (very successful for Ashton Ide) and Ripple, and still use his stored semen from time to time.

Nightdance is sire of multiple Champions across Australia at a very high level, the most well known being Chalani Tempo, a full sibling to Ashborns Style and Grace, ASHBORNS NIGHT MOVES, ASHBORNS VOLARE, and Chalani

Skylark, all out of the mare Chalani Pivot. This whole family have been exceptional performers both led and under saddle, and are very versatile, winning in multiple disciplines.

Photo gallery of Chalani Nightdance progeny.

ASHBORNS LADY JANE, ex BROUGHTONVALE ECLIPSE, 2008 blk m.

Ashborns Lady Jane, consistent winner ASH and Royals. Shown here winning Novice Draft, Strathalbyn 2020, after a run-off, ridden by Melanie Austen for owner Lindy Launer.

ASHBORNES STYLE AND GRACE, ex Chalani Pivot, 2008 blk m.

Grace has been a consistent Champion led and under saddle in ASH and ANSA classes, then eventing and drafting. She is now a broodmare at *Galcodi* stud, SA. She and the next three are all full siblings, to Chalani Tempo, p239.

Ashborns Style and Grace, Mildura 2022, with Breah Marston.

CHALANI SKYLARK, ex Chalani Pivot, 2009 blk m, 15.1h.

Chalani Skylark (left) Team Penning, Quorn, SA 2013.

Chalani Skylark (2009) as a yearling, Mt Pleasant Show, Mar 2011.

ASHBORNS NIGHT MOVES, ex Chalani Pivot, 2010 blk h.

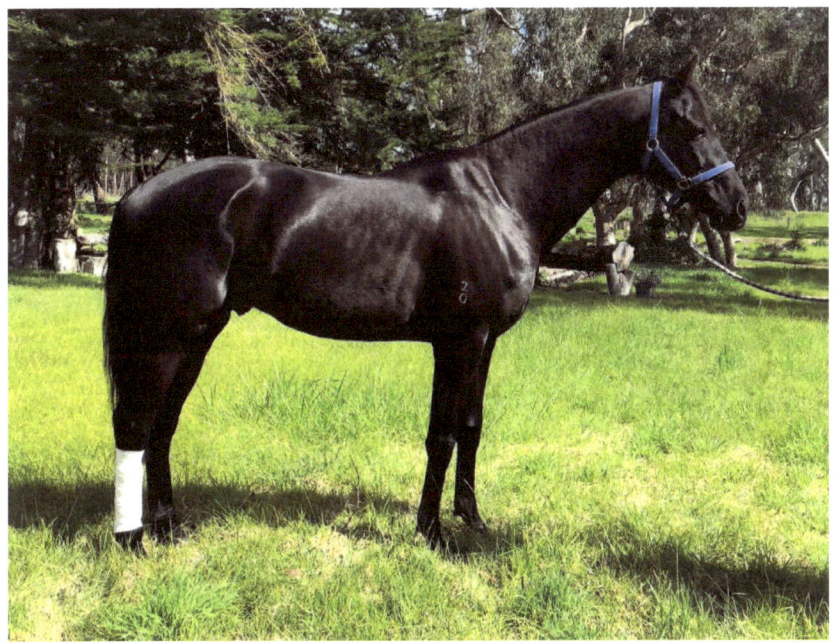

Ashborns Night Moves, stallion owned by Melissa Prior, Naracoorte SA.

ASHBORNS VOLARE, ex Chalani Pivot, 2011 blk m.

*Ashborns Volare, Ch Led ASH mare Adelaide Royal, 2016 with owner
Catherine Agius.*

LOCHNESS DANCING REJOICE, ex Puzzle, 2013 blk m.

Lochness Dancin Rejoice, was second overall in the ASH Nation-
al 3yo Futurity, 2017, for Jodie Middleton-Clark, and multiple
winner for junior, Karen Christensen, in Gippsland area and the
National Youth Shows 2018-2019. Photo Julie Wilson.

KYALLA AUTUMN NIGHT, ex KYALLA GITANA, 2014 blk m.

In dressage, Kyalla Autumn Night, has had consistent results with
junior Maddie Collins, including 2023 High Point Jnr ASH
Dressage of Australia, in ASH classes, and Pony Club events.

SKYVIEW ETERNITY, ex GOLDMINE CHAMPAGNE BLUSH, 2012 buck m.

Eternity was so named as she was the last foal from Blush, a miracle foal, after her dam was diagnosed with Type 3 Endometriosis, and not likely to fall pregnant again. She was the result of Paula Talbot-Taylor of *Ashborn Park's* kindness in reaching out to Jenni Phillips from *Skyview Stud*, and offering live cover, saying "if anyone can get Blush in foal, it will be Nightdance".

Skyview Eternity, Adelaide Royal 2017. PYT Photography.

Blush (1989) was out of KEANDRA BALLERINA, a full sister to KEANDRA DAZZLER, an SA stallion which did very well in ASH and Open competition for Keith Menzel in the 1970s. They were in turn by PEREZ, an exceptionally quiet and beautiful Thoroughbred horse, owned by Irene Wilson, which stood primarily on the West Coast of SA, so didn't get a lot of opportunity.

Blush was arguably one of the two best palomino mares in Australia, with a track record of winning Led Melbourne Royal six years in a row, a feat that is yet to be repeated by any horse, of any breed or colour. Blush's sire was CLAREDALE CHAMPAGNE CHARLIE, possibly the most decorated palomino stallion ever in Australia, and his lines feature prominently in palomino Australian Stock Horses.

L. Keandra Dazzler, with Keith Menzel, R. Keandra Lara, dam. Photos Lorraine Micke.

GOLDMINE MIRAGE, Blush's third foal, a cremello stallion, is highly prized in Skyview Stud's breeding program. Blush also produced the incredible mare, GOLDMINE LATTE, which remains the most highly awarded and performed cremello mare in Australia, owned by Skyview Stud since a weanling, so the stakes in this breeding were high.

Just after midnight, Eternity was born. There was a very special moment the next morning, when Blush, as an aged mare at 22 years old, rounded the filly up, and pushed her towards Jenni as if to say "There you go, you wanted a dilute filly, here she is, and now she is both of our responsibilities." In 2014, at 24 years of age, Blush unexpectedly passed away peacefully, leaving Eternity, then a yearling, to carry on the family as Blush's last foal.

Skyview Eternity, Adelaide Royal, 2017. Photo by Kangra.

In 2016 as a 3yo, Eternity competed in the Royal Adelaide Show for the first time, and was sashed Royal Champion Junior Buckskin and Royal Champion Junior (Dilute) Ancillary. At her fourth show in December 2016 as a 4yo, Eternity was awarded the Dilutes Australia State Champion Led Buckskin and Supreme Led Exhibit, was the winner of the Betty Hosking Memorial Trophy for Supreme Led of Show with Dilutes Australia, and the 2016 State Champion Buckskin and Supreme Led Exhibit of Show for the SA Buckskin Association.

In January 2017 judged by a panel of 5 from all State Champions, Eternity was awarded the first ever Dilutes Australia Ltd Annual Australian National Video Supreme Champion Led Exhibit for 2016, a huge and unexpected honour.

In April 2017 as a 4 year old, the Adelaide Royal Autumn Breed Show, Eternity went Champion Led Australian Stock Horse Mare / Filly, and in the Judges words, "had there been a Supreme Led Australian Stock Horse this year, she would've won." Eternity was also sashed Champion ANSA Exhibit, Reserve Champion Buckskin and Reserve Champion Ancillary. During 2018 and 2019, Eternity competed under saddle, which included 4 Supreme Awards, culminating in winning at the National Horse of the Year in Ridden Mare, Champion Hack, Champion Open Performance, Champion Mare under saddle, and overall Led and Ridden, in both associations.

Eternity was awarded multiple Australian National and State Horse of the Year Awards, Overall Supreme leds, and High Point Led awards in Buckskin and Dilute events, from 2014 to 2018.

Skyview Eternity with Jenni Phillips. In Motion photography.

Eternity had a short ridden career, due to a significant accident which resulted in an almost indiscernible injury to both her cervical spine and sacroiliac. The decision was made in 2019 to retire her for breeding, as one of Skyview's most valuable breeding assets. To date, she's had two foals, a cremello filly,

SKYVIEW INFINITY (2021), and palomino colt, SKYVIEW ORION (2023), by Chalani Sunstream, giving the foals a double cross of Master Herbert.

Eternity is one of those very special mares that Skyview Stud has been fortunate to own, one of those horses that just seeing her in the paddock through the house window, or driving past in the farm vehicle, fills your heart with joy. Right from the beginning, Eternity didn't go through the traditional young horse 'ugly' stages. She just always took your breath away. Accordingly, Latte and Eternity take pride of place in Skyview Stud's logo.

CHALANI MAWSON, ex MOSSROSES GALICA (Chalani Mystic), 2010.

Chalani Mawson, bred by Jodi Penna and sold to WA to be a Clerk of the Course horse. He was lightly shown for Championships as a hack until he broke his pelvis in a freak paddock accident.

Kyalla Moon Dance

Kyalla Moon Dance, gelding from Warmblood mare, produced by Finnis Dressage Stables and now owned by Heidi Van Meerveld.

CHALANI MAIA, ex Chalani Aurora, 2009 brn m 15.2h.

Maia was leased out as a young green-broken horse in 2013, to Kelsey Stafford *Tarrawonga*, then at Mt Sanford Station, Northern Territory. Maia was used primarily for mustering cattle and Kelsey described her as a "kind mare, lovely and sensible ride, clever on cattle and cowy". Maia was lightly shown in the Northern Territory, for Champion Led ASH on each occasion, including an All-Breeds Supreme Led Mare.

"Maia came to me through a very fortunate twist of fate. Upon enquiring about a foal by first season sire Chalani Sunstream, I was offered the lease of Maia by owner/breeder Kim Ide of Chalani Australian Stock Horses, due to the impending expansion of her family at the time. Without even thinking twice I accepted the offer. It was a really huge thing for Kim to do. I was a complete stranger living on the opposite end of the country, but Kim said she had a good feeling about it. Part of the lease agreement with Chalani, included me being allowed to breed a foal from Maia, and this was something I was very keen to do.

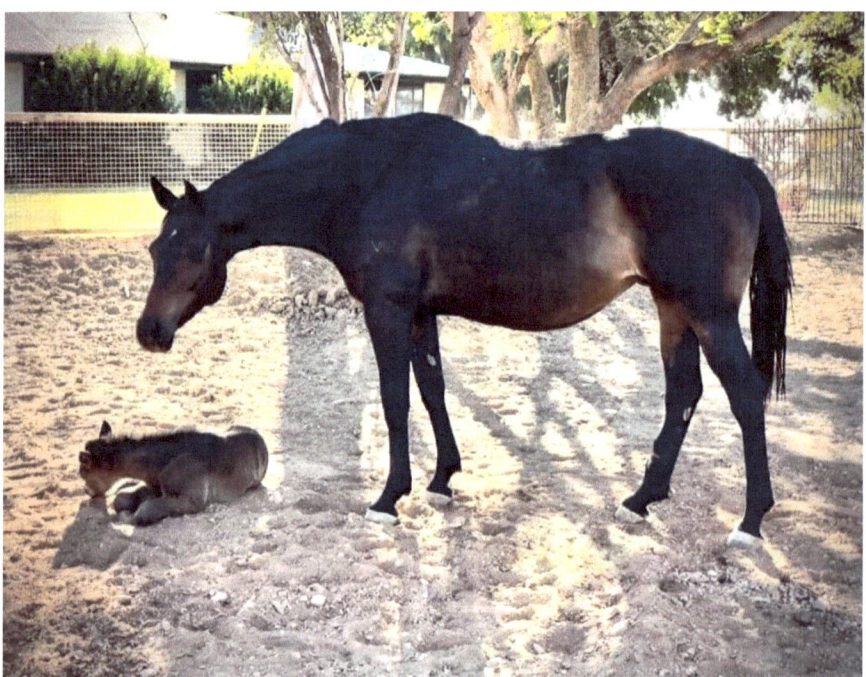

Chalani Maia at Mt Sanford, NT. Photo Kelsey Stafford.

"A lot of thought went into the cross that produced Maia. Kim said of Maia's parents that both were nice types and the bloodlines in the pedigree had crossed successfully before, plenty of times. She was aiming for an attractive, sensible all-rounder stock horse type. Chalani Minerva is by Master Herbert, who Aurora crossed brilliantly with, however he died the year Minerva was born, so she couldn't repeat the mating. Nightdance being out of a Master Herbert mare, was the closest next best she could use to try to breed a similar one.

Chalani Maia at Chalani 2023. Photo Teresa Thomson-Jack.

"Maia won Champion Led ASH, at Kununurra (NT) in 2014, followed by Champion ASH Mare, Champion Led Mare and Supreme Led Exhibit All Breeds, and repeated this at Katherine the following year. She also won Champion ASH Ridden Mare in 2015. At Pussy Cat campdraft 2015, her first ever run, she finalled in the Ladies, but injured herself shortly after that, so she was put in foal.

"Maia herself has been a wonderful horse to ride and learn with. Her temperament is second to none, and she is a cowy, bold mare with a massive heart. I was subsequently able to purchase CHALANI ATHENA, a half sister to Maia but by Chalani Sunstream. Such was my liking of Maia and her line, I was keen to acquire my own." – Kelsey Stafford.

Maia has since had 3 foals by KIRKBYS STUD CREDIT, all showing lovely big movement. The filly TARRAWONGA LA NINA, broke in well and is being retained by Kelsey. Maia returned to *Chalani* in 2021 and produced the striking pinto colt CHALANI SIROCCO in 2023, by YINBARUN CONMANCHE.

Chalani Sirocco, 2023, ex Chalani Maia, future sire for Chalani.
Photo Theresa Thomson-Jack.

Chalani Nightdance has been away from the spotlight his entire career due to his owner's circumstances, but the performances of his progeny from limited opportunity, has been nothing short of extraordinary. He has not been standing at a 'name' stud, but in private ownership of one dedicated lady, with only two mares of her own. Paula has simply wanted to enjoy her horse, see him thrive and pass his genes on to the next generation, so has welcomed outside mares, when many would not have. With progeny all over Australia, he has definitely left a mark.

Chapter 20

Chalani Tempo

The life-changing horse

(Chalani Nightdance x Chalani Pivot), 2011 blk 15.2h.

Adelaide Royal 2016 win, followed by Champion, with Janita Edwards. Photo by Kangra.

Said owner Janita Edwards in 2019:

"Tempo has been a life-changing horse for me. We have had a hell of a ride and there is still more to come. I first saw Tempo as a several month old foal, still on Pivot at *Chalani*, when I visited with Helen Grantham, who was considering leasing Skylark (full sister) to get back into riding. I took one look at him and had to have him. I have bought and sold weanlings and yearlings for many years in the Thoroughbred industry and the minute I saw him I knew what an amazing type he was. So what started off as keeping a mate company on a drive, ended up with me with a stud colt. We have been Australia-wide campaigning him, with Royal Champion wins at Canberra Royal (twice), multiple Supremes, and Champions at Adelaide Royal, and Reserve Champs at the ASH Nationals in Led and Ridden.

"He is a one in a million horse and I am now looking forward to showing his progeny which have his wonderful temperament and type. When the opportunity came up to buy Pivot as well, I jumped at it. She produced two foals for me, both fillies, KIAHGLENN ALLEGRA and BOUNCE, both by Chalani Sunstream."

Chalani Pivot

(Chalani Paper Man x Chalani Skelter) 1996, blk 15.1h.

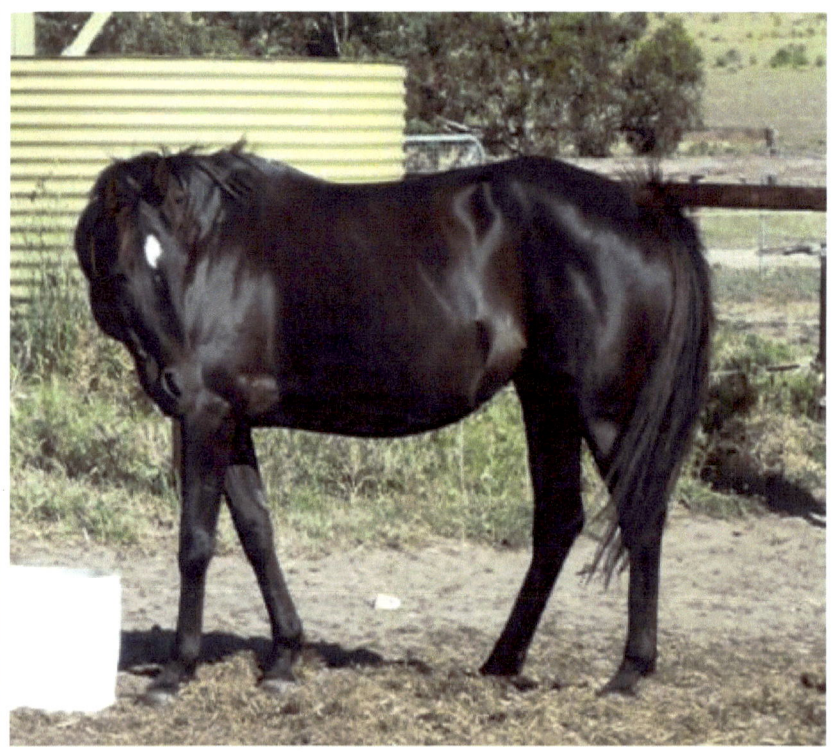

Pivot was an exceptionally beautiful filly and a much loved favorite for the stud. As a yearling being prepared for the Dubbo Breeders Championships, she was also the companion to her full brother, CHALANI REVELLER, orphaned at only 10 days old, He quickly adapted to taking his milk from a bucket. Soon we realized that Pivot was drinking it too. No wonder her coat was so shiny!

Reveller turned out to be a very safe and versatile mount for a number of families, particularly eventing/showjumping, and always ridden by juniors.

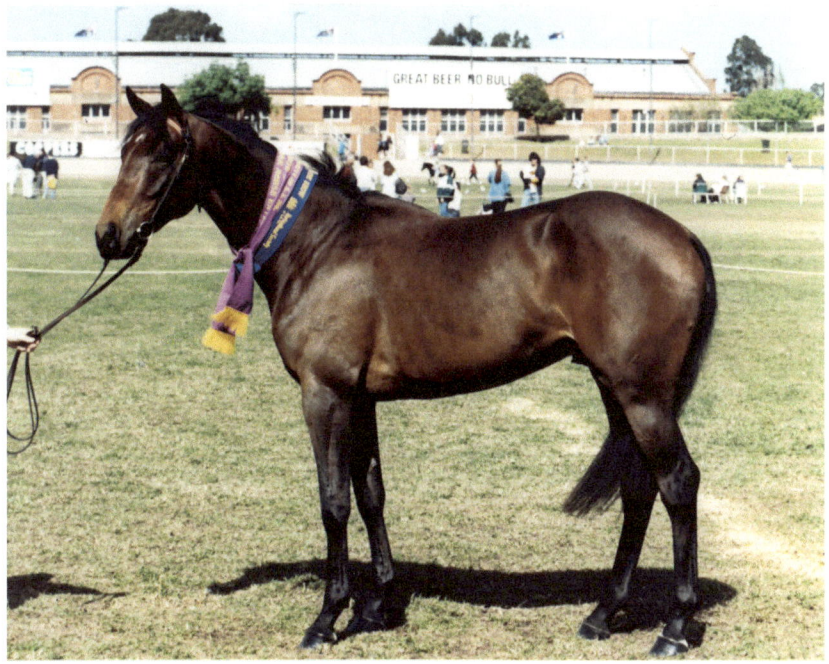

Chalani Paper Man (Fintona Artist x Chalani Paper Tiger), 1993, b h. Sire of Chalani Pivot, shown here as a three year old, Reserve Champion ASH male, 1996 Adelaide Royal. He sired very quiet and useful progeny, before being sold to Noal Day in NSW, where he sired polo and polocrosse horses.

From limited showing, Pivot was very successful winning awards as a yearling and two year old. This included 3rd at Dubbo 1998 Breeders Championships Yearling Futurity, a very big class. She was Reserve Champion Led Mare 1998 Adelaide Royal Show (to stablemate Chalani Aurora), and first 1997 2yo Filly Futurity SA Central Branch. She was easy to break in and placed under saddle at ASH Branch Shows. But for me, she was more valuable as a breeding horse with her unique bloodlines, so I chose to breed her early, the first foal being Chalani Chipper, by Chalani Pacesetter.

As a broodmare, Pivot excelled, being the dam of 14 foals, 12 to be shown, of which 11 have been Led Champions at Royals and Futurity Winners. The biggest plus was their temperaments, which have been outstanding in all respects. Most have been by Splashdance. Others by Chalani Nightdance are listed under Nightdance's chapter (p 227.)

Some of Chalani Pivot's Splashdance progeny are:

*CHALANI ZEST, 2004 blk m, SA
Yearling Futurity 2006, for owner Ian
Bishop, Geelong, Vic.*

*CHALANI JESTER 2005, b g, with Danielle De Barro.
Danielle said "he's the horse you'd always put on the truck
because you knew you'd always come back with a ribbon."*

CHALANI WALKABOUT, ex Pivot, 2006, Res Champ Gelding, Ad Royal 2013, Photo by Kangra.

Walkabout was very successful for several years, in a number of disciplines at major events in the Mid-North of SA.

CHALANI ACTION, ex Pivot, 2003, Royal Melbourne Show Champion 2011, for Felicity Chafer, and Barastoc winner.

Barastoc Nationals 2011, winner ridden ASH mare class.

Chalani Ripple, ex Pivot, 2014, winner SA Yearling Futurity 2016.

Ripple being broken in by Kim Ide, 2018.

*Ripple Above and below, 1917 Adelaide Royal Led winner with
Jeanette Gower, photos by Kangra.*

Following on from Tempo's successes in young horse classes, he was sent to Mt Sanford Station in the Northern Territory with Kelsey Stafford, for 5 months of mustering experience. When it was realized the potential he had, Kelsey strongly suggested he be seriously campaigned in the campdraft arena. In the meantime, he continued showing for wins at major Royals and the ASH Nationals, both led and under saddle, including Reserve Champion Working Stallion 2021.

Chalani Tempo at Mt Sandford Station, Kimberleys, N.T.

Melbourne Summer Royal 2015, with owner Janita Edwards.

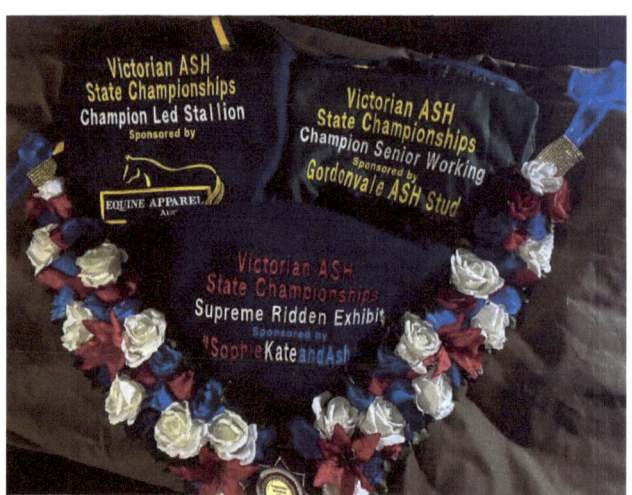

Tempo continued with major wins first with Kim Ide, then David Murphy.

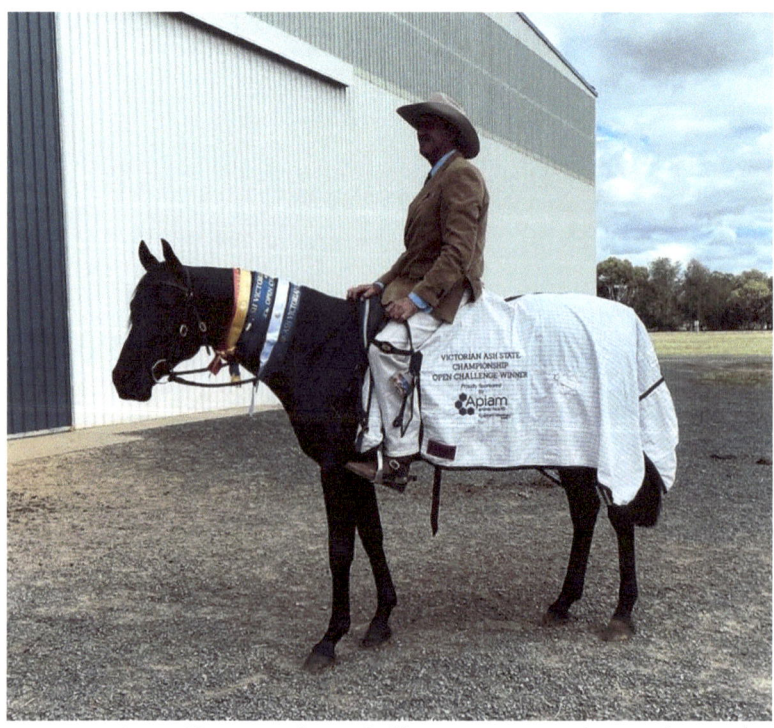

Victorian State Championships Challenge winner, with David Murphy.

Tempo has taken to drafting like a duck to water. Under the training of David Murphy, he has been brought along slowly to become seasoned for some big events. It is early days, but he has moved quickly up to Open level, consistently scoring 89 to 91 across the Southern Campdraft circuit and camp scores of 22. He was SCA Maiden Horse of the Year, and Runner up, Horse of the Year for 2019/20.

Chalani Tempo, ridden by David Murphy, photo by Jo Thieme.

His results speak for themselves, with a number of wins and placings drafting in 2022, including winning the cattle section of the Abbey Open Challenge, and 4th overall draft at ASH Nationals.

In 2023, he won the prestigious Stallion Draft, at Goondiwindi ASH Campdraft Championships, placed equal 5th in the Second Round of Willinga Gold Buckle Draft, equal 8th from 645, in round 1 of the Warwick Gold Cup and finalled in the Stallion Draft. He recently won the Open Draft (after a runoff) at Lucindale SA from some 150 competitors, in the lead up to his 2024 campaign.

Such a fabulous partnership has been forged by David Murphy and 'Toad' as he is affectionately known, over a four year period, which is still going from strength to strength. His bloodlines present an important outcross opportunity for mainstream lines, and there is no doubting the consistent stamp on his progeny.

Chalani is proud of Janita's vision and successes with Tempo. She said "he is a testament to your breeding programme – a once in a lifetime horse."

Chalani Tempo wins National ASH Stallion Campdraft with David Murphy, July 2023. Photo by Created By Kiwi.

Chalani Tempo

Foaled 2012
Blk stallion 15.2h

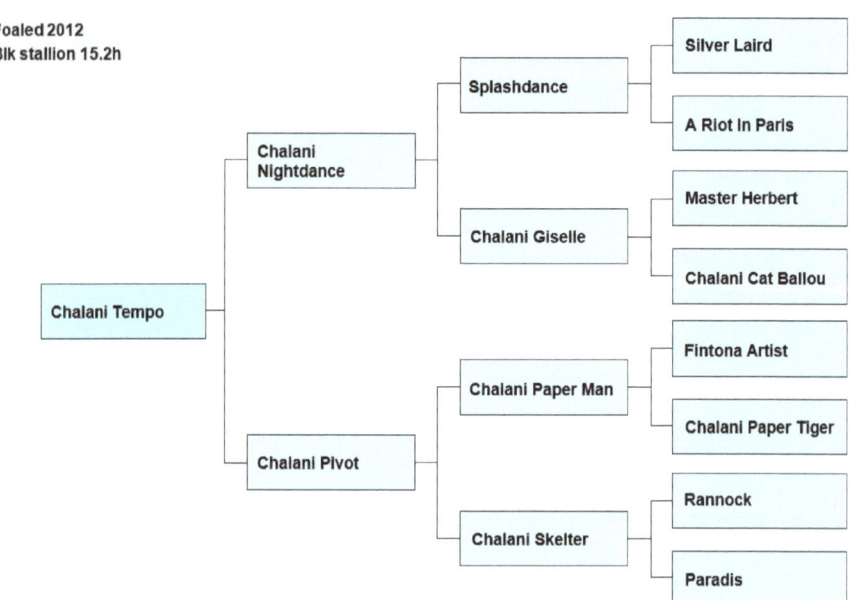

Chalani Tempo progeny gallery

KIAGLENN FOXTROT, ex LIBERTEPARK JEWEL, 2021,
blk g, Reserve Champion ASH gelding at Adelaide Royal, 2023.

KIAGLENN DESTINY, ex TARRAWONGA RHYTHM,
2019, blk m, with David Murphy.

*BALLANDOWN LOTUS, ex BALLANDOWN LILLY, 2017, b
m, Kirsty Foster, Moot Yang Gunya Stockmen's Challenge, 2020.*

*Inverdale Mahvellous Melody, Supreme Arabian Stockhorse at the Na-
tional Arabian Championships 2021. Photo by Dee Kelly.*

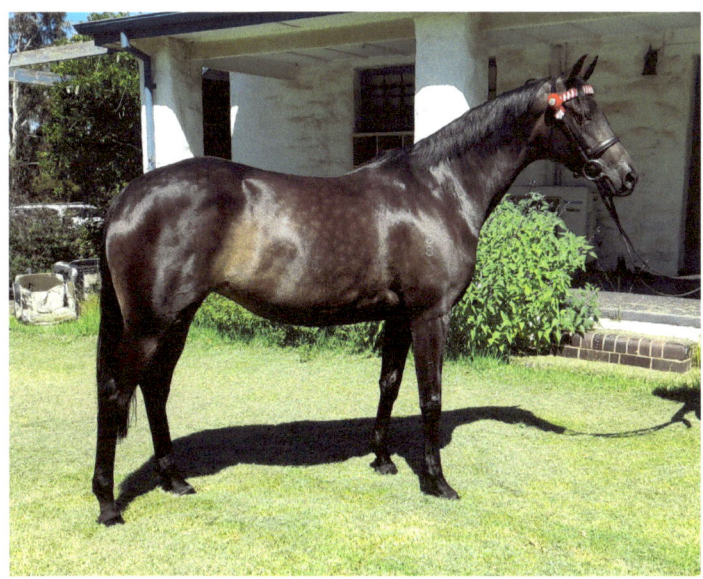

CHALANI ARIEL, ex Chalani Minerva, 2018, brn m.

BALLANDOWN ARMANI, ex BALLANDOWN
CALAMITY, 2019 ch m, with David Murphy, photo
Equine Promotions.

Chalani Sunstream, photo by Paws and Pose.

Chapter 21

Chalani Sunstream

One-of-a-kind

(Tintaras Chandra x Yooroona Rapids) 2010, Pal h, 15.1½h.

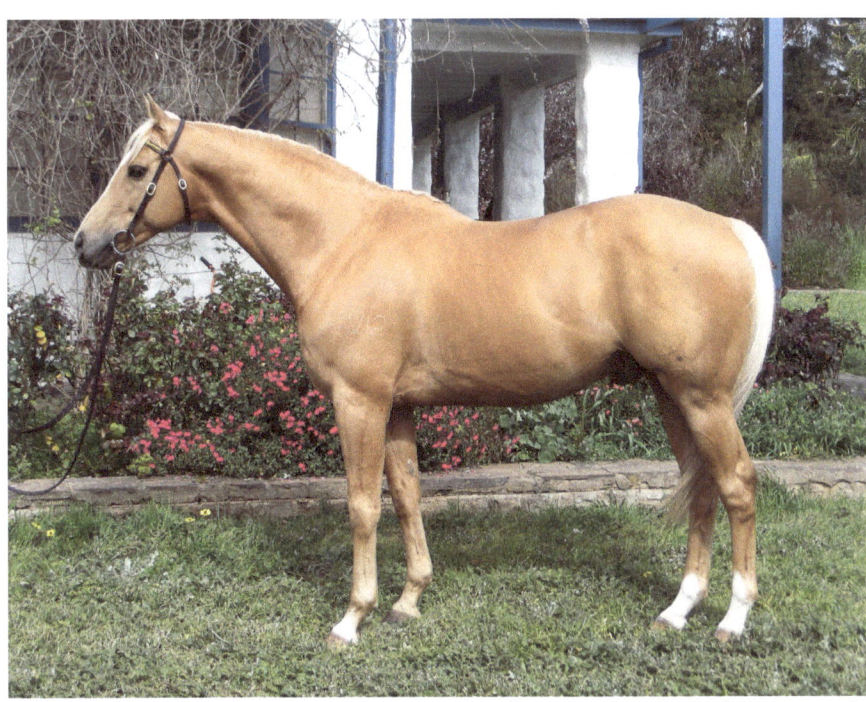

Chalani Sunstream epitomises the strength, balance and quality of the Rannock line, generations down the track.

Chalani Sunstream (Sunny) was produced after a careful selection of a complimentary outcross stallion for his dam Yooroona Rapids (by Master Herbert) who was leased by Kim Ide from Chris Roberts, of Spalding SA. Rapids played

A grade polo, and her story is in the Master Herbert chapter (p154).

Rapids' dam is the TB/reg ASH mare EXPRESSA by Green Line Express. Expressa was shown as a hack in Tasmania under the name English Rose. She was then used by Margot Maitland at Willowcroft Stud (Claire, SA) to breed a foal which hacked with success. Her pedigree contains two crosses to the famous racehorse Star Kingdom.

Chalani Sunstream's sire was the cremello stallion TINTARAS CHANDRA, which was bred in Western Australia, by Janet Forster, before being sold to Leanne Owens in Queensland. Sunny is one of his first foals. Chandra was bred on thoroughbred bloodlines, ideal for siring jumping and dressage horses, show hacks and of course Australian Stock Horses with speed.

CHALANI SUNSTREAM

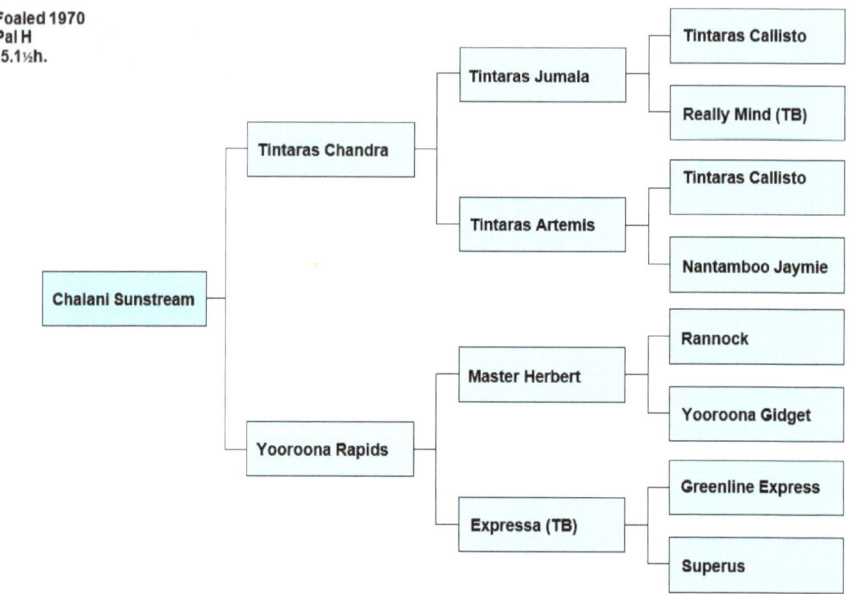

Foaled 1970
Pal H
15.1½h.

Chalani Sunstream
- Tintaras Chandra
  - Tintaras Jumala
    - Tintaras Callisto
    - Really Mind (TB)
  - Tintaras Artemis
    - Tintaras Callisto
    - Nantamboo Jaymie
- Yooroona Rapids
  - Master Herbert
    - Rannock
    - Yooroona Gidget
  - Expressa (TB)
    - Greenline Express
    - Superus

In 2013, Chandra was exported to Japan, after the Japanese owner's world-wide search for a suitable dilute stallion. Chandra is one of only a few ASH stallions exported internationally. He was purchased to be put over high class Thoroughbreds for the breeding of International-standard show-jumping, dressage and eventing horses, but died only a few years later.

We have tracked down Tikki, which has just moved up to Japanese National Level in showjumping, with Amy Tsuda. Amy's mother says "the competition is filled with super expensive European imports, super rich kids and big name riding clubs. Here we come along, Amy's first time at National level, winning with the smallest, cheapest, barefoot homebred!!" Another, Adonis, is used as a lesson horse and in wedding ceremonies at the popular Northern Horse Park.

Tiki, by Tintaras Chandra, in Japan, with 15yo rider Amy Tsuda.

Chandra's pedigree contains three crosses to the palomino stallion NANTAM-BOO GOLD SHINE. Gold Shine is by Waveney Goldbine, which sired top SA performance and showjumping horses Australia-wide, by Melbourne Cup winner Comic Court (TB). Nantamboo Gold Shine, in turn sired KIRBY PARK NANTAMBOO, owned by Olympian Megan Jones, Hahndorf, SA. Megan used this stallion to sire top class eventers, several of which went overseas to represent Australia.

Tintaras Chandra (2005) in Qld, 2012.

Of TINTARAS CALLISTO, Janet Forster says "Although very lightly used, he has proven to produce consistently good types from a range of mares with conformation, temperament, natural ability, movement and colour. His progeny are competing in a variety of disciplines; combined driving, campdrafting, pony club, high level Parelli, dressage and so on."

As you can see, a lot of thought has gone into the breeding of these horses, and to all extent, they could be considered blood horses. Fortuitously, in Chalani Sunstream, these bloodlines have returned to South Australia.

Waveney Goldbine

(Comic Court (TB) x Waveney Goldbrae), 1965, Pal 17.1h.

Goldbine, Nailsworth Show (1972), with breeder Louis Thring.

With the recent focus on Heritage-bred stock horses, Janet Forster noted Jessica carried 2 crosses back to Silver Lyn (Pearlyn x Creamy), a palomino stallion renowned for his jumping and performance abilities, and the sire of a number of exceptionally good performance horses, including Goldie, a 13.3h palomino stallion born in 1934 and registered with the Australian Pony Stud Book Society (APSB).

Goldie himself, was the sire of a number of well known dilute performance horses, including East Lynn, Golden Dawn (sire of Golden Flash who was the cornerstone of Louis Thring's palomino breeding program) and Gold Ray. (He was sire of Golden Ranger, who was the sire of Golden Paleface, the foundation stallion of Ken & Betty Hoskings' Nantamboo Stud). It is through Golden Dawn and Gold Ray, that Jessica goes back to Goldie and Silver Lyn.

NANTAMBOO GOLD SHINE, 1970 Pal h, owned by Ken and Betty Hosking circa 1975. Back in the day when white coats were compulsory at Adelaide Royal.

NANTAMBOO GOLD SHINE

Foaled 1970
Pal H
15.3h.

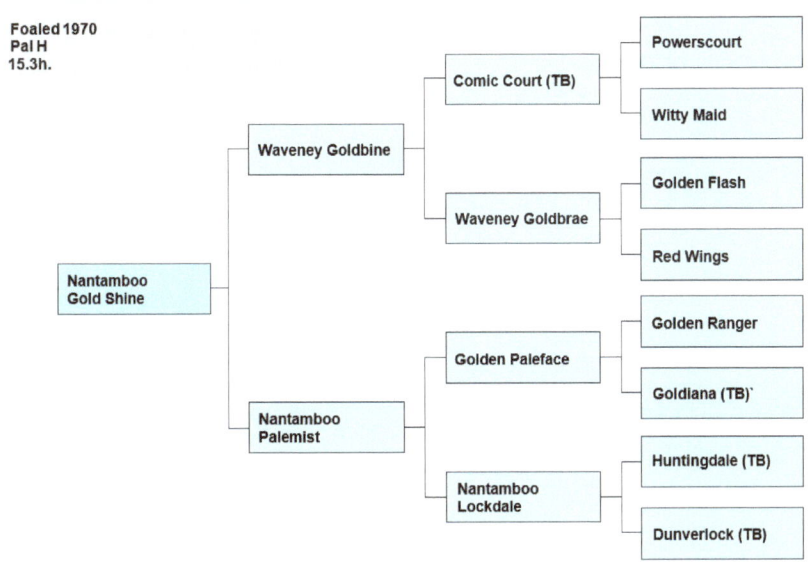

Comic Court (Powerscourt x Witty Maid) TB, 1945 b h.

Golden Dawn was a palomino stallion by Goldie out of a mare of now unknown breeding called Mousie. The line of modern day dilutes that trace directly back to him about which much is known predominantly come down through his son **Golden Flash**, a palomino out of a Thoroughbred mare called Flash By (by Passing By out of Abstainer). Golden Flash was the sire of a number of palomino Tb crosses bred by Louis Thring of the famous Waveney Stud in SA. Probably the most notable of these was the mare **Goldbrae**, a palomino mare out of the thoroughbred mare Red Wings who was by *Soltoi out of Gay Wings* (and not to be confused with several other mares of the same name, including one by Star Kingdom and another who was the dam of Claredale Champagne Charlie!!). Goldbrae in turn was bred to Melbourne Cup winner Comic Court several times to produce a couple of palomino offspring and it is primarily through these horses (**Waveney Goldbine** and **Comic Gold**) that the family survives today in horses bred by Westbury Park, Kirby Park, Beauleigh, Kilmaine, Tintara, Chalani, Davien Park and so on.

Gold Ray was also by Goldie out of a now unknown mare and his major sire son seems to have been Eric Campion's stallion **Golden Ranger** (out of an Arab Tb x mare) who produced another famous SA sire in **Golden Paleface,** owned by Nantamboo Stud. Golden Paleface sired a large number of foals for Nantamboo Stud, many of which were sold interstate where they founded their own dynasties of dilutes

Bengal Shah, by Golden Ranger, was seen many a time jumping out of his paddock.

*Bengal Shah (14.3h), winning Puissance at Adelaide Royal, clearing 6'6",
with Jeff Evans riding, photo Keith Stevens. Bev Schutz (nee Mangelsdorf) his
regular rider, had a big crash two days before when he nosedived on landing
over a huge spread. "I only got out of hospital in time to see this event. The Golden
Ranger horses were 'natural jumpers.' I had Magician and another very handy
Goden Ranger, Desert Ranger. He was a full brother to Desert Sun. I won an
Adelaide Hunt Club Ladies Point to Point on him."*

NANTAMBOO JESSICA

(Nantamboo Gold Shine x Halloshine (TB)) 1987, pal m.

Appearing twice in Tintaras Chandra's pedigree is Nantamboo Jessica. This ASH mare was a multi-Champion both in hand and under saddle. Janet showed her quite extensively in led classes as a youngster and she always came home with either Champion or Reserve. There were some extremely nice mares being shown at the time, yet she held her own against them.

She was twice winner of the Prince of Wales trophy for High Point All-Round Stock Horse of Australia 1993 and 94! – an incredible achievement.

She also won Directors Awards for High Point ASH Hack 3 years in a row 1993, 94, 95, and High Point All Round ASH for 1994 and 1995, High Point Junior and Senior Performance Palomino of WA etc.

Jessica suffered a bout of Ross River virus which is another one of those things both horses and humans can catch. Janet got it at the same time, so Jessica was retired. Her only foal was Tintaras Callisto, which was a Perth Royal Show Supreme Champion led palomino, and is Chandra's grandsire on both sides of his pedigree.

Nantamboo Jessica, 1987, owned by Janet Forster WA. Jessica's taproot female is by Aurum (TB) a leading Broodmare Sire, which stood in SA.

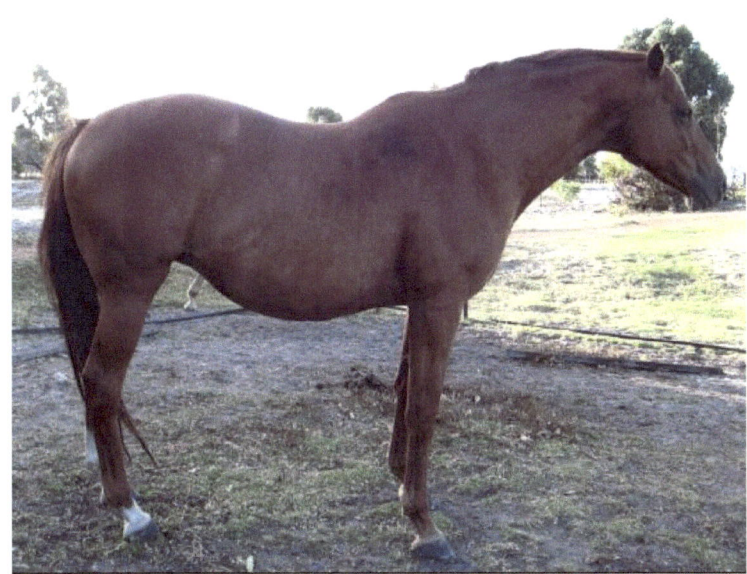

NANTAMBOO JAYMIE, 1994 ch m, full sister to Nantamboo Jessica and dam of Tintaras Artemis.

Aurum (Aureole x Golden Gulf) 1957, ch h.

TINTARAS CALLISTO

Foaled 1999
Pal H
15.2h.

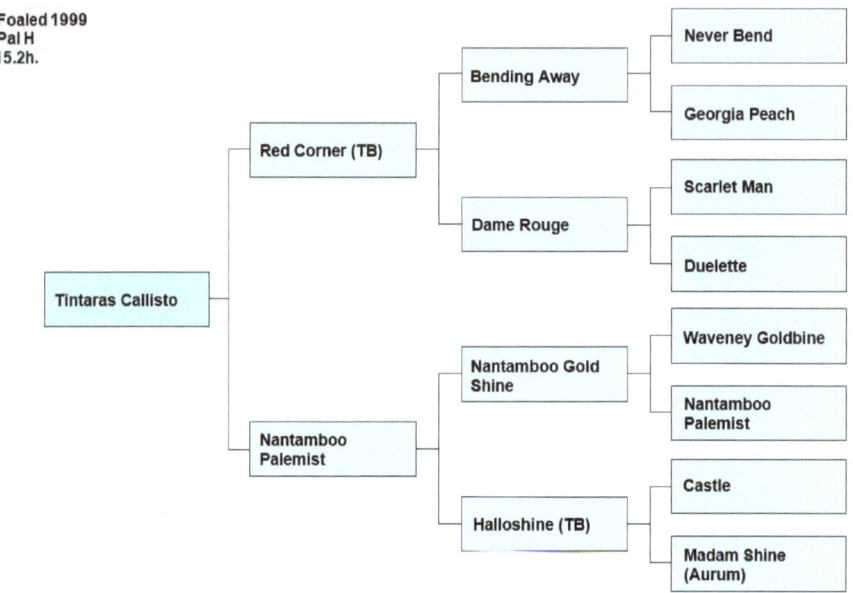

Janet Forster calculated that the famous Carbine (TB) appears in Chalani Sunstream's pedigree some 41 times. You can see the resemblance here:

Carbine

In March of 2013, Sunny was started under saddle by well known Victorian horseman Colin Byron. Col used him as a demo horse at a 'colt starting clinic' where he showed his breaking procedure with Sunny. Col described him as a "beautifully soft horse to ride, with great length of rein and a great type. I love him."

Col did 5 weeks of riding with Chalani Sunstream before he was spelled. See more photos on the Chalani page. https://www.chalani.net/sunstream.php

Sunny leading his son, Chalani Tussock, yearling colt, with Kim Ide.

"Chalani Sunstream is a quick learner and gentle natured. He is a striking 'palomino version of Rannock', a true gold palomino all year round, with striking coat iridescence which draws comment wherever he goes. He has plenty of presence under saddle, with his swinging movement and self-carriage. Though he is extremely gentle, he gives 100% when the going gets tough.

"Sunny is a gentleman to show, compete and train with. He demonstrates immaculate behaviour at very busy competitions, with judges and competitors commenting on his good manners and calmness. He has been used to lead the kids' Shetland pony mare on trails, lead breakers off, and give schoolmaster rides to Ashton and Xander Ide when 10 years old. He attended an Ian Francis clinic and was so quiet that Ian didn't realise he was a stallion, until the second day when he was sitting on a chair and could see underneath him!

"I've had people come and tell me how amazed they were at seeing Sunny in the stables at ASH Nationals, where they saw people had pulled up their mare next to his box, and not realise he was a stallion, as he just remained relaxed.

"I can ride mares past his paddock at home, and he knows they are not worth paying attention to, as they are being ridden, not led. He is a very 'thoughtful' horse and tries very hard, as he hates doing the 'wrong thing,' never needing to be reprimanded." – Kim Ide.

Chalani Sunstream has been shown very successfully in ASH and Dilutes Australia classes, with a highlight being Champion Novice Hack at the ASHS National Show as a 4yo in 2015, under judge Lindy Walker. He has won in dressage (twice) at the ASH Nationals, with many placings in Led, Hack, Pleasure, Working, and Station horse.

Kim Ide from South Australia had a great day yesterday with her homebred stallion Chalani Sunstream. The combination was declared Champion Novice Hack from a huge number of horses and won the class for 4 year old stallion hack. Today the young stallion performed well again taking second place in the Working Stallion 4 year old.

From The Horse Deals Gallery, 2015, Julie Wilson.

He was the winner of the ASH 4yo Maturity at the ASH SA State show in March 2015.

He has had multiple Supreme Champion wins at Adelaide Royal 2015,- Supreme Champion Led ASH under judge Larry Cutler, from Victoria, Champion Ridden ASH, Supreme Champion Led Dilute, Supreme Champion Ridden Dilute (winning Champion Ridden Dilute, Champion Dilute Hack and Champion Best Educated Dilute, as well as 1st Pleasure horse) under Queensland judge, Cherie Devenish-Edwards.

Adelaide Royal Champion ASH, 2015, with Kim Ide, stewards (who all wanted to be in) and judge, Larry Cutler.

He was High Point Horse of the show at the Dilutes Australia National Championships, Easter 2015, winning multiple Champions Led and Ridden, including Supreme Led Palomino. He was 1st and 2nd in the Prep and Prelim dressage tests, with the highest percentage on the day (72%).

Supreme, National Dilutes Championships 2015

He has won back to back Supreme Led and Ridden Dilute at the Dilutes Australia, SA State Championships, in 2018 and 2019. Then the Led Supreme of Australia for the Dilutes Australia-wide video competition from all state winners in 2018. (The ridden video unfortunately corrupted and due to rider injury was unable to be re-filmed before the due date).

Sunny has been lightly campdrafted. "We do not own any cattle to develop skills, however Sunny demonstrates cowiness and has made maiden, novice and open finals, as well as achieved placings. At Strathalbyn Campdraft 2018, Sunny scored 86 in the first round of the Sunday Maiden draft (personal best score for his rider at the time). He had not seen a cow for 12 months.

"At Strathalbyn Campdraft in Feb 2019 he placed 3rd in the Novice draft. At McArthur Campdraft in March 2019 he placed 6th in the Ladies draft. He placed 4th in the Ladies draft at Fleurieu Campdraft 2021, again after not seeing a cow in 12 months. He followed this up in Feb 2021 with 3rd in the Novice at Fleurieu Campdraft. He has had camp scores of up to 22 on several occasions." – Kim Ide.

In keeping with his jumping ancestry, Sunny shows tremendous talent over jumps, with great lift, scope and style, and is passing this on to his progeny. Chalani Sunstream is truly a 'one-of-a-kind' stallion from unique bloodlines.

It takes a long time for a stallion to become recognised, often not until after his death, which is a potential loss for the breed. Chalani Sunstream is on the right path to fulfilling his promise as an outstanding sire for 'the breed for every need.' He provides a valuable outcross. It can be genuinely stated that he combines outstanding, unique, versatile bloodlines, with international reach!

Photo gallery of Chalani Sunstream

Keith (SA) Novice Challenge Winner, 2017, with Kim Ide.

Photo Beauty and the Huntress.

Perfect Partners photo.

Photo by Marscar.

Horizons Photography.

Champion Novice Hack ASH Nationals, 2015.

With young Ashton prior to the dressage. Photo Flash Pony.

Kerri Afford Photo

Patiently waiting, with Kim

Ride-outs with the children, Xander Ide at 5yrs.

Strathalbyn Campdraft, 2018.

Time trial, fastest horse wins.

Chapter 22

Chalani Sunstream Progeny

Chalani Sunstream's ability to pass on his type, athleticism and colour is expected from his strong ancestry and evident when crossed over a range of mares, including ASH, TB, QH, Paint, Riding Ponies, Warmblood and Sportaloosa.

His progeny are proving versatile, being used by competitors, leisure riders and junior riders. They have competed in ASH led, hack and working classes successfully, made Cloncurry Novice Campdraft final, won and placed in campdrafts in the Victorian and South Australian regions, and qualified for Royal shows in Open Hack and Open Show Hunter classes, with Horse of the Year places at Show Horse Council shows. They have been used on long distance trail rides, for barrel racing and won at dressage and show jumping, with wins in open jumping competition. One was also an Adelaide Royal mounted steward's horse for several years.

CHALANI TUSSOCK, ex CHALANI CLOVER, 2013 buck g.

In 2012, Kim leased the 19yr old Fintona Artist mare Chalani Clover, to return some Artist blood to the stud. A colt was the result, rather than the wanted filly. He was so nice, she used him over the mare Chalani Trivia (see p 213), before gelding him. CHALANI CARD TRICKS was the result.

Tussock was then broken in. He proved to be very successful in young horse classes, both led and under saddle in the 2016/2017 show season, in ASH and Show Hunter galloway competition, qualifying for Adelaide Royal 2017. He was Runner-Up Newcomer Show Hunter Galloway, SA SHC HOY Show Oct 2016, an Encourage Challenge Winner, Coonalpyn Ag Show Oct 2016 (working pattern, obstacle course and whip crack) and multiple championships. He was very successful as a 3yr old at the March 2017 ASH National Championships in Tamworth, winning two classes and placing in five others. He was then sold to Tanya Stuart.

Tussock as a 3yo, in the pleasure hack with Kim Ide.

Station Horse event, at the ASH Nationals 2017

Tanya viewed Tussock at the ASH Nationals in 2017. "We travelled to Tamworth to view Tussock and ride, to ensure he was suitable. I purchased him on the spot and organized for him to catch a ride home to Northern NSW, with a friend who was competing at the show. From there our journey began.

"At this point Tussock was 3 years old and I was a very amateur rider. One of our first outings under saddle was a dressage day at Bangalow where we competed in the Preliminary test, for a score of over 65% and placed highly. Tussock was a very balanced, rhythmical horse and was very easy to ride. He always responded to my aids (even when they weren't delivered correctly). His temperament was that of a 'bloody good horse'.

"Over the next few months we competed at local agricultural shows competing in the Stock Horse ring as well as the ANSA, Hunter Galloway and colored rings. Tussock achieved huge success in these events, always coming home with multiple champions in both led and ridden classes. We continued with our dressage days scoring very highly in every test, and taking home overall Preliminary championships. We even entered the masters games in the dressage section and came home with 3 gold medals!

Tussock with Tanya Stuart.

"In 2019 after many riding lessons and clinics, I decided we had grown together and our partnership had developed enough to enter some bigger shows. Toowoomba Royal was the first on the agenda, where he received Champion

Tanya with Chalani Tussock at Qld Country Hack Championships, 2018, photo Lisa Gordon

Buckskin exhibit and placed in the Novice and the Open Hack classes. He placed in the Child's Hack piloted by Lucy Sidney. Lucy also took him to Pony Club where he showed his willingness to jump, and sporting events, and won many admirers.

"During that year we also tackled Maryborough, Caboolture and Northern NSW Hack Championships which are Grand National Qualifying shows. We were up against the big guns, all the professional riders. It was a bit scary and I was very nervous, however Tussock didn't disappoint and worked beautifully in his open classes and was also awarded Smartest on Parade at every SHCA event. (Yes he grew, and was now being shown as a hack.) Tussock would stand in the line up perfectly collected and would not move a muscle, no matter how long it took the judges to look over the horses.

"From memory, the biggest class had 32 Hacks which we were competing against at these SHCA shows. I also won my rider class on 2 occasions.

"Late 2019 we ventured to the QLD Dilute Championships where Tussock took out the Supreme Led Dilute horse. This was one of our biggest achievements. Then in 2020 Chalani Tussock was awarded the National Supreme Champion Dilute Horse of the Year.

"In 2020, after 2 bouts of pneumonia, I decided I had achieved as much as I could with Tussock, so due to my health, I made the heart-breaking decision to sell him to someone who could take him further and reach even higher goals. Tussock was sold to the very best of homes in the Sydney area, to a 12-year-old girl, and is still with her. They first competed in Interschool competitions, winning Novice dressage at state level, among many other achievements. He enjoys having a spell at his owners' prestigious property *Luskin Park* in the Hunter Valley. Tussock and Claudia have developed a very special and successful partnership."

***

Sunstream progeny lined up in the ASH 3 years and under class at Breed O Rama, SA 2023. From Left, Chalani Pocket Rocket, 3yo, Chalani Skydancer, 2yo (both ex Chalani Skylark), Wanjohi Catseye, 1yo, Wanjohi Sun Seeker, 2yo, (both ex The Echo Gemima) and far right, Chalani Galaxy, 2yo. Photo SRS Imagery.

CHALANI CARD TRICKS

(Chalani Tussock x Chalani Trivia) 2016, buck m 16h.

'Trixie', as she is affectionately known, is a most versatile mare, having drafted, hacked, done Pony Club, and excelled in ASH events. She would have to be one of the most talented horses bred at Chalani. (See p 215.)

Adelaide Royal 2022, results for Trixie and Nova. Kim and 12 yo Ashton.
Photo Jenni Phillips.

CHALANI CARD TRICKS

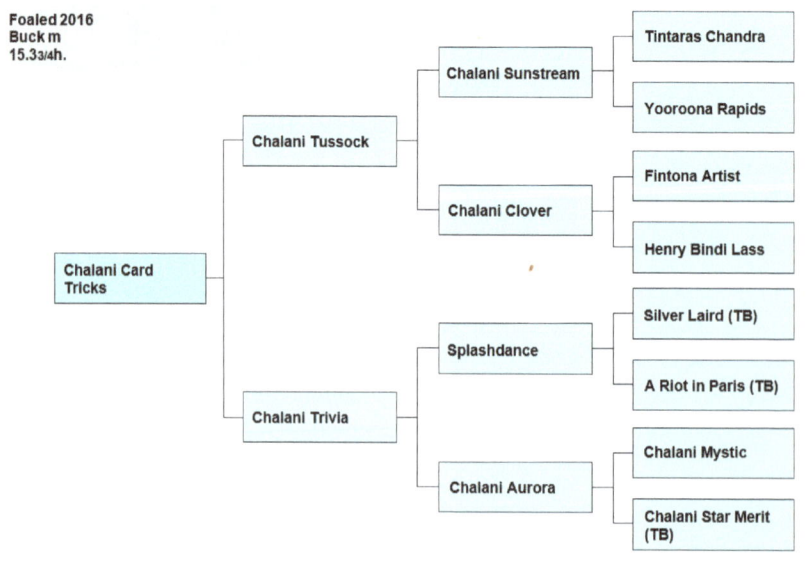

Foaled 2016
Buck m
15.3¾h.

- Chalani Card Tricks
  - Chalani Tussock
    - Chalani Sunstream
      - Tintaras Chandra
      - Yooroona Rapids
    - Chalani Clover
      - Fintona Artist
      - Henry Bindi Lass
  - Chalani Trivia
    - Splashdance
      - Silver Laird (TB)
      - A Riot in Paris (TB)
    - Chalani Aurora
      - Chalani Mystic
      - Chalani Star Merit (TB)

Card Tricks is known for her exceptional, rythmical, floating movement, and brilliance. Photo Lisa Gordon.

Kirstie Murch photo.

Ashton and Card Tricks won the Pony Clubs National Subjunior Preliminary Dressage, 2023.

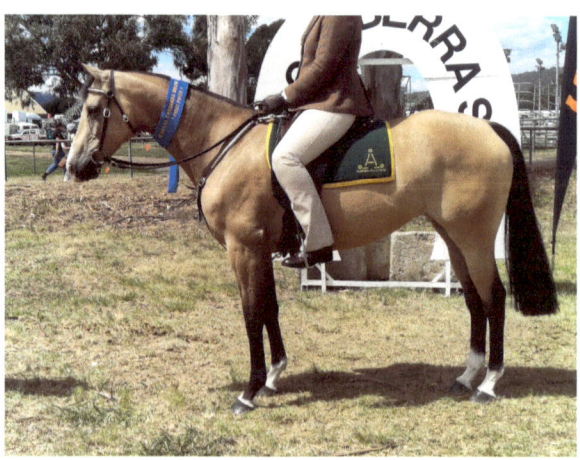

Canberra Royal 2023, first ASH Hack mare o 15h.

CHALANI ATHENA, ex Chalani Aurora, 2013 ch m.

This is another beautiful foal of Chalani Aurora. She was sold as a weanling to Kelsey Stafford. In Kelsey's hands, they won the Led ASH mare at 2016 Darwin Royal, and second Katherine, NT. She continued mustering on Mt Sanford and

started to score regularly. She finalled at her third draft with Kelsey in mid 2019, scored multiple times with Kim Ide at Mt Isa, and then finalled in the Novice at Cloncurry with Kim in 2019. She was super consistent, fast and cowy, and never heated up. She would just walk away on the buckle after every run.

Athena with Kelsey Stafford, Darwin Royal 2016.

The story continues with Kelsey. "Today I said goodbye to Chalani Athena, at least for the next few years. It's almost 9 years to the day since that little (big) weanling filly headed north to me in the NT from SA, a massive trip for a six month old! I will never forget the transport driver ringing me to say "you forgot to tell me it's a foal!" He said she loaded beautifully, and continued to do so all the way to Katherine in the NT, where we picked her up from a dear friend, and headed home with her in a questionable station float.

Athena with Kim Ide, Mt Isa, 2019.

"Halfway home on the 6 hour trip from Katherine, the bearing went in one wheel, but we persevered - until only about 30 k from the nearest community to the station, said wheel went flying past us and down the bitumen at 100 miles an hour! By this stage it was dark because we'd been creeping along hoping exactly this wouldn't happen.

"Once we found the missing wheel in the 10 foot high peabush, about 100 metres off the road (still not entirely sure how we managed it in the dark) we chained up the axle missing the wheel, and kept going, with the thought that we could maybe leave the filly in Kalkarindji with people we knew for the night. However, upon arriving there, we figured what was another 65k, so headed home on the very rough gravel track that was the station driveway. And through all of this, that little filly stayed calm, fuss free and beautifully mannered.

"Nothing has changed in the following almost 9 years. Athena has remained an unflappable, sweet and stoic mare. Still one of my all time favourite horses to ride, she has cow sense in spades, movement in buckets and sweetness in truck loads. The only other person I think who could appreciate her and her lines more than me is the lady who bred her, so I have leased her to Kim, and will be watching with bated breath, every foaling." – Kelsey Stafford.

In 2023, Athena foaled an elegant bay colt in SA by ROHAVEN REGAL BANQUET (TB/reg ASH), named CHALANI TROOPER.

KIAGLENN ALLEGRA, ex Chalani Pivot, 2016 pal m.

Said Kelsey Stafford, "I had had my eye on Allegra from the get go as she had an exquisite head, a beautiful depth of girth and just a presence about her that had you looking twice, even without the palomino colouring, and not to mention I liked the idea of getting a close pedigree mix of my two favourite Chalani stallions.

Allegra, above and next, with Dave Murphy, 2021 Vic State ASH Champs.
Equine Promotions photography.

"In late 2018, Janita Edwards decided she would sell her, as she was understandably more interested in marketing half-brother, Chalani Tempo. I dreamed a lot about possibilities, but never went any further with it because I couldn't see any way at the time to afford buying her outright, and then paying for transport to north-west QLD from SA. However, as women tend to do, we got talking and when I was offered a payment plan, bam, all of a sudden those possibilities were within reach!

"Allegra came north to me at Cloncurry in March 2019. She was left to grow out, with a led class in June, and then while Kim was visiting in July, she offered to break her in and show me her process for doing so. She broke in easily and well, and was left to continue growing out for the rest of 2019, except for a short stint with Daisy Robertson in October 2019.

"Allegra competed in the Central Qld ASH branch show in early October and she took out Supreme Led Exhibit there. Early 2020, I dropped her off to Daisy to prep for the Three Year Old Futurity at the ASHS Nationals. Of course with Covid, it wasn't to be. At the end of 2020, she headed off to David Murphy for training for the Four Year Old Maturity at the next ASH Nationals.

"Murph took her to the Victorian State champs at Elmore in March 2021, where she won and placed in multiple led and ridden classes the first day, and then won the Four Year Old Maturity the next day. (photo below).

"On to Nationals 2021, and Allegra came second in the cattle work section of the 4 Year Old Maturity, and finished highly enough in all the other sections to place 5th overall, hugely exciting after all the naysayers who liked to tell me she was too pretty for anything except a hack class!

"Murph thought she showed enough talent on cattle, to compete in the newly-minted 5yo Challenge at the Nationals the next year, so we continued. But first I showed her at the SE of SA ASH branch show at Penola in November 2021, where she again took out Supreme Led Exhibit, pipping older brother Chalani Tempo for the win. I also rode her to placings in a couple ridden classes.

"This stint with Murph saw her really set up for drafting. Nationals was cancelled in 2022 because of all the flooding so he took her to two drafts, for 5 scores of 87 in a row - an excellent start for a still green horse. She then came home to me and although I continued riding her, almost every event in 2022 was cancelled due to wet weather.

"In late July, I carted her to Goondiwindi for the inaugural ASH Society Championship Draft where Murph, after a four month hiatus, finalled her in both drafts entered. She went home with him from there, as it had been announced that the ASHS were going to run a Feature Events Show in December, so the aged event horses didn't miss out, particularly in the case of the 5 Year Old Challenge.

ASH Nationals 2021, Dave Murphy with Allegra, photo Flash Pony.

"Murph continued drafting her in Spring 2022. Her first draft back she placed 5th in a maiden with, you guessed it, another 87! In early November she cracked her maiden win at Keith in SA, breaking the 87 jinx for an 88 first round run, and an 86 in the final, still averaging 87!

"In December we made our way to Inverell in northern NSW for the ASH's Feature Events Show. Allegra won the Hack section of the 5 Year Old Challenge, which I was stoked about.

She was travelling very well over all events and only needed a very low score in the cattle work to take out the overall win. But as we know, cattle work is the great equaliser. You can quickly go from the penthouse to the outhouse if an ordinary beast decides to not play the game. I was still absolutely rapt when she managed to finish 8th overall.

"She also finalled in the Maiden Series draft with, yep, an 87!

"This beautiful pally mare had been such a joy to see go through the levels. She is a lovely horse to watch travelling outside, very fast and athletic. Murph was the perfect partner for her, and managed to bring out her very best, where many others would've only succeeded in frying her. She's sensitive and smart but does not suffer fools lightly. Hopefully, there's still some more drafting and showing success in the future." – Kelsey Stafford.

CHALANI CHARISMA ex CHALANI FORTUNE, 2016 buck m

Campaigned by Kate Merritt, this attractive mare won all before her in junior classes in both ASH and Dilutes, most often with Supremes or Championships, including Adelaide Royals. She is now a broodmare for Capehawke Stud, Forster NSW,

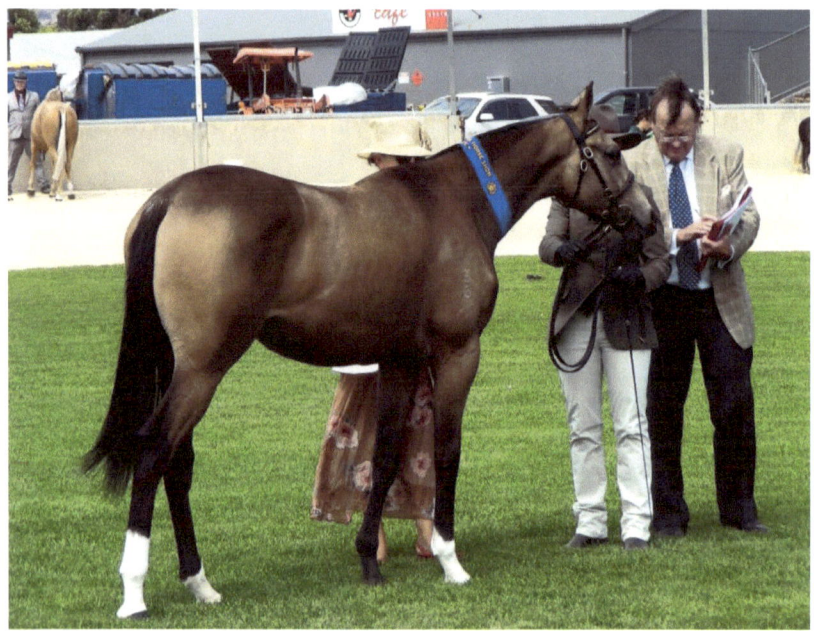

Adelaide Royal 2018

Chalani Charisma with Kate Merritt, Adelaide Summer Royal 2019 alongside her sire, held by Jeanette Gower.

CHALANI SCOTCH, ex Chalani Sangria, 2018, buck g.

Ridden by Cody Wilson, Scotch won in Working Equitation as a 2-3yo colt and was admired by many. He sired a small number of foals before being gelded.

Chalani Scotch with Cody Peterson, photo Kim Peterson.

BLACKSPRINGS ROLEX, ex Escholar Time Flies, 2018 pal h.

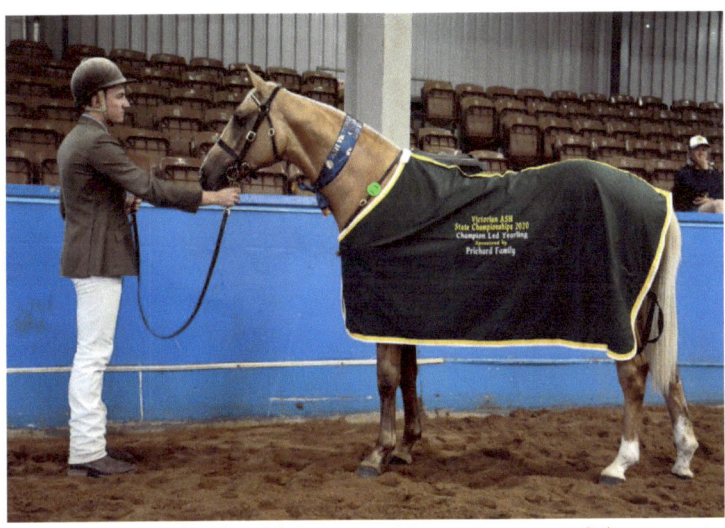

Blacksprings Rolex, bred by Lynette Meyer, Springton SA, a promising sire for Noal Day, Qld (who owned the stallion, Chalani Paper Man.) He reports Rolex has a wonderful nature, and his first foals are outstanding.

CHALANI GALAXY, ex Chalani Minerva, 2021, b h.

This fellow was of standout quality, a 'head turner' the minute he was born, and has been retained as a colt. He carries five crosses of Rannock in his pedigree.

From his only showings as a 2yr old in Led ASH events, he has been Supreme Led Exhibit and won the SA ASH State Two Year Old Futurity 2023, Penola, from a large class. Galaxy was recently broken in by Kim showing a lot of promise. He goes calmly under saddle, proving to be light of tread, free moving and soft to ride.

On his 13th ride, during a photo session, 10 year old Xander had a walk, trot and canter, and declared "This is the horse I am going to ride next. He has a very smooth canter!"

Galaxy was the standout foal, very closely resembling the ASH Society Standard of Excellence painting.

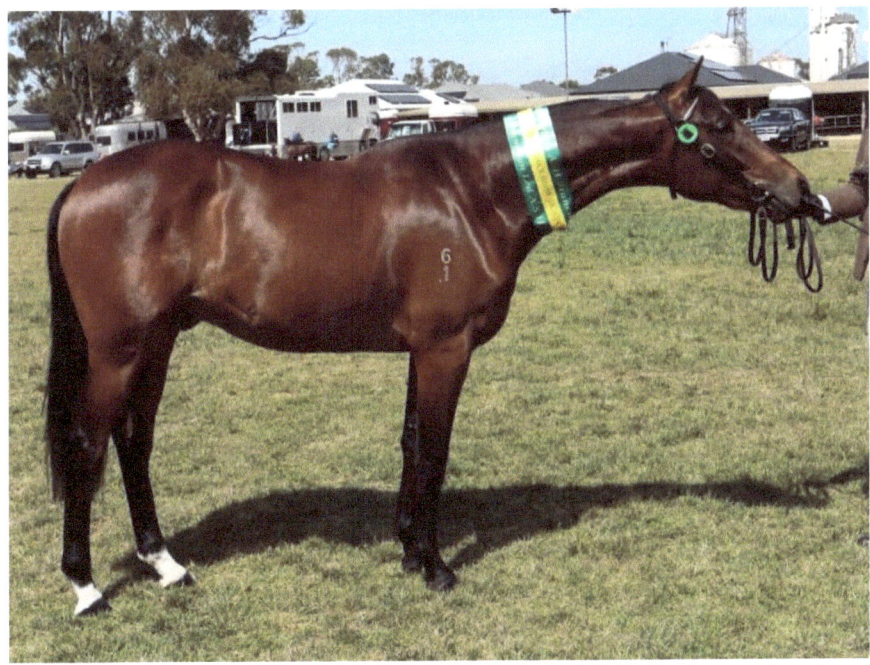

Galaxy, Supreme Champion Led ASH of show, Breed o Rama, Strathalbyn 2023.
Photo by Jenni Phillips. Below: April 2024.

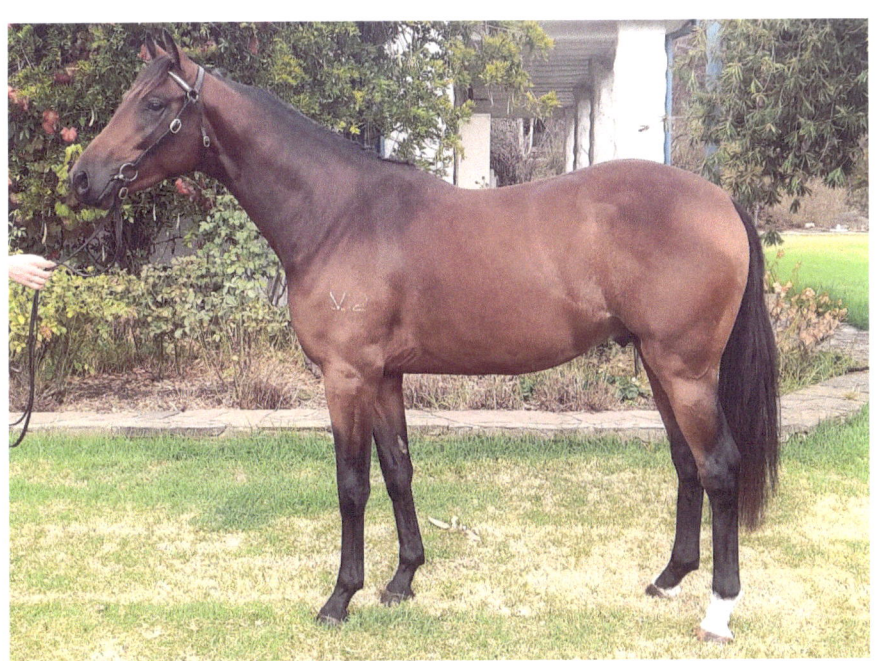

WANJOHI SUNSEEKER, ex THE ECHO GEMIMA, 2021 p g.

The Echo Gemima was bought from Lindy Launer after a successful show career, in the hope of breeding three foals for the Davie family, one for each family member. She is by THE ECHO RIVOLI RELIC. All her foals to be shown, have been successful in Led ASH and Dilutes Classes. Sun Seeker won all before him in Dilutes and SABA classes often taking out Best Youngstock and Supreme all ages, in additional to his win at the SA State ASH Yearling Futurity 2023.

Wanjohi Sun Seeker, with owner Janet Davie, and judge Helen Grantham, photo by Airtime Images, and below SRS photography.

CHALANI TOPAZ, 2020 buck m, full sister to Wanjohi Sun Seeker.

TARRAWONGA SEQUIN, ex Chalani Chiffon, 2015 ch m.

Tarrawonga Sequin, with Kelsey..

"Sequin's had lots of ribbons as a led horse, and placings ridden. We've competed at the Nationals, and she's drafted consistently well. She's very cowy and very athletic. She will never say die! In 2024, I leased her to a young girl and they're beginning a promising career in showjumping. After only 3 months, they won and placed at their first competition at State level." – Kelsey Stafford.

Chalani Sunstream now has progeny in the USA from frozen semen.

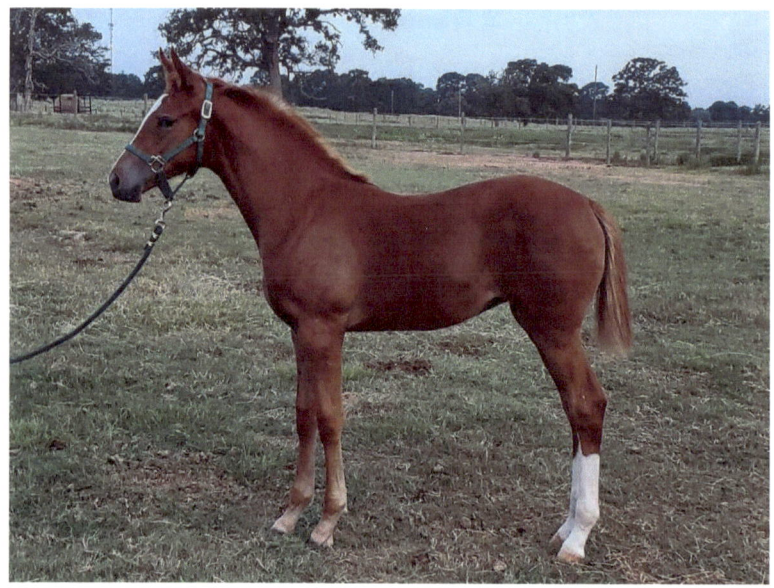

Sandhaven Sienna - The Sandhaven prefix is owned by Kellee Campbell who imported the semen to Texas.

Sandhaven Oro Escondido

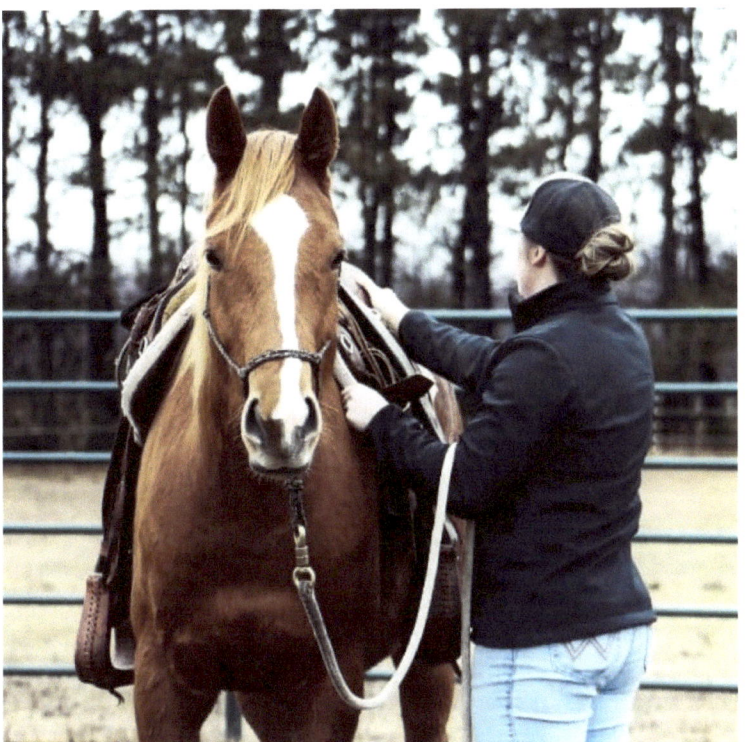

*This is Sandhaven Oro Escondido (USA) and his owner Bailey Rigg.
She started him herself and has done all of his training. "Escondido is a
very willing horse that has been very easy for me to bond with. He's quick
and athletic yet responsive, calm, and connected. I can envision myself
accomplishing anything I set my mind to with this talented horse."
Maggie Rigg photo.*

Contact the Stud

Chalani can be contacted by email chalani@chalani.net or via our Facebook page. Photos and video on the *Chalani* Facebook page, the *Chalani* website or You-tube channel. Live cover or frozen semen only. Also standing Chalani Galaxy.

Chalani Sunstream HSH is available by frozen semen in USA by contacting Kellee Campbell, Sandhaven Stud Facebook page.

Chapter 23

Final Words

What is the legacy?

Candid moment with Trixie and Ashton, Adelaide Royal 2022.

How does one evaluate the legacy of a horse, especially that of a sire?

Would it be the number of successful progeny in a specific discipline, or across multiple disciplines, or the ratio of those to the number of progeny produced? Would it be prize-money earned? Or total sale prices? How would one know the average performance value of progeny, if statistics aren't kept by either the Society, or the umbrella organizations for other disciplines, or even their owners?

Is it by numbers? HAZELWOOD CONMAN has 1485 registered progeny. He is a 'pinnacle horse,' an all-time great and a modern sire. With stored semen, that will increase over time. Stored semen was not even possible 50 years ago. Different eras, different access to proven mares, different location, and the like, all bring about differences in the numbers of resulting progeny.

Would it be the number of progeny out there performing for amateurs and kept for life by their owners because they were a valued partner, or enjoyed by all the family? No matter how good a horse is, it may never get the opportunity to show its talent if it is a much loved friend, safe for one to enjoy and sound to last. These may never get an opportunity to be put in a breeding band, to pass on their genetics to the next generation.

Rannock stood at stud at a time when there were no Australian Stock Horse events, no Australian Stock horse mares to come to him, and few working-style events in South Australia for him and his progeny to compete in. For some 50 years, there were only two campdrafts in SA, hardly an opportunity to spotlight stock. Hence they had to find their way into existing and varied disciplines.

South Australian-bred horses have been very successful on the polo field, in showjumping, eventing and dressage, and have even played their part in producing Olympic horses. Think CROWN LAW, Erica Taylor's stallion which competed at Seoul, 1988, to name just one. See https://www.equestrian.org.au/erica-taylor

We also had an amazing birthplace for some of the greatest Thoroughbreds in the nation. All this was happening as the introduction of exotic breeds, professionalism and money was poured into growing the disciplines in other states, and the Australian Stock Horse Society was taking off.

I am proud to have been around at this amazing time, to witness our own horse Rannock measure up and his descendants play their own part in this growth. I am proud that 55 years on, Chalani Sunstream is available to play his part in preserving South Australian bloodlines which were at the fore, during that time.

I am proud this line is also finding a path internationally. It is amazing to think there have been Rannock progeny and descendants in every state and territory of Australia, and overseas in New Zealand, America, England, Dubai, Argentina, Canada and Taiwan. I am sorry I could not have covered more horses in depth. So much I had to leave out.

I am proud that the narrative involves the recognition by breeders of the quality of their stock, and their desire to preserve them, rather than follow fashion. At the heart of a great breeder, is the need to preserve those qualities they find necessary in a good horse, using the best of their lines by testing and performing them, before putting them into the breeding band. The story of Rannock cannot be told without the inclusion of these families who owned, rode and bred good horses.

Throughout this story, the fondness of the owners for their horses is evident. This then is my tribute to them and their remarkable horses.

Chalani Minerva, end of workout Melbourne Royal, type so evident countinues down the generations..

A 'pinnacle' horse, is a horse which takes a huge positive leap towards a more ideal type of the breed. There are only handfuls of those horses. The type then changes from that horse onwards. They are always a real quality individual, (and in a very high %, is usually a line bred horse.) Going forward that horse is always referred to in bloodlines as a 'game changer' . – Trudy Hamilton-Irving.

Addenda

CHALANI CAT BALLOU

(Quarter Master x National Velvet) 1971, blk m, 15h.

The story I will share occurred when one of our ASH Board of Directors was passing through and he asked to visit our stud. I showed him around and came to our best mare. I showed him with great pride but I could see he was rather hesitant to comment. I asked him what he was holding back. He said "well pardon me for saying this but she is...... mmmm....rather ordinary. I far prefer this one over here."

I explained that that was her daughter. He walked over to the next one and said, "my gosh this one is absolutely lovely. What's she done?" I explained that she was led Champion at Adelaide Royal, then an A Grade polo pony for many years, as well as at the same time, the whipper-ins mount for the Adelaide Hunt Club for some 8 years. That too was a daughter. I then went on to show him Paper Tiger, who had placed second in the All Australian Futurity, was a Champion led QH mare and was a top rated sprint mare in SA for two successive seasons. He adored her and was amazed when I said, she too was a daughter of the original mare.

Finally, he went to the last few mares and said how he really loved these mares, they were the pick of the bunch. I said they were all daughters or granddaughters of the original mare. He was totally gobsmacked. My light bulb moment! She may have looked like the worst mare, but in outproducing herself, she had provided us with a broodmare band that anyone could spend a lifetime building up and trying to achieve. This mare had done it all on her own and was still producing!

The fact that she was still there was testimony to the fact that she was a truly GOOD mare, a rare mare, that not only outproduced herself but was the stuff that all good studs are made of and are to be treasured.

That mare, Chalani Cat Ballou was honoured by the ASH Society by being placed on their Wall of Renown and her picture hangs in their office. She was pregnant with her 17th foal when she died peacefully of natural causes. She was a trouble free mare in every way and a delightful temperament, that even beginners could ride. Her progeny could all jump. She too left a legacy of very nice stallion descendants, though her greatest influence has been through her daughters and their daughters. Kitty, as we called her, was only the second horse I ever bred, so if she had come along now, I possibly wouldn't have kept her, and a great opportunity would have been missed.

Kitty had a marvellous temperament, and was
totally safe for anyone to ride.

I think it is all sheer luck sometimes. At the time I kept her because I liked her breeding and loved the real quality in her eye, something that is very hard to come across. I believed the first moment I saw her that she was something 'special'. Funnily enough I was only a poor teenager when I bred her so without a horse float and being cash strapped, I only managed to take her to one show. It was the first year of Quarter Horse classes in South Australia and I was asked to take her along. I didn't believe she would get anywhere because there were experienced exhibitors participating. However, the judge Charlie Beard, from USA, put her first.

I was in so much disbelief, that I went up to him afterwards, particularly as she had beaten a well-known stallion. His answer was prophetic - "I believe a horse such as her will have a lasting influence. That other fellow will likely disappear," he suggested. I'll never forget that. All as it turned out, true.

When Chalani decided to stick to breeding Heritage Australian Stock Horses, this mare and her descendants were the only ones with Quarter Horse in them which we kept in our breeding programme, as we couldn't bear to part with them. Her name appears in some of the significant lines mentioned in this book.

About the stud

Chalani (pronounced sh-larn-i) began in 1967. The name is aboriginal for 'place of cockatoos.'

The three most influential mare lines at Chalani have been Paradis, Chalani Cat Ballou, and later Chalani Aurora. The mares we retain are special to us and difficult to replace. Once a mare enters our broodmare band, we rarely sell her. Because they are proven under saddle (except through injury) we prefer instead to sell colts or proven stallions.

We are only a small stud, having bred on average over the past 55 years, 5-6 foals per year. Chalani strongly supports the Heritage Australian Stock Horse (HSH) as we believe no other horse in the world comes with the stamina, grace, heart and athletic ability of 'the breed for every need.'

The stud could not have progressed with the times, without the input from my daughter Kim, who now runs the stud. She has taken it to a higher level, with support from her family. Andy developed the HorseRecords pro- gramme which we use to record all our data. (Check it out https://horserec ords.info/) Two of the boys, Ashton and Xander are promising young riders themselves. I still breed a couple of foals and get to participate by handling youngsters and being strapper at events.

If you would like to buy from us, you nearly always need to buy a youngster. If you register an expression of interest, you will get an option to purchase ahead of us advertising. Sale horses are placed on our website, but you can always check in with us as to what we might have coming up. We do promote sales of client's Chalani-bred horses on the few occasions they come up for sale. They don't come up very often, so watch out for them on our FB page.

Chalani Sunstream is of course, available at stud. Check him out on the Chalani website, and for other stallions we may have available from time to time. See also our terms and contracts there.

https://www.chalani.net/

For horse sales, bookings or general enquiries, please email **chalani@c halani.net.au** or phone Kim on **61 4130 280 444**.

The Rannock Legacy Reviews

Thank you for the opportunity to read *The Rannock Legacy - The Story of a Remarkable Horse*. This was an insightful experience on a history and lasting legacy of a less well known, yet significant sire.

The book details insight into Rannock's origin, life, and future impacts on the Australian Stock Horse. However, the book offers more than the tale of one horse and his legacy. It reinforces the importance of breeding from proven lines, which offer diversity to the gene pool, guaranteeing an outcross as more fashionable lines dominate, creating potential for a bottleneck.

The book reinforces the mindfulness of breeding from good bloodlines, and the fragility of lines. I would highly recommend *The Rannock Legacy*, not only for its history content, but as a lesson for current and future breeders of horses.

A very enjoyable read. Thank you.

David Ricketts
Board Member, Australian Stock Horse Society

***

The Rannock Legacy is a must read, not only for those interested in the heritage of Australian Stock Horses or horses in general, rather all Australians, as it takes us upon the journey of the building of our Nation.

The evocative personal stories and stunning photographs capture the moment so intrinsically that the reader is quite simply transported back to the time and place to feel the emotion 'first hand'.

The book is superbly written, meticulously researched and flows beautifully. Jeanette Gower is already an accomplished author and you can truly feel the passion and admiration in her writing.

This is a book you will read over and over again as it is an invaluable reference for future generations of equine enthusiasts and breeders alike.

Congratulations on the book. It is truly remarkable.

Darren de Jong
Ophir Australian Stock Horse Stud
Former Senior Vice Chairman of the Australian Stock Horse Society.

Also by Jeanette Gower

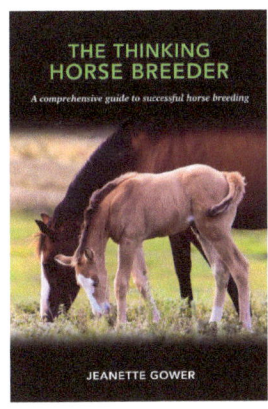

The Thinking Horse Breeder

Horse breeding is more complex than you think. Set yourself up to succeed in your passion for horses. Are you breeding horses and want to take it to the next level? Do you want to make better choices, breed better horses, improve your results? How would you go about establishing a horse stud?

It can be a lonely journey without someone to learn from, to show you how to lessen the mistakes along the way, and to steer you in the right direction. *The Thinking Horse Breeder* is a step by step, treasure trove of practical information for those who want to thrive and succeed doing what they love.

This book discusses selection of foundation stock, planning matings, breeding methods, genetic diseases, conformation and temperament, foaling down, raising foals, young horse training, common problems, financials, promotion, photography and ethical considerations, in an easy-to-read, authentic style.

Each chapter can be read and re-read for new insights. It will challenge your thinking and give you the art, science and tools for success. Everything you need to know is here in a simple, non-technical format based on the author's experiences and reflections over 50+ years. For aspiring, hobby or serious, established breeders, this will be an invaluable guide to be read over and over, so you too can master the inevitable challenges and be successful.

The Thinking Horse Breeder can be ordered direct from the author at the below QR code or

https://thinkinghorsebreeder.chalani.net/or from bookstores worldwide.

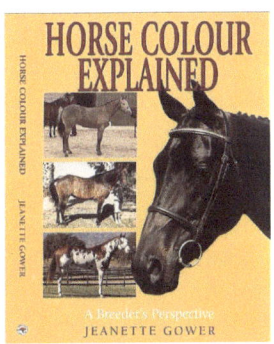

A classic of its time, it is now out of print. It is of collector/historical value only. You can order from me while stocks remain, by going to the below link.